S.F. EDGE

MAKER OF MOTORING HISTORY

Published in August 2022

ISBN 978-1-910505-79-3

Published by Evro Publishing, Westrow House, Holwell, Sherborne, Dorset DT9 5LF, UK

Printed and bound in Malta by Gutenberg Press

Edited by Mark Hughes
Designed by Richard Parsons

www.evropublishing.com

Front cover: Gordon Horner of *The Autocar* drew this charcoal and gouache depiction of S.F. Edge winning the 1902 Gordon Bennett Trophy in his Napier. The drawing hangs in the Segrave Room at the Royal Automobile Club in Pall Mall, London.
Back cover: caricature of S.F. Edge. *Brooklands Museum Trust*
Contents page: S.F. Edge manoeuvres his 80hp Napier before the start of the 1903 Gordon Bennett Trophy race in Naas, Ireland. *Grand Prix Library/Maurice-Louis Branger*

Author

Simon Fisher grew up in Surrey, not far from Tilburstow Hill, scene of some of S.F. Edge's early competition successes. After university, he trained in London as a chartered accountant, using a 1934 Alvis Firefly as his everyday car. A few months after qualifying he signed a six-month contract to work for his employer in Addis Ababa, Ethiopia, at the end of which he forgot to return home. The rest of his career has been spent in Eastern Africa, mainly in Kenya, where he and his wife Catherine now live. That has not prevented him from pursuing his passion for early motoring. He has been a member of both the Vintage Sports-Car Club and the Alvis Owner Club for over 50 years and the Veteran Car Club for almost as long, and has maintained a succession of elderly cars in England, including two Napiers, while his Alvis Firefly spent many years with him in Nairobi.

Michael Sedgwick Memorial Trust

S. F. Edge, Maker of Motoring History is published with the financial assistance of the Michael Sedgwick Memorial Trust. The MSMT was founded in memory of the motoring historian and author Michael C. Sedgwick (1926–83) to encourage the publication of new motoring research, and the recording of Road Transport History. Support by the Trust does not imply any involvement in the editorial process, which remains the responsibility of the editor and publisher. The Trust is a Registered Charity, No 290841, and a full list of the Trustees and an overview of the functions of the MSMT can be found at www.michaelsedgwicktrust.co.uk

MICHAEL SEDGWICK
MEMORIAL TRUST

S.F. EDGE

MAKER OF MOTORING HISTORY

EVRO PUBLISHING

SIMON FISHER

Contents

COMMERCIAL
MOTOR RACE
CARS

APPRECIATION

He was one of those men who provided the inspiration for drivers-to-come and for many years he was the greatest figure in all our racing — the one man who fought hard, to keep our colours in the forefront of every great battle in the heroic age of racing. There is nobody who had a better knowledge than S.F. of what racing means and how its effect best could be obtained. Also he was the greatest figure Brooklands has known.

In fact, there is much sound truth in the statement that he made Brooklands by unceasingly organising races and records on the track with Napiers or A.C.s. When Edge won the Gordon-Bennett race in 1902 he started serious British competition in foreign events. His world's 24-hour record was the curtain-raiser for Brooklands, the series of records he then organised with Napier, A.C. and Spyker mightily encouraged competition as a whole, and all the time he was absolutely ready to carry on any argument of interest to the very end, wheresoever and whensoever he could.

His keen grey eyes, the bushy eyebrows and the hawk-like face, always supposed to be typical of racing drivers, made him a notable figure in any assembly and the character of the man fitted the face.

S.C.H. 'Sammy' Davis
Writing in The Autocar *under the pseudonym 'Casque', shortly after S.F. Edge's death in 1940*

S.F. Edge in an early Napier.
Brooklands Museum Trust

FOREWORD

I was born shortly after the death of my grandfather, Selwyn Francis Edge, so did not know him, but I did know his wife, my grandmother, up until her death in 1969. My late mother, Selwyn's younger daughter, Sonia, never spoke much about my grandfather when I was a child but I found that I had many interests in common with him, such as cycling and farming.

I am told I have a striking family resemblance to him and on more than one occasion strangers have come up to me at motoring events and said I must be a descendent of 'SF'. In later life I have made an effort to learn more about him and have visited many of the places mentioned in this book. I have also inherited some of SF's trophies and medals and a number of family photographs, some of which are reproduced in this book.

My grandfather led a very active life, with a career progressing from selling bicycles, then tyres, then motor vehicles before switching to farming on a large scale and then back to cars, but this time as a manufacturer. Parts of this career have previously been recorded in some detail but other parts have barely been touched upon, so I am glad that, for the first time, the full story of my grandfather's life is being told.

I am grateful to Simon for spending so much time researching and writing this accurate and balanced record from which I have learnt a few things that I did not know before.

Michael Cooke
Grandson of Selwyn Francis Edge
Caister-on-Sea, Norfolk

PREFACE

Selwyn Francis Edge, known to his friends and colleagues as 'SF', was a national hero in the early years of the 20th century. Having been a successful racing cyclist in the 19th century, he played a significant part in the birth of the motor industry in Britain through his close association with the Napier company. As a natural publicist and salesman, he recognised the importance of success in racing as a means of advertising his product and was the first driver to win an international motor race in a British-built car — a Napier — in the Gordon Bennett Trophy in 1902. He was the instigator of the first successful six-cylinder car and went on in 1907 to set a record for the longest distance to be covered by one driver in 24 hours, in a six-cylinder Napier, at the newly opened Brooklands track.

From a relatively modest, middle-class background, he was a wealthy man by the start of the First World War, but in the 1920s, which was a volatile period for the motor industry, he invested and lost much of his fortune in trying to sustain the AC car company. By the time of his death in 1940, when the country was in crisis, he was almost forgotten.

Between 1895 and 1905, the motor industry in Britain was created by a relatively small group of individuals, most of whom had known each other as racing cyclists. Besides SF, the cyclists included Harry Lawson, Harvey Du Cros, Montague Napier, the Hon Charles Rolls, the Hon John Scott-Montagu and H.O. Duncan. The first two of these had become wealthy from involvement in the cycle industry. The non-cyclists included the Lanchester brothers, Herbert Austin (General Manager of Wolseley before starting his own company), and Henry Royce. More in the background, as supporters of the cause, were the Hon Evelyn Ellis, Sir David Salomons and Frederick Simms. These men were from very different backgrounds, ranging from the wealthy aristocracy (Charles Rolls and John Scott Montagu) through competent engineers who could turn their skills to producing motor cars (Montague Napier, Henry Royce and the Lanchester brothers) to entrepreneurs such as SF, but most of the time they worked together as a

team to promote automobilism in Britain. At the end of the 19th century, French firms — notably Panhard et Levassor, De Dion-Bouton, Peugeot and Renault — followed by two German firms — Daimler and Benz — dominated the motor industry internationally. SF was a key player in making sure that British firms could compete with them.

Much had been written about SF while he was alive. SF himself was a prolific letter writer and author of many short, published articles. In the late 1920s, a cycling friend, G.H. Smith, wrote a short biography that focused mainly on SF's cycling achievements, and in 1934 SF published a memoir entitled *My Motoring Reminiscences*. This stuck strictly to the subject of the title, revealing nothing about his family life and very little about his activities after 1912. We are lucky that his one-time business partner, H.O. Duncan, filled in some of the gaps in his marvellous tome *The World on Wheels* published in 1926. Since SF's death, little has been written about him until recently save for occasional articles in motoring magazines.

The author stands proudly with his 1913 30hp Napier Landaulette, displaying the Brian Dinsley Trophy awarded for the best Edwardian Car at the Brooklands Reunion in 2007. *David Marles*

My interest in SF started when I acquired my first Napier car. Soon after, I obtained a copy of *My Motoring Reminiscences*, which immediately left me wanting to know more about him. Perhaps I was subconsciously attracted by the fact that he was known by the same initials as mine! I was also struck by his physical presence, which is so evident in photographs of him, especially in his bushy eyebrows above penetrating eyes and his efforts to ensure that he was always smartly and fashionably dressed. Later, I was lucky enough to acquire St John Nixon's copy of Smith's small book. I met, very briefly, SF's younger daughter, Sonia, at a Napier Power Heritage Trust event in 2008, but this was before I had decided I would write a biography of him and, sadly, she passed away in 2012. I only had the chance to ask one brief question on the spur of the moment: 'Was SF a good father?' to which the answer was a definite 'Yes'. Since then, I have been fortunate to meet Sonia's son, Michael Cooke, and his wife, June.

This biography is my attempt to help ensure that SF and his achievements are not forgotten, and to cover the whole of his life from his birth in New South Wales in 1868 to his death in Eastbourne in 1940.

ACKNOWLEDGEMENTS

I must give grateful acknowledgement to the Veteran Car Club of Great Britain. SF, from an early age, paid a company to collect cuttings of any mention of him in the press. His widow, Myra, who was appointed a Vice President of this Club in 1947, donated these press cuttings, covering the period 1887 to 1940, to the Club, and I am very grateful to the Club, its Secretary, Stephen Curry, and its Librarian, Simon Moss, for allowing me to spend many hours in their library perusing these.

Especial thanks go to Michael Cooke for letting me view the various memorabilia of his grandfather, checking my draft, and providing the foreword to this book.

My thanks also go to Penny Morris for permission to quote from the cycling diary of her great grandfather, G.H. Smith, and for the photo of GH on his wedding day.

I am also grateful to the National Motor Museum, Beaulieu, their librarian, Patrick Collins, and Jon Day of their Motoring Picture Library; the Brooklands Museum Trust and their librarian, Andrew Lewis; The Royal Automobile Club and its Librarian, Trevor Dunmore; and the Vintage Sports-Car Club and its Librarian, Ian Ferguson, for help in sourcing photographs and access to their libraries and archives. I am also grateful to the Institution of Mechanical Engineers for allowing me access to the Minute Books of D. Napier & Son.

Dr Craig Horner, author of *The Emergence of Cycling and Automobility in Britain*, has provided me with much advice and encouragement, as have Peter Card, Anders Clausager and Michael Edwards of the Society of Automotive Historians of Great Britain. I have also benefited from Michael Barton's insight into the life of Dorothy Levitt. Clive Boothman, Chairman of the Napier Power Heritage Trust, has assisted by providing some of the photographs.

Other sources that have provided much of the material in this book include the contemporary motoring journals such as *The Autocar, The Automotor Journal, The Motor* and *The Car Illustrated*, digital copies of which are available through Grace's Guide to British Industrial History, *The Times* archive, *Veteran and Vintage Magazine*, Ancestry.com, and Wikipedia.

I have tried as far as possible to acknowledge the source of the images reproduced in this book. If I have inadvertently breached any copyright, I offer my sincere apologies.

I would also like to acknowledge the contribution of two very long-standing friends and fellow early motoring enthusiasts, Hugh Corby and David Marles, for helping to keep alive my passion during my long absences overseas. David has also provided helpful editorial assistance.

Finally, my thanks go to my daughter, Jean, for much needed 'tech support'.

CHAPTER 1
EARLY LIFE
1868 TO 1883

Selwyn Francis Edge was born in Concord near Sydney in New South Wales on 29 March 1868, shortly before his parents, Alexander Ernest Edge and Annie Charlotte Sharp, married. Alexander had been born in New South Wales in 1843, while Annie was born in Lincolnshire in 1840,[1] but her family emigrated to New South Wales in 1844. In 1871, when SF was three years old, and probably with his and his siblings' education in mind, his parents moved to England.[i] Even at that age, SF demonstrated the combination of a sense of adventure, fearlessness and luck that was to bring him fame. On the long sea voyage to England, in a large sailing boat, he nearly came to an untimely end: he clambered over the side of the ship and was later found playing quite happily on a small ledge about a foot wide, with nothing to prevent him falling into the sea. A sailor had to clamber down a rope to rescue him, an act that had to be achieved without distracting the boy lest he fall from his perch.[2] Later on the same voyage, he fell through a skylight and might have been killed had he not been lucky enough to fall into the lap of an elderly lady sitting beneath, reading.[3]

SF was the first-born of seven siblings, the others being Kelburne (born in 1869, before the family left New South Wales), Seaton (born 1872), Mary (born 1873), William (born 1875), Randolph (born 1876), and Marguerite (born 1883).[4] His parents settled in South London, and the 1881 census shows the children living with their mother, Annie, but with Alexander absent, at 80 Belvedere Road, Upper Norwood, South London. Alexander, who was a merchant in the City of London, was probably travelling at the time. The house in Belvedere Road, known as Odessa House, was a substantial property, on three floors with a basement, which Alexander had taken on a 21-year lease.[5]

After a brief spell with private tutors, SF was educated at nearby Belvedere House College,

i SF is often referred to as an Australian. At the time of his birth, New South Wales was a self-governing British colony (Australia did not exist as a nation), so he was always a British citizen. It was not until 1901 that six colonies joined together to form the Commonwealth of Australia.

➢ SF's father: Alexander Ernest Edge (1843–1924). *Michael Cooke collection*

in Upper Norwood, until he was 16. In 1910 he wrote:

> As a child, I was very delicate, having very weak lungs, and being altogether anything but a robust specimen of human nature. These drawbacks naturally prevented me from taking part in many outdoor games which I have always loved. At first I could not understand how it was that I should be debarred from taking a share in harmless pastimes in which other boys indulged to their hearts' content. My inquiring mind pondered deeply on this subject, and when it was explained to me that my weak lungs were the cause of my having to sit down and look on instead of taking my own part in violent exercises of any sort, I there and then determined to strengthen these offending organs as rapidly as possible.[6]

He was not strong academically, and on leaving school his headmaster is reported to have told his father that the boy was so dull and incapable that he was afraid he would never succeed at anything.[7] He did, however, have an inquisitive mind, and took a close interest in anything new that presented itself. SF's own recollection of his school days, written in 1927, was somewhat at odds with his headmaster's opinion:

> I loved school because to me it was all play. While some of the boys struggled to learn, I got through the minimum amount of work with the minimum amount of effort because I took to such things as geography, history and mathematics as readily as a cat laps milk. I claim no credit; credit is due to those who overcome obstacles, not to those who find no obstacles to overcome, and the things that did not come easily to me I evaded, my chief ambition all the time being not to be kept in![8]

SF's home in Belvedere Road was less than one mile from the Crystal Palace. The 'Palace', a giant glass and iron structure built in Hyde Park for the Great Exhibition of 1851, had been dismantled soon after and rebuilt in Sydenham Hill, where it was to be destroyed by fire in 1936. SF described it as 'a happy hunting ground' and declared that he learnt more there than at school. He recalled, in 1927:

> When I was thirteen I picked up a lot of knowledge about electricity at an Exhibition which was held at the Palace, and in the same year I studied the original Edison phonograph there, to such good purpose that I made a similar phonograph myself. I learned about telephones, electric bells, electric coils, and all manner of things.[9]

While still at school, his main pastimes were fishing and shooting with a catapult, and he claimed to have designed a new type of catapult: 'very small, very light, and capable of extreme accuracy and great penetration, which was so effective it frequently landed me in trouble'.[10] One example of such trouble was when he had to appear before Mr Biron, QC, at Lambeth Magistrates Court in August 1883 accused of killing or injuring valuable birds (such as swans) belonging to the Crystal Palace Company.

A witness who said he had seen SF fire the catapult stated that at first the 15-year-old had denied that he even had a catapult but later admitted that he did. SF then declared that he had been firing at a tree, but this was not accepted by Mr Biron. The miscreant was ordered to pay a fine of 10 shillings plus costs and told that if the offence were repeated the punishment would be far more severe.[11]

A more serious offence was allegedly committed on 14 December 1883. An explosive device was detonated in the front garden of 76 Belvedere Road, next door but one to the Edge's residence. The elderly resident, Miss Mary Chetwynd, had been sitting in her downstairs parlour when its front window was shattered by the explosion. The incident left her shaken and confused. A witness, who had been standing opposite the house when the explosion occurred, claimed that he saw SF, whom he knew, run along in front of the railings in a crouching position and enter the gate of Odessa House.

Alexander Edge told Croydon Magistrates Court that he remembered the evening in question and that at the time of the explosion he had been in the dining room at Odessa House with SF, two other sons, and his sister-in-law, Catherine Sharp. He said that after the explosion, SF was the first to run out into the street to find out what had happened. Kelburne, one of SF's brothers, and Catherine both corroborated this version of events, as did a nursemaid in the family's service, but it was suggested that the family had been 'talking the matter over to her'.[12] The hearing was adjourned and evidence was later produced of SF having bought two ounces of gunpowder from a shop in Anerley Road. Despite this, the magistrate concluded that there was insufficient evidence to convict the youth.

▲ The Edge family home in South London, at 80 Belvedere Road in Upper Norwood, pictured as it looks today. SF grew up here from the age of three. *Author*

Few 15-year-olds at that time can have had their name published in *The Times*, and many other newspapers, twice in one year, and maybe this led to SF's later addiction to seeing his name in print.

CHAPTER 2

CYCLING DAYS

1882 TO 1895

The latter part of the 19th century was the age of the bicycle. Motor vehicles powered by petrol internal combustion engines had not yet been invented. Early attempts to develop road-going steam locomotives, particularly as coaches, had been crushed in Britain by the Locomotive Act of 1865, which limited their speed to 4mph. So the primary forms of transport at this time other than the railways remained horse-drawn.

Velocipedes, or 'hobby horses' — two wheels connected by a frame on which the rider sat and propelled the machine forward by pushing on the ground with his feet — had been in use since 1790, but one could not travel any significant distance in this way. SF described them as machines one would push up slopes then ride down. In Paris in the 1860s, Pierre Michaux and his son Ernest started fitting pedals to the front wheels of velocipedes, which made them much more viable as a means of travelling.

Early bicycles, such as those built by Michaux et Cie, had a front wheel only slightly larger than the rear wheel, but as higher speeds became possible it was found

Early cyclist Herbert Liddle Cortis with his 'ordinary' bicycle, better known today as a 'penny farthing'.

Author's collection

that the front wheel needed to be much larger to achieve the right gearing. Such bicycles became known as 'ordinary' bicycles but are now better known as 'penny farthings' due to the pedalled wheel being much larger than the trailing wheel. The pedals at this stage were connected directly to the axle of the driving wheel, with no intermediate gearing. Only the length of the rider's leg limited the size of the driving wheel on an 'ordinary'. One rider, Herbert Liddle Cortis (1857–1885), who was over six feet tall, was able to ride a machine with a 62-inch wheel. The rear wheels were generally about 18 inches in diameter.

Riding such high machines was dangerous, so 'geared ordinaries' (allowing the front wheel to be smaller) were developed, and then 'safety' bicycles. The latter, like modern bicycles, had wheels of equal size, with the pedals connected to the rear wheel by chain, allowing the necessary gearing. Nevertheless, 'ordinary' bicycles remained popular for several years.

A Sparkbrook tricycle of 1884, as purchased by SF when he was 16. *gracesguide.co.uk*

Bicycle races were being held in France as early as 1868, the year of SF's birth, and in Britain not long after. A cycle manufacturing industry soon emerged in Coventry, pioneered by James Starley of Starley & Son, and George Woodcock, owner of the Rudge Cycle Company.

As cycling became popular in Britain, numerous cycling clubs sprung up. Every major town would have at least one club and cities such as London had several. The Anerley Bicycle Club, close to where SF lived, was founded in 1881 and is still going strong. Other London-based clubs included the Catford Cycling Club in south-east London and the Bath Road Club in west London, both founded in 1886. To the north of the city, in Hertfordshire, the North Road Cycling Club was founded in 1885.

SF's father and an uncle were both keen cyclists. His uncle, Arthur Edge, bought a 54-inch Humber ordinary, and his father, Alexander, acquired a tricycle soon after. This tricycle had two 56-inch wheels, between which the rider sat, and was steered by a small trailing wheel. While his father and uncle were on a voyage, SF could not resist trying out the tricycle. He found it difficult to steer, and when going downhill he braked too hard and lost control. The tricycle hit a curb and buckled a wheel. SF was terrified about how his father would react, but fortunately found a 'kind of mechanic' who 'by skilful application of knees and hands, sprang the wheel back true'.[13]

SF decided that the way to good health, contrary to his doctor's advice, was through exercise, and he found cycling an appealing way of achieving this. He started in 1882, at the age of 14, on a primitive 'boneshaker' that he hired out on the terrace of the Crystal Palace.[14] He progressed to a tricycle and finally to an 'ordinary' bicycle.

In 1884, aged 16, SF bought a Sparkbrook tricycle[ii] and soon after joined Anerley Bicycle Club. He remained an active member of this club for the rest of his life and was elected its President in 1929.[15] He also bought a Rover 'safety' bicycle but was happy riding anything with wheels. When riding an 'ordinary' bicycle, his preference was for a 52-inch wheel.[16]

One evening in the summer of 1886, SF was riding his Sparkbrook tricycle between West Wickham and Elmers End when he met another cyclist on a rear-steering Meteor tricycle. They rode together for a while, chatting as they went, and even raced each other for a short distance over Elmers End railway bridge. Before parting, they exchanged addresses and SF asked his fellow cyclist whether he was a member of a cycling club. On receiving the answer 'No', SF offered to propose him as a member of the Anerley Bicycle Club. The other cyclist was G.H. Smith, who duly joined the club and went on to serve as President, in 1914.[17] He and SF became lifelong friends.[iii]

SF had been expecting to join the army and had even started studies for admission to Sandhurst,[18] but what he described as 'family reverses' changed his plans, and being the eldest in the family he felt the need to earn his living.[19] His first employment after leaving school was in his father's business,[20] but he was so keen on cycling that he left to join a bicycle firm in Holborn, London, which sent him out as a commercial traveller to sell its machines. It soon occurred to him that he would do better business if he were to become known as a successful racing cyclist, and he set out with determination to train himself.

Cycle Racing

SF was soon entering cycle races and won his first race in August 1887, aged 19. It was the Westerham Hill Climb organised by the Catford Cycling Club.[21] Westerham Hill in Kent is a long, steep climb, and most cyclists would find it hard to reach the top without dismounting at some point. SF stormed up on his Marriott & Cooper Humber solid-tired safety bicycle in 6 minutes 24 seconds, three seconds faster than the next competitor. When practising in the previous

ii A new Sparkbrook tricycle cost between £18 and £24 at that time, equivalent to between £2,000 and £3,000 today. As this was around the time SF left school, presumably his father stumped up the money.

iii Many years later, G.H. Smith wrote of this chance meeting: 'It brought me into the Anerley Bicycle Club, of which I have now been a member for 44 years, made me associated with the cycle press, the Dunlop Co. from which sprang my remarkable travels, led on to the motor industry, made me one of the earliest British motorists, gave me nearly all the friends I ever had outside the family circle, and indeed I can trace direct association of almost every event of my adult life with that quiet little spin with the dark stranger on that calm summer evening in Kent.'

week he had ridden up the hill four times in one evening. G.H. Smith attributed this success not so much to SF's strength as to his 'beautiful ankle action' and to his strategy, which enabled him 'to quickly see the thing to do and to do it'.[22]

Two months later, on 25 October, riding with G.L. Morris on an Olympia tricycle tandem, SF set a new record for a tandem by covering 100 miles in 6 hours 57 minutes 32 seconds, beating the previous record by more than nine minutes. His time included a stop of five minutes for refreshments.

By now he was a very enthusiastic cyclist, constantly training, touring and racing. In the absence of motor cars, he probably cycled to most of the races, although possibly his longer journeys were by train. In 1887 his recorded rides amounted to 7,201 miles, mostly in Surrey, Sussex and Kent, but also on the Great North Road, now the A1.[23] During training, SF would often stay at The George in Buckden, Hertfordshire, on the A1, or the Fisherman's Joy at Selsey, on the West Sussex coast (both establishments continue to provide hospitality to this day).

H.O. Duncan described how The George attracted cyclists, quoting from an article published in a cycling journal in 1890, the author probably being Tommy Edge: 'Buckden I know but slightly but hope to be better acquainted. I know the dining room where ye cyclists do congregate. Everything looks so cosy at the George. Men go down to train and have been known never to get on a bicycle during their sojourn there. It would take wild horses to drag them from the charming company they meet with and get them to scorch. To persuade them that going out for a ride was pleasanter than bathing in the river or fishing and other amusements, would be madness. And I solemnly swear that there are fish in the river. I caught one. So did my namesake, S.F. Edge.'

This montage captures scenes of SF riding in Anerley Bicycle Club events. *Bicycling News (7 July 1888)*

1888

In 1888, SF won a medal in a 25-mile tricycle race held in Coventry and a few weeks afterwards, on 30 June, he won the one-mile tricycle championship of the National Cyclists Union held in Halifax. Then on 22 September he beat a strong field of 46 competitors to win the North Road Cycling Club 100-mile race. Starting just north of Hitchin, the route took the riders as far as Peterborough before turning back towards London. At the halfway point there was a close struggle between SF, Hale, Lea, Holbein, James and Turvey, all well-known cyclists at that time. SF won in 6 hours 33 minutes, fully eight minutes ahead of the next competitor. Amazingly, a rider on an 'ordinary' bicycle, G.R. White, completed the course in 6 hours 48 minutes, a new world record for that type of cycle.[24]

A month later, on 18 October, the Bath Road Club held its annual 50-mile open handicap race, also on the Great North Road. J.G.H. Browne of the Anerley Bicycle Club won on handicap, but of those starting on scratch, SF won by a small margin after a fiercely fought contest with C.A. Smith on a safety bicycle, and M.A. Holbein and G.P. Mills on a tandem.

1889

In June 1889, SF tried his hand at a quarter-mile sprint riding a tandem with F.J.B. Archer and set a new record of 35.8 seconds, but his favourite distance was 100 miles. He again won the North Road Cycling Club's 100-mile race, which saw more than half the starters retire, exhausted from battling against a 'cruel' wind. SF completed the course in 6 hours 55 minutes, seven minutes slower than his time the previous year, suggesting that the conditions must indeed have been a lot worse.

The Speedwell Bicycle Club ran its first open race near Worcester in October. At one point the cyclists speeded up their pace when they were chased by a group of angry gipsies on horses.[25] The result was a dead heat between SF and J.E.L. Bates, Chairman of the Anerley Bicycle Club, in 8 hours 33 minutes. The conditions were dreadful, with riders becoming soaked with rain, and mud getting everywhere. For sustenance, SF was carrying some cold chicken in one of his pockets but had to wash the dirt off it before he could tuck in.[26]

The Anerley Bicycle Club was a social club as well as a sporting club, and H.O. Duncan related that in 1889 'most of Edge's evenings were spent in the clubhouse and always in company with his dog'. SF was a dog lover and was frequently accompanied by one, this particular dog being a Bull Terrier known as *Bully*.[iv] A cycle journal at the time recorded that *Bully* was often getting into fights with other dogs and that he had 'an uncontrollable desire to sample each gentleman's leg'.[27]

1890

London to Brighton was already established as a route on which records could be set. In 1888, one J. Selby, driving a coach and horses, had achieved a time of 7 hours 50 minutes for the round trip of 108 miles starting from the White Horse Cellar in Piccadilly, winning a bet of £1,000 in the process.[28] The Surrey Bicycle Club decided to offer a substantial prize to any member who could beat this coaching record. Frank Shorland, who had competed against SF in the Speedwell Bicycle Club's race the previous October, comfortably

iv *Bully* either lived to a great age or SF owned other bull terriers named *Bully* in later years.

▲ This portrait of SF was taken when he was 21. *The Cycle Record (18 January 1890)*

▲ SF poses on a Marriott & Cooper 'Olympia' Tandem Tricycle with J.E.L. Bates at the front. *gracesguide.co.uk*

beat the record with a time of 7 hours 19 minutes in June 1890, but he was ineligible for the Surrey Bicycle Club's prize because he was not a member.

SF, determined to improve on Shorland's effort, assembled a large team of volunteers— timekeepers, pacemakers, feeders and other helpers — for his own attempt the following month. Shortly before the appointed day, heavy rain washed out much of the road between Hand Cross and Brighton — a large part of the route was unsurfaced in those days — but SF nevertheless went ahead, riding a Marriott & Cooper safety bicycle fitted with rubber-cushion tyres. He started from the Hatchett's Hotel, Piccadilly, at 9.00am, reached Croydon in 38 minutes, and the top of Hand Cross Hill, part of which he had to walk up, in 2 hours 5 minutes. E. Dangerfield, a small, wiry speed cyclist who later became proprietor of the magazine *Cycling*, paced him down the long descent from Hand Cross.[29] After reaching Brighton in 3 hours 18 minutes, SF paused at the Gloucester Hotel for six minutes to eat and remove some mud before setting off back along the same route. He completed the distance in 7 hours 2 minutes 50 seconds, bettering Shorland's time by 16 minutes 10 seconds and achieving an average speed of 15.3mph. He also won the Surrey Bicycle Club's prize.

In October, SF was able to put up a fast time in another 100-mile race, this time on an

Another image of SF at this time was published in *The World on Wheels*, which, in its caption, described him as a member of Surrey Bicycle Club. *The World on Wheels*

Olympia tricycle tandem with J.E.L. Bates over a route that started near Lincoln and ended near London. The pair covered the distance in 5 hours 30 minutes 31 seconds at an average speed of over 18mph. T.A. (Tommy) Edge (no relation) from Manchester paced them over the first stage and, realising that he was going well, carried on and completed the full course with a slightly better time, by 2 minutes 53 seconds, on his pneumatic-tyred Ivel bicycle.[30] At this time, pneumatic tyres were just beginning to become available from The Pneumatic Tyre Company, which had been founded in November 1889 and was run by Harvey Du Cros, with whom SF was to become closely involved in later years.

1891

In May 1891 SF took part in his first continental road race, from Bordeaux to Paris, a distance of 358 miles, again paced by Tommy Edge. There were 38 competitors, of whom four others were British: G.P. Mills, M.A. Holbein, J.E.L. Bates and P.C. Twentyman. The conditions were rough, with a 150-mile stretch of hilly country and the road made worse by heavy rain. Twentyman did not finish, but Mills rode very well and came in first, with Holbein, SF and Bates taking the next three places. Mills, whose time was 26 hours 34 minutes 57 seconds, must have been totally exhausted but he was assisted by a large team, including no fewer than 40 pacemakers.[31] Holbein's organisation was less effective and his second place was 1 hour 16 minutes slower. Tommy Edge, acting as pacer for both SF and Bates, was unable to continue after 70 miles, so the two competitors then stuck together, pacing each other in effect, and came in 3 hours 39 minutes behind the winner. Despite it being May, they encountered a snowstorm at Rambouillet and resorted to warming themselves by pouring whisky into their shoes.[32] They did not carry food and were at the mercy of roadside cafés and restaurants for hastily eaten meals along the way, hampered by the fact that few, if any, of the English team spoke much French. In 1909, Bates reminisced about this race, the interviewer recording:

Five British competitors took part in the Bordeaux-to-Paris road race of May 1891. From left: J.E.L. Bates, G.P. Mills, M.A. Holbein, P.C. Twentyman and S.F. Edge. *Peter Card collection*

> As he [Bates] approached Paris, the desire for a rest became overpowering. Both S.F. Edge and he were so fagged out that they could not resist the sleepy feeling any longer. Rolling, rather than dismounting, from their machines, they threw themselves down in a wet field by the roadside, not far from Versailles, oblivious to every consideration on earth, excepting only that rest which was so sweet and necessary.[33]

Later in 1891, SF won the open 50 handicap run by the Poole Bicycle Club, and he also travelled to Scotland for the Waverley Roads Club open 100, which he won in a record 6 hours 32 minutes 30 seconds. The Bath Road Club's 100 was again run on the Great North Road, with a mixed field of safeties, ordinaries and tricycles, and SF was beaten, but only by one second, by the Club Secretary. In the North Road Cycling Club's open 100, SF was again beaten, surprisingly, by J.F. Walsh of the Bath Road Club riding a pneumatic-tyred ordinary. The same two riders drew in a dead-heat for longest distance covered in the Catford Cycling Club's open 12-hour event on the North Road, both covering 166 miles.

In between these competitions, SF managed to

S. F. E.

THE prominent place which S. F. Edge holds among the road-riders of to-day is sufficient excuse for presenting our readers with his portrait. A hundred miles is Edge's pet distance on the road, but that he is a sterling wheeler for even longer distances is evidenced by the sample of his riding powers which he gave the Frenchmen just recently. Next week S. F. Edge intends making an onslaught on C. A. Smith's Brighton and back record. Edge was born in Australia, andwas one of the very earliest riders of the rear-driving safety.

< Published by an unknown source soon after the Bordeaux-to-Paris road race, this cutting provides ample testimony to SF's cycling prowess. *Author's collection*

^ Fred Cooper built a pedal-powered boat, also known as a hydrocycle. SF is in the centre in this photo, with Fred Cooper leading. *Illustrated Sport and Kennel (March 1929)*

find time to 'mess about in boats' on the Upper Thames, although this must have represented a 'busman's holiday' since the main task was that of pedalling, a friend, Fred Cooper, having built a pedal-powered boat. Three crew sat one behind the other and drove a two-bladed screw through cranks and chains. SF's friend, G.H. Smith, recounts how one Sunday afternoon in the summer of 1891 he volunteered to be a member of the crew, sandwiched between Cooper in the front and SF to the rear.[34] From his description, it sounds like the crew got involved in informal races with oarsmen and Smith acknowledges that he was not as fit as the two athletes, and only the respite afforded by having to pass through locks saved him from total exhaustion.

SF was now 23 and still working as a commercial traveller, at this time with the firm of Marriott & Cooper, which sold cycles made by the Rudge Cycle Company of Coventry, amongst others.[35] Given the number of races in which he competed, and the training and travelling that would have been required, he can hardly have had enough time for a regular job, but his time spent racing must have been considered as good publicity for the company, especially when he was racing on one of its machines.

1892

On 1 June 1892, SF set out to regain his record for London to Brighton and back after C.A. Smith had taken it from him. He chose to ride one of the new geared ordinary bicycles, a Marriott & Cooper, of course, fitted with Dunlop tyres. This time he started from Purley, heading north to London to begin with. Even in those days there could be traffic that might hold him up. The roads were also slippery, and on turning at Piccadilly at 6.44am, he fell from his high cycle. One of the spectators who saw him fall was M.S. Napier, an enthusiastic cyclist and member of the Bath Road Club, who would have a close business relationship with SF in later years.[36]

Only a few yards further on, SF fell again and grazed his hip, and had to be assisted by a policeman before setting off again for Clapham, reaching Purley at 7.44am. Heading towards Brighton he faced a strong headwind, which slowed his pace. One of the pacers on this stretch was his brother, Seaton, and he turned at Brighton at 10.22am. When SF stopped briefly at the Gloucester Hotel, his face was licked by a dog, the same one that two years earlier, as a puppy, had sprung up and licked him at the same spot.[37] SF considered this a good omen. Somehow he managed to recover his strength and put in a very good time for the last hour back to Purley. His total time of 6 hours 51 minutes 7 seconds beat the record by just 1 minute 8 seconds. He was perfectly fresh at the finish and quickly engaged in his usual humorous banter.

A few weeks later, on 25 June, SF also broke the London-to-York bicycle record, again on a geared ordinary with pneumatic tyres. The record had stood at 14 hours 22 minutes for the 197-mile route, and SF knocked 1 hour 33 minutes off this, averaging 15.35mph,[38] despite being hampered by rain between Grantham and Newark. Just before Selby a tyre punctured but he was able to switch to a similar machine so as not to lose time.[39] Just 100 yards from the finish, the pacer stopped to embrace a spectator and SF collided with them. He remounted so hurriedly that he crossed the line with the front wheel of his geared ordinary turned round the wrong way. By the end, he was covered in black mud from head to foot, his dark eyes just being distinguishable by a fierce gleam.

SF then tried the geared ordinary on a track, and at Herne Hill on 11 July he broke all records from 64 miles to 100 miles, his time for the 100 miles being 5 hours 6 minutes 51 seconds, which equated to an average speed of 19.55mph. He was back at Herne Hill on 22/23 July for a 24-hour track race for the Cuca Cocoa Challenge Cup, with a prize of 100 guineas. However, his intensive racing programme over the previous few weeks had taken its toll, and he retired after 227 miles.[40] The Cup was won by Frank Shorland, who covered just under 414 miles in the 24 hours.

In the North Road Club's open 100 of 1892, SF was beaten into second place by a sturdy pair of brothers, A.J. and R.J. Ilsley, on a tandem. Flanders was third and the fourth man was M.S. Napier, soon to acquire the family engineering business, D. Napier & Son.

1893

For 1893, SF reverted to a safety cycle, a Rudge with Palmer tyres, on which he won the Bath Road Club's 100-mile Open on the North Road

The 12 best road riders of 1891, as selected from votes cast by the readers of Cycling. *Michael Cooke collection*

on 2 September in a time of 5 hours 24 minutes 57 seconds. He broke the world record for 100 miles on the road at the same time.

Just a few days later, on 12 September, he was tackling the London-to-Brighton return trip again to win back his record, which had been taken from him by E. Dance. He was successful, completing the slightly modified route, now of 106 miles, in 6 hours 13 minutes 48 seconds. Dance sportingly rode as one of the pacers for SF on this occasion.

Within just a few days, however, C.A. Smith reclaimed the record once again, so SF wasted no time in making yet another attempt, on 22 September. This time he made a dramatic improvement, achieving a time of 5 hours 52 minutes 30 seconds, despite three falls on a greasy stretch of road between Dale Hill and Brighton. He went on to win the Bordesley open 100 in Tewkesbury, a 100-mile track event in Leeds, and the Yorkshire Road Club's Open 100 run on the West Riding track before the year was out.

Eleanor Rose Sharp

When not racing, SF, still living at Odessa House, enjoyed touring on his cycles with friends, and would often visit Selsey, on the south coast. On these tours a regular companion was Eleanor Sharp, herself an energetic cyclist, who also lived in Belvedere Road, at number 31.

Eleanor Rose Sharp, known to friends as Nellie, was born in Lewisham on 29 April 1872. Her mother, Theodosia Hann, had married John Sharp in 1864, and Eleanor was the youngest of their five children. However, the marriage was an unhappy one, and Theodosia divorced her husband in 1874, citing the fact that he had wilfully communicated a venereal disease to her and at one point had thrown a knife at her and threatened to murder her. He also had an affair with Theodosia's younger sister, Isabella, and was cohabiting with her at the time of the divorce. Because of the scandal created by the divorce hearing, John and Isabella were forced to leave England and settled in New Zealand.[41]

Theodosia remarried in 1882, to a doctor, Samuel Walter, and in 1892 they were living in Belvedere Road together with Eleanor and her older sister Alice.

SF and Eleanor married in July 1892, the ceremony being held at St Pauls, Hamlet Road, Upper Norwood. SF's Best Man was G.H. Smith, who also had to 'give away' Eleanor, as she was not on good terms with her stepfather. Eleanor was 20 years old when she married SF, who was four years her senior. It would seem to be just coincidence that her surname was the same as the maiden name of SF's mother.

SF's mother, Annie, had died in October 1889, at the age of 49.[42] Catherine Sharp, Annie's unmarried younger sister, had been living at Odessa House, at least since 1881, and now presumably acted as mother to the younger children (the youngest, Marguerite, was only six years old at the time of Annie's death). It is possible that she and Alexander also became partners, although they never married. Another of Annie's sisters, Stella Sharp, had died at Odessa House in March 1887, aged 37.

Just a few months after the wedding, on 5 October 1892, SF's father, his aunt, Catherine, and all of his siblings other than Kelburne, set sail for Sydney, Australia, on board the *Macquaria* to settle back in New South Wales. Kelburne may have left for New South Wales slightly earlier.

In 1892, SF had been appointed manager of the Marriott & Cooper shop at 65 Holborn Viaduct, London, but by the start of 1893 he had left the business and taken up the position of manager for a new cycle manufacturer, the New Howe Machine Company in Glasgow, living in Helensburgh during the summer months. This probably explains why he did not race in the summer of that year, although curiously Smith's diary (see below) records cycle rides with the Edges at least once a month throughout 1893, so they must have regularly travelled by train between Glasgow and London.

While in Scotland, SF went out for a ride one evening with Eleanor in Dumbarton. SF had gone on ahead of her when she was accosted by four young men on cycles, one of whom attempted to kiss her. Outraged when learning of this, SF returned down the road and, finding four likely cyclists, held them up with his revolver, threatening to shoot them. Unfortunately, it appears he had picked on four innocent young men, as Eleanor subsequently failed to identify any of them as the culprit. As a result, SF was handed a fine of £5 plus costs but received a certain amount of sympathy in the cycling press for his chivalry. Whether he always carried a revolver when out cycling is not known.

At New Howe, SF worked with one R.L. Philpot, whom Smith describes as restless and talkative, but who taught SF much about advertising. Neither of them got on with the Managing Director, 'who knew little of cycles and less of advertising',[43] and both left within a matter of months to join Rudge & Co. in Coventry. There, SF met Harvey Du Cros, who took an interest in him and offered him a position, which he accepted at once, as racing manager in the London branch of his company.[44]

As mentioned, Du Cros had realised the potential of the pneumatic tyre and quickly set up the Pneumatic Tyre and Booth's Cycle Agency, Limited, which had purchased John Dunlop's patent for £500, in Dublin, in 1889. SF could also see that the pneumatic tyre would soon oust solid and cushioned tyres for bicycles. However, neither of them at that time could have realised the scale of the market for pneumatic tyres that would develop following the introduction of the motor car.

SF was now 25 and had perhaps reached his peak as a racing cyclist, but in any event the demands of his new job resulted in him withdrawing from cycle racing and, as we shall see, he was soon to become involved in motor racing and business. He never lost his love of cycling, however, and for many years afterwards liked to take an early-morning ride, accompanied by his dog.[45]

Cycling with G.H. Smith, 1891 to 1895

As already mentioned, G.H. Smith had joined the Anerley Bicycle Club and was a good friend of SF. Although not as competitive as SF, Smith was also a very active cyclist and between 1891 and early 1896 kept a detailed diary of his cycling trips, many of which were in the company of SF and often Miss Sharp/Mrs Edge. He recorded the mileage covered on each trip and added it up at the end of each year, the mileages covered being:

➢ SF's wife Eleanor in 1896. At this time they had been married for four years. *The Lady Cyclist*

1891 — 3,992; 1892 — 4,660; 1893 — 4,461; 1894 — 4,760; and 1895 — 5,066.

The trips were mainly within Surrey (Godstone, Horsham and Crawley being common destinations), but also further afield to Brighton, Worthing and Selsey. Eleanor must have accompanied SF on many of the trips to Selsey, and Smith records that on one of them SF, who was a strong swimmer, had to rescue her from being swept away by a strong current around Selsey Bill.

On 15 April 1894, Smith, SF and Eleanor cycled 68 miles from Coventry, passing through Warwick and Kenilworth, which Smith described as a 'grand ride'. Presumably they had travelled to Coventry by train.

On 26 May 1895 Smith cycled 172 miles, despite being involved in an accident with a horse and cart when his cycle was crushed. He describes it as a 'narrow escape of self and Edge'. Smith had to borrow another cycle to complete the journey.

Smith and SF were particularly active in July and August of 1895, Smith recording:

7th July	In evening to Westerham to meet Edge party. Nice quiet ride home with them.
14th July	With Edges and Linley. Quiet riding round Godstone, Titsey, Saltbox, etc.
18th July	Evening run with SF to Horley.
23rd July	Evening run to Crawley with Edges.

◅ Pictured with their friends in the Anerley Bicycle Club during 1895, SF and Eleanor (third and fourth from right) often rode to Selsey on the Sussex coast and stayed at the Fisherman's Joy Inn. *Cycling*

3rd August	Met Edges at Selsey. Big party down there.
5th August	To Emsworth with the Edges and others.
11th August	Grand ride home from Selsey in party of 8 including the Edges and the Wridgways.
13th August	Evening ride with SF.
17th August	Met Edge at Purley and on to Crawley.
21st August	To Reigate with SF and others.
25th August	Loxwood with SF Edge 'and usual mob'.

Writing in 1929, Smith had this to say about their trips to Selsey:

> At Selsey there used to be only the choice of 'The Crown' or the 'Fisherman's Joy', both in their time have done the Club well and at both we have found the Selsey Bill a very moderate one; particularly in view of the huge dishes of baby lobsters that always graced the dinner table, and no-one has learnt what a lobster can really be unless he has had two or three babies of the clan at a sitting. Now, of course, there is a big hotel on the front, boarding houses, bungalows galore, and we dare say a cinema, but 30 years ago Selsey was an undiluted straggling village inhabited by lobster fishermen, and it may be a smuggler or two; a place for a real holiday.'[46]

Eleanor Edge was interviewed by *The Cycle* in 1895, which described her as 'a pretty rider, with an easy and pleasant style of riding, which shows a tall and graceful figure to advantage'.

Within a few years of getting married, SF and Eleanor moved to an apartment in Tavistock Chambers, Bloomsbury, not far from the British Museum, pictured here as it looks today. *Author*

She told the interviewer that she did 'most of my riding on a tandem safety in company with my husband, though I rode a very long way last year on a single' and 'I like cycling immensely, and can compare no other pastime with it. The reason, I think, why it does not become more popular, is because many girls have no one to advise them on the choice of machine, etc.'

Given the frequency of their trips with Smith it would be reasonable to assume that SF and Eleanor were still living in South London. The rest of the family had left England at the time that the 21-year lease of Odessa House ran out, so SF and Eleanor probably were not living there. By 1896 they were living in a flat at 7 Tavistock Chambers, Bloomsbury, but the date on which they moved in is not known.

CHAPTER 3

INTRODUCTION TO MOTORING

1895 TO 1898

'The motor vehicle has dominated the world. It has altered the whole aspect of our lives. It is, in fact, part and parcel of the great order of things which matter and count in our everyday existence.'

Charles Jarrott, writing in 1928

It is generally acknowledged that the development of the first practicable motor vehicles propelled by internal combustion engines was by both Gottlieb Daimler and Karl Benz working independently, in Germany, around 1885. Daimler built a motor bicycle in that year, while Benz built a motor tricycle. Then in 1886, Daimler made a four-wheel vehicle, which was the first practical motor car. The French, however, soon moved ahead in development, and one Frenchman in particular, René Panhard, took the lead. Initially using Daimler engines, Panhard started to build cars around 1891 in the configuration we know well today: radiator in front with engine immediately behind, driving the rear wheels through a clutch and gearbox.

The pneumatic tyre, patented first by Robert William Thomson in 1847 but not developed, then patented again by John Boyd Dunlop in 1888, was being produced for bicycles, as we have seen, by Harvey Du Cros's company, and had even been tried on horse-drawn carriages. Again it was left to the French, and the Michelin brothers in particular, to develop pneumatic tyres for motor vehicles.

The world's first motoring competition (a trial rather than a race) for self-propelled vehicles was held in France in 1894, between Paris and Rouen, a distance of just under 80 miles.[v] The Panhard and Peugeot entries, all powered by 3½hp Daimler engines, tied for first place, and a De Dion steam tractor completed the course at an average speed of 12mph.

Very little was being built in Britain, however, since the Locomotive Act of 1865 (the 'Red Flag' Act) was so restrictive, requiring self-propelled

v Rose points out that a 'competition' had been held in 1887, but only one vehicle took part, a steam quadricycle driven by Count de Dion, so it was not very competitive.

vehicles (mainly steam-driven at the time the Act was passed) to be preceded by a man on foot carrying a red flag, with a speed limit of 4mph (2mph in towns). The Highways and Locomotives (Amendment) Act of 1878 repealed the requirement for a red flag to be carried, but all vehicles still had to be preceded, by at least 20 yards, by someone on foot. Because of these restrictions, SF had still never seen a motor car by the end of 1894 despite the many thousands of miles he had travelled on Britain's roads. However, through his involvement in the cycle trade he had kept in touch with developments and could already see the potential of the motor vehicle, given that pressure was now being put on the Government to amend the legislation. SF had tried, without success, to interest Harvey Du Cros in the commercial possibilities presented, so instead he took matters into his own hands.

A former racing cyclist, Fernand Charron gave SF his first experience of a ride in a car, a Panhard et Levassor, in Paris early in 1895. *The World on Wheels*

1895

SF had previously met, on several occasions, a successful French racing cyclist named Fernand Charron, whom he described as 'a small, dapper little man, with a quick way of talking which gave the suggestion that he was a bundle of nerves'. In 1890 Charron had been the Paris manager of Humber, the cycle manufacturer, but early in 1895 SF heard that Charron had left Humber and was running an agency in Paris selling Panhard et Levassor, Peugeot and De Dion-Bouton cars, in partnership with two other racing cyclists, Léonce Girardot and Émile Voigt.[vi] So in his usual direct manner, SF wrote to Charron in February 1895 asking if he could be given a run in a car if he came to Paris.[47] Charron's reply was very welcoming, so SF lost no time in crossing to France to visit him.

He dined first with his old cycling friend, H.O. Duncan, who was living in Paris. Duncan had not yet driven a car but had ridden on many, and was most enthusiastic about them. He helped SF understand the basic principles of their design and operation, since at that time SF had only superficial knowledge, gathered from reading.

SF met with Charron the following evening. Initially they had great difficulty communicating,

vi In 1901 these three set up their own automobile manufacturing company in Paris, which became known as CGV.

neither knowing the other's language, but Charron soon led SF to the rear of the premises where, for the first time in his life, he saw a motor car.[48] It was a two-cylinder 6hp Panhard et Levassor with tiller steering and pneumatic tyres. SF watched intently as Charron prepared the car for a run. Ignition was by 'hot tube', so burners had to be lit first to heat the igniters, before swinging the starting handle. They then climbed up onto their high seats and Charron took SF for a drive around the streets of Paris for over an hour. SF returned to England the next day, 'convinced that the death-knell of the horse, as a means of locomotion, had been sounded' and determined to advance the cause of the automobile in Britain.[49] But the law was going to have to be changed before this could happen.

SF was not alone in his resolve to introduce the motor car to Britain. There was a growing lobby of individuals committed to the cause, amongst them Harry Lawson. Lawson had been heavily involved in the cycle trade, including transforming the Haynes & Jefferis company in Coventry into the Rudge Cycle Co. He was also involved in the reconstruction of the Dunlop Pneumatic Tyre Company, Ltd, and had taken out a patent for a motor car as early as 27 June 1880.[50] In 1885 he registered the British Motor Syndicate and successfully raised a large amount of capital, which he used to buy up any motor car patent that he could get hold of, with the hope that he could create a monopoly of motor car manufacture in Britain. SF is quoted as saying that Lawson would pay anything for the 'so-called patent rights' to some motoring invention.[51] Lawson raised £150,000 as capital for the British Motor Syndicate Ltd, then bought up the Daimler Motor Co. (which was licensed to manufacture Daimler cars in Britain).

Others furthered the cause in a less commercial way. Sir David Salomons, a keen amateur mechanic, organised a horseless-carriage exhibition at the Agricultural Show Grounds in his home town of Tunbridge Wells on 15 October 1895. Only five self-propelled vehicles attended: Salomons exhibited his own Peugeot, fitted with a Panhard engine; The Hon Evelyn Ellis, one of the first people to import a car into England, a 4hp Panhard that he had purchased four months earlier, brought along his new acquisition; Frederick Simms appeared with a fire engine powered by a Daimler engine; and Marquis Albert de Dion, Baron de Zuylen and Georges Bouton brought a steam tractor and a De Dion-Bouton motor tricycle over from France. To add one more exhibit, Salomons had a bit of fun by removing the horses and pole from a horse-drawn carriage and placing a placard on it with the words 'Horseless carriage, made in England'. Surprise was apparently expressed at the clever way the engine had been concealed and, according to Salomons, no one saw through his practical joke.

As soon as SF heard of the Tunbridge Wells exhibition, he was determined to attend and rode there from London on his bicycle.[52] It was very well attended — some 10,000 invitations had been sent out — and helped further the cause of the motor car in Britain.

The exhibition was followed by a meeting at the Cannon Street Hotel that November at which the Self-Propelled Traffic Association was formed. The political lobbying had been successful and on 17 June 1895 George Shaw-

Lefevre had introduced the Light Locomotives Bill in the House of Commons, emancipating the over-restrictive Locomotive Act of 1865. Unfortunately, Lord Rosebery's Government, of which Shaw-Lefevre was part, was defeated in a motion four days later and resigned before the Bill was passed. So it had to wait until the next session, and it was not until 14 November 1896 that the Locomotives on Highways Act, as it was by then called, became operative. This Act prescribed a maximum speed for motor cars of 14mph but gave the Local Government Board the power to reduce this, which it promptly did, to 12mph, which remained the legal limit until the Motor Car Act of 1903 increased it to 20mph.

1896

Meanwhile, late in 1895 or early in 1896, while still working for Du Cros at the Dunlop Tyre Company, SF had approached Harry Lawson, whose offices were at 40 Holborn Viaduct. Lawson's British Motor Syndicate also had a depot at 366 Euston Road where several cars were kept, including Daimlers, De Dion-Bouton tricycles, Bollée tri-cars, and a 6hp Panhard et Levassor, all in anticipation of the time when they could be legally driven on the roads.[53] Lawson had bought the Panhard et Levassor car that had won the Paris–Bordeaux race in 1895, which was known as 'Old No 5', the number it carried in that race. He went on to buy the three Panhard et Levassor cars that came first (No 6), second (No 8), and third (No 5) in the Paris–Marseille race of 1896. The latter car became known as 'New No 5'. Lawson paid 30,000 francs for each of the four cars.[54]

SF asked Lawson if he could be allowed to work on these cars in his spare time, to gain as much experience of their design and construction as he could. He was surprised to be told by Lawson that another young man had recently asked the same question. So it was that 27-year-old SF and 18-year-old Charles Jarrott met, and soon they were spending much of their time together, working on Lawson's cars. SF would go over to the Euston Road depot after finishing his work at the Dunlop Tyre Company, and work there, with Jarrott, often until the small hours of the morning.

At this time, SF would often spend the weekend as a guest of Du Cros at his house, Cornbury Park, in Oxfordshire, but would otherwise spend his weekends experimenting with Jarrott on the cars at Euston Road. SF recounts how one evening they were refused admission to a nearby restaurant because they were covered in grime from working on the cars, so the two had to walk back to SF's flat to get something to eat. SF later described these days as 'some of the most interesting and enjoyable in my life'. It is doubtful that Eleanor felt the same way.

Lawson organised an International Motor Exhibition at the Imperial Institute[vii] from 9 May to 8 August 1896. Being in the heart of London, this reached a wider audience than Sir David Salomons' exhibition and did much to smooth the passage of the Bill through Parliament. SF attended this exhibition several times and tried out many of the cars. With the experience he had gained, he was also called upon to explain

vii The Imperial Institute was in Exhibition Road, South Kensington, and the buildings now form part of Imperial College, London.

how they worked to some of the onlookers. One of the organisers of this exhibition was Claude Johnson, who later became the Secretary of the Automobile Club of Great Britain and, later still, Managing Director of Rolls-Royce Limited.

On 14 October 1896, SF was initiated as a member of the Freemasons' Upper Norwood Lodge. His fellow cyclist, J.W. Stocks, joined the same lodge a year later.[55]

The coming into force of the Locomotives on Highways Act on 14 November 1896 was celebrated by the Motor Car Club, founded by Harry Lawson, by organising a run from London to Brighton. The run started after breakfast from the Metropole Hotel in Whitehall, with a stop planned for lunch at the White Hart Hotel in Reigate. The cars would then gather at Preston Park in Brighton before forming a procession to the Hotel Metropole, Brighton, where a dinner was to take place, starting at 7pm.

SF, then 28, did not yet own a car but had more than one offer of a seat in a participating vehicle. Instead, however, he decided it would be

Harry Lawson stands beside his wife in the Panhard et Levassor 'Old No 5' outside the Hotel Metropole on arrival in Brighton at the end of the first Emancipation Run in 1896. The car behind is 'New No 5'. *Royal Automobile Club*

better to follow the cars on a bicycle. For this he teamed up with his old friend from cycle racing days, R.J. Mecredy, who was then editor of *The Irish Cyclist* and a director of the Dunlop Tyre Company. Mecredy was later to admit that he had not been an enthusiast for the motor car at this time, but that it was SF who eventually converted him.

No fewer than 58 vehicles were entered for this 'Emancipation' run, which continues to be re-enacted annually in November each year (now with around 500 entrants). These included Panhards, Daimlers (Gottlieb Daimler himself rode as a passenger in one of the cars), Bollées (one driven by Léon Bollée, one by his brother Camille, and a third driven by H.O. Duncan — Lawson had bought the patent rights for Bollées for £20,000, and Duncan was employed by him), Duryeas, Rogers, an Arnold, and a Pennington (driven by Mr Pennington, an American). There were also Bersey and Britannia electric cars, and one 'steam bicycle' (it is difficult to imagine quite how a water tank and boiler could be carried on a bicycle). The Panhard et Levassor cars included 'Old No 5', which had won the Paris–Bordeaux race in 1895, as well as 'No 6', 'No 8' and 'New No 5' which, as mentioned, had finished first, second and third in the Paris–Marseille race in 1896.

At the breakfast at the Metropole Hotel in London, the Earl of Winchelsea dramatically tore up a red flag. SF described the scene outside the hotel as being like a Lord Mayor's Show, with the streets teeming with people, while others were standing on roofs and balconies, or watching from windows.[56] Once the cars had set off, SF and Mecredy followed the procession on their bicycles, passing many of the entrants that had broken down along the way.[57] The two Bollées driven by the Bollée brothers were the fastest, but Duncan in the third Bollée had an unpleasant accident in which his passenger, riding in front, was thrown out into a muddy ditch. The car was severely damaged but the two of them carried on until it began to rain heavily. Rain and grit got into the carburettor and brought their journey to an end. Only ten cars completed the run, Leon Bollée reaching Brighton in 3 hours 45 minutes while the last car to arrive, a Panhard, took 6 hours 22 minutes.

1897

Up to this point, SF had not yet driven a car himself, but in May 1897, some six months after the 'Emancipation' run, he persuaded Lawson to lend him a De Dion-Bouton tricycle to drive to Canterbury and back.[58] He spent many hours preparing the car and set off in high spirits early one morning. His experience as a cyclist helped, and he knew the road well. The machine went very well and, once out of London, he timed himself between two milestones at just over 20mph. He reached Canterbury in time for lunch at the Crown and Mitre. There he met some cyclists who were amazed when he told them he had travelled all the way from London that morning. On the return journey he managed to top up with two quarts of benzene bought at a chemist's shop in Sittingbourne, and he reached home without encountering any difficulties.

SF was so impressed with the De Dion-Bouton on that trouble-free journey to Canterbury that within a day or two he placed an order for one, together with a Coventry Motette.[59] Soon after, he also bought a French Bollée. The De Dion-Bouton was a motorised tricycle, and hence a single-seater, with its engine slung between the rear wheels. The Bollée had two front wheels and one rear wheel. It could carry a passenger in front (more exposed to the elements and 'closest to the accident') and was driven from the rear. The Motette was the English version of the Bollée, manufactured by Lawson in Coventry. SF's was specially built for him with a more powerful motor.

It must have been on his new Motette that a photograph was taken of him with his wife, Eleanor, and a friend that he published in *My Motoring Reminiscences*. *The Autocar* dates this photograph to 1897[60] and Duncan reports that it was taken near Brighton.

SF travelled over 1,500 miles in the De Dion-Bouton in 1897 and described the vehicle as an unqualified success. The Bollée was not always as reliable:[61] Jarrott described it as 'experimental to a great degree, unreliable in every degree, and full of peculiarities'.[62] Soon after SF acquired it, he invited his old friend, G.H. Smith, for a drive to Norwich. Leaving his flat in Bloomsbury, they drove only a few miles before the engine stopped. He swung the starting handle as many times as he could, but with no sign of life from the engine, so as darkness fell they pushed the car into a stable.[63] Next morning SF called on an employee of Lawson, C.H.E. Rush, to come and help. SF describes finding him dressed 'as if he were going to be married', but without changing he willingly turned out to help. It was another five hours before SF and Smith were able to resume their journey to Norwich, leaving a very dirty Rush behind. But they only managed a further two miles before the Bollée skidded and collided with a brick cart. The damage to the car was such that they had to abandon their journey.[64] Smith observed wryly that it had taken them 24 hours to cover five miles.

SF had a similar experience with a Bollée that he borrowed from Jarrott, although it is not clear whether this was before or after the trip with Smith. This time he wanted to take Harvey Du Cros to his home in Oxfordshire. They set out early on a Saturday morning and reached as far as Hounslow, where the engine stopped. Nothing SF could do would persuade it to start. Jarrott recounts that at this time SF was not a skilled mechanic and 'knew but one gospel — "winding"' (cranking the engine with the starting handle).[65] Eventually they had to leave the little car in a stable and proceed to Oxfordshire by other means.

The owner of the stable was insistent that they leave a deposit, so Du Cros had to leave his best overcoat, although the car itself, of course, was worth very much more than the coat. Jarrott heard nothing from them until the Monday morning, when SF telephoned and asked if he could send someone to collect the car. He went out with a mechanic and they found a small piece of grit blocking the carburettor jet: after it was removed they were able to drive it back to London, carrying Du Cros's coat with them.[66]

It was around this time that SF started his regular letter writing to *The Autocar*, which had been first published in October 1895. At this point he had nothing to sell but was keen to pass on his experience to others. One of his early letters included the prophecy: 'To tell you the truth, it has almost made me give up cycling,

➤ SF drives his Coventry Motette in Brighton in 1897. The photo appeared in *The Autocar* of 13 November 1897 and again in the issues of 24 November 1906 and 4 November 1916. It was also published in *The World on Wheels* and *My Motoring Reminiscences*. The passengers are SF's wife Eleanor (left) and a Miss Wright of Upper Norwood. *Royal Automobile Club*

as at present there is a good deal to be learnt in driving these cars… I have absolute faith that we shall see them running about in thousands in a few years' time.'[67]

The Automobile Club of Great Britain, later to become the Automobile Club of Great Britain and Ireland and eventually the Royal Automobile Club, was founded in 1897 by Frederick Simms. The first meeting was held on 10 August 1897 and SF was probably present, as he was recorded as a founder member.[68] The next meeting was held on 8 December 1897 at the Club's new premises at 4 Whitehall Court, preceded by a luncheon at the Hotel Metropole, after which there was 'a demonstration of the most recent types of motor-cars'.[69] Over 20 vehicles — steam, electric and petrol — were demonstrated: SF attended with his Coventry Motette, Simms brought his Cannstadt-Daimler, and the Hon Evelyn Ellis and the Hon Charles Rolls came in British-built Daimlers.

1898

In January 1898, Jarrott and SF made a trip to Brighton, Jarrott in the Panhard 'new No 5', and SF in his Bollée. They left at 8am and reached Brighton by 3pm. They spent some time servicing the cars, and it was not until 7pm that they set off back to London. It was a dark night and Jarrott's car was lit only by candles. Jarrott was

Eleanor Edge pictured in *News of the Wheel* in 1898. *News of the Wheel*

following SF but could not understand why he was not catching up, the Panhard usually being quite a bit faster than the Bollée. When Jarrott eventually caught up, he discovered SF's secret was that whenever he came to a hill he would jump out and run alongside the car. SF was alone while Jarrott had a passenger, so the difference in weight was enough to render the Bollée faster than the Panhard. When Jarrott caught up, however, SF was totally exhausted.[70]

They nevertheless reached the outskirts of London by 11pm, but before reaching home the Bollée broke down. After rolling in the mud under the car they found that the exhaust valve had broken. They found a new valve, albeit of the wrong size, and repaired the car in the street, not setting off again until 2.45am. Near the Mansion House, Jarrott's Panhard emitted two loud backfires and stopped, at which point policemen appeared from all directions, SF speculating that they thought he was trying to blow up the nearby Bank of England.[71] They eventually reached home at 4.30am and enjoyed a hearty meal in SF's flat.

SF arranged to stay at Cornbury Park over Easter that year and persuaded Jarrott to visit in the Panhard 'No 8', which SF was interested in buying. Shortly before arriving, Jarrott turned a sharp corner and came upon a coach full of people travelling in the same direction. The suddenness of his appearance caused the horses to shy and created some confusion. Jarrott then found that SF was one of the passengers, and very happy to jump in the car for the rest of the ride to Cornbury Park. For the journey back to London, SF rode his De Dion-Bouton tricycle while his wife, Eleanor, rode with Jarrott in the Panhard. They had a narrow escape going down Dashwood Hill. The Panhard was on solid tyres and had tiller steering, and the road was muddy with deep ruts. Jarrott lost control in a skid but managed to bring the car to a halt just before going over a drop at the side of the road. However, by the time they reached London, SF had made up his mind to purchase this car.

In July 1898, SF travelled to France again to watch the Paris-to-Amsterdam race. In a letter to *The Autocar* he observed: 'There is no doubt that this motor business will be the boom of the next century, compared to which the cycle era will seem but a small thing' and 'Another thing I noticed was the almost universal use of pneumatic tyres'.[72] Whilst the Dunlop company for which he worked had pioneered the use of pneumatic tyres on bicycles, it had been slow to exploit the potential for their use on cars, believing that the much greater weight would place too much strain on such tyres.

The young Automobile Club of Great Britain organised an autumn tour of the south-east starting on 28 October 1898 in which SF and Eleanor participated in his newly acquired Panhard ('No 8'). They stopped at Maidstone that night, and Hastings the following night, with lunch in Tunbridge Wells before heading home.[73]

In January 1899, SF, Jarrott and Stocks went to watch a play at Drury Lane theatre. Stocks had to return to Birmingham, 110 miles away, that night, so they skipped the last act of the play, and SF and Jarrott volunteered to accompany him part of the way. It was a bitterly cold moonlit night, so they had to put on so many clothes that they could hardly pedal their motor tricycles to start them. The three travelled together for about 50 miles before SF and Jarrott turned back, reaching home at 7am.[74]

CHAPTER 4

EARLY MOTOR TRICYCLE RACES
1898 TO 1901

The first motor race in which SF competed was on 14 November 1898, organised by the Motor Car Club at the old Sheen House track. Charles Jarrott was the Secretary of this club at the time and also competed. This was not the first motor race in Britain because Jarrott had organised a similar event the previous year, in which only he, Duncan, and F.T. Bidlake had taken part.[75] This time SF rode an Ariel motor tricycle, made by a company of which he was a director.[76] He described it as a considerable improvement on his De Dion, with better and quieter gearing.

Three races were run that day. The second was for tricycles only, over a one-mile course, and SF found himself competing against Jarrott and another famous cyclist, C.G. Wridgway. SF won this in 2 minutes 13 seconds, with Jarrott second. Jarrott, as the organiser of a run in the morning as well as the races in the afternoon, had had difficulties with his car on the run, making him late for the meeting. His motor tricycle also gave him problems, and he later claimed that 'had I been riding up to form, I should have won'.[77] The third race was a two-mile event for the Motor

Charles Jarrott, pictured in Motor Car Club uniform, organised the earliest motor races in Britain and competed in them. *Clive Boothman collection*

➤ This is the start of a race during the second race meeting held in Britain, at Sheen House on 14 November 1898. Charles Jarrott (centre) had competed in the first race meeting but SF (right) and C.G. Wridgway (left) were new to it. SF won. The onlookers are mostly quite formally dressed, with a few even sporting top hats. *Mary Evans Picture Library*

Car Club Championship. Competing with SF were Jarrott, Wridgway, Stocks, and Gorton. SF led to start with, pursued first by Wridgway and then by Gorton. In the second half Gorton took the lead for a while, but on the last lap he and SF were neck and neck. SF managed to win by a length in a time of 4 minutes 18 seconds (an average speed of 27.9mph).

This experience left SF 'determined to enter for every such competition which was open to me'.[78] He also realised that he needed to obtain a vehicle that would be competitive.

1899

The next races were in May 1899, at Crystal Palace. SF and Jarrott were hoping to compete on De Dion-Bouton racing tricycles, which they had both ordered from the factory in Paris. Jarrott's arrived about half an hour before the race, but SF's failed to materialise.[79] The only other competitor was Wridgway, whom Jarrott beat by a narrow margin after a fast and hard-fought race.

SF's De Dion arrived soon after and he and Jarrott took the two machines to Paris by rail later in May, hoping to compete in the Paris–Bordeaux race on 24 May 1899. They were both guests of Paris Singer and stayed in his apartment in the Champs Elysées:[80] Paris Singer was the 22nd child (out of 24) of Isaac Singer, of sewing machine fame, and SF had worked with him briefly in 1898 (see Chapter 5). SF's and Jarrott's machines were taken to the factory to prepare them for the race, with SF's car needing more work than Jarrott's. SF, however, went back into Paris and left Jarrott to ensure that his machine was ready in time. The work was not finished until 11pm, so Jarrott got very little sleep before being woken early by SF to get ready for the race. Nevertheless, they both got there in time for the 3.15am start. The starters numbered 37 motorcycles that all set off together in somewhat chaotic fashion and 28 cars that departed 15 minutes later. The instructions to the competitors were brief: 'Gentlemen, this is Paris and there is Bordeaux: there is but one thing for you to do — get there as quickly as you can. Are you ready? Go!'.[81]

SF's motor tricycle was not run-in and started

losing power within five miles of starting, so he had to slow his pace. Jarrott pushed on ahead. SF passed through Tours and reached Poitiers, where it began to rain very hard. Soon after, soaked through, he came across Jarrott pulled up at the side of the road. SF stopped and found that Jarrott's engine had come to a halt in the rain, probably due to shorting of the ignition circuit. When SF tried to start his engine again, he found it was suffering from the same problem. They waited a while for the rain to stop, then decided to try pushing their tricycles to the next village, 11 kilometres away. Soon the rain ceased, and Jarrott found his engine would start, so rode off to the village, leaving a miserable SF to push his machine the entire distance. Jarrott walked back from the village to meet him, having first ordered some food at a café, but SF was unimpressed when he was given nothing more than bread and a bottle 'containing some kind of liquid', which they started to drink. It turned out that the liquid was vinegar.[82]

Both engines were now working, and they set off again for Bordeaux. Some of the villagers, however, were not in favour of these new-fangled noisy machines racing through their tranquil streets and had placed boulders in the road. One of these knocked a hole in the crank chamber of SF's engine, such that it lost all its oil. This took them some time to repair, and they decided to spend the night in Angoulême, reaching Bordeaux without further incident the next day.

The race was won by SF's friend Charron in a Panhard in a time of 11 hours 43 minutes for the 351-mile course, and neither SF nor Jarrott were listed as finishers. Rose's *Record of Motor Racing* does not even record their participation (perhaps feeling the cars were more interesting than the motor tricycles), but this was probably the first continental motor race in which British competitors took part. Jarrott explained that the two of them went over in the spirit of explorers, 'to see whether the sport of motor road-racing was all that had been claimed for it, and whether we could successfully play the game'.[83]

On 1 July 1899, SF took part in a motor tricycle race meeting organised by the Motor Car Club, again at his 'home' venue of Crystal Palace. His rivals were Jarrott, Stocks, Wridgway and six others. The races included one- and two-mile handicaps, a five-mile scratch event and a one-hour contest for the Brassard Cup, the last of which SF was particularly keen to win. He had so many tricycles at that time that he was in a quandary as to which to use for this race, but he eventually settled for the 2¼hp De Dion-Bouton tricycle he had ridden in the Paris–Bordeaux race.

SF won the one-mile handicap in 1 minute 50 seconds with Jarrott second and Wridgway third. In the five-mile race, SF and Jarrott traded the lead for most of the distance and, as the bell sounded for the last lap, SF trailed by 60 yards. Both were pedalling as hard as they could to assist the engines, which was allowed, and SF passed Jarrott on the final turn to win 'by a wheel'. In the two-mile handicap race SF led from the start and won in 3 minutes 28 seconds, with Jarrott again second and Stocks third. SF had won a hat trick so far, but it was still the Brassard Cup that he coveted.

Again, the only serious competition in the hour-long race came from Jarrott, and the lead alternated through the early stages. However, after five miles SF had established an advantage

that he increased over the next five miles, by which time he had almost lapped Jarrott. By the 30th mile, SF had lapped him twice and went on to cover 34 miles 540 yards, which was a new British one-hour record.

SF was understandably extremely pleased with his performance so far, but there was one race remaining, for motorised tandem cycles. These were even more dependent on the degree of pedal assistance that could be provided by the riders. SF teamed up with Jarrott for this one-mile event against only one other competitor in the form of Stocks and Wridgway. The latter pair got off to a good start, but SF and Jarrott passed them on the second lap and won in 1 minute 44 seconds. All in all, SF had had a most successful day and received many congratulations.

The following Saturday, 8 July 1899, at the International Race Meeting at the New Brighton Tower grounds near Liverpool, SF found himself competing against a French 'crack' rider called Henri Béconnais, and was less successful. This

▲ Jarrott (left), Wridgway (centre) and SF at the start of the Motor Car Club Championship at Crystal Palace in 1899. *Alamy*

time SF chose his Ariel tricycle, which by now was fitted with pneumatic tyres, while Béconnais was using a Phoebus-Aster. There was again a one-hour race, in which SF hoped to break his record of the previous week, but after 48 minutes a rear tyre burst. He switched to Jarrott's machine, which happened to be lying idle nearby, but still lost a lot of time to Béconnais, who completed 37 miles 485 yards to SF's 35 miles 470 yards, which was still better than his previous record.

During subsequent weeks there were several more motor races at various cycle tracks, with most being won by SF or Jarrott, who were usually on identical machines.[84]

SF competed against Jarrott one final time in September that year, for the Motor Car Club Championship. It was another closely fought race, but this time Jarrott won — by three inches.[85]

CHAPTER 5
IN BUSINESS
1893-1901

Contrary to how it might seem from the previous chapters, during the closing years of the nineteenth century SF did not spend all his time driving and racing motor tricycles. He was also active in business. As recounted in Chapter 2, after very short spells with the New Howe Machine Company in Glasgow and Rudge & Co in Coventry, he had accepted an offer from Harvey Du Cros in the autumn of 1893 to work for the Dunlop Pneumatic Tyre Company Limited, first as Racing Manager, then as London Manager. SF's appointment proved such a success for the Dunlop Company that Du Cros moved the Head Office from Coventry to London and appointed SF as General Manager.[86]

This is SF's office at 160 Clerkenwell Road, London during his time as General Manager of the John Griffiths Cycle Corporation. *The Wheelman (9 January 1897)*

At this time the company was mainly supplying tyres to the cycle trade. Du Cros had also set up the John Griffiths Cycle Corporation Limited in Dublin at the end of 1893, to establish a foothold in the cycle retail trade and therefore protect the pneumatic tyre business. This company performed poorly in its first two years of operation, losing about two-thirds of its initial capital of £155,000. Against his better judgement, SF agreed to take on the position of General Manager of this company in addition to his responsibilities as the London Manager of the Dunlop Pneumatic Tyre Company. The offices were at 160 Clerkenwell Road, where he was in charge of about 150 employees. Among them was one Harry (H.T.) Vane, manager of the 'travelling department', who went on to hold a key position in SF's own business in the early years of the following century. During this period, SF had tried to persuade Du Cros of the potential of the motor car, and the business prospect it presented. SF had even explored the possibility of the John Griffiths company becoming an agent for importing Roger-Benz cars. However, this was before the Emancipation Act had been passed, and Du Cros's mind was still focused on cycles.

There was a temporary boom in the cycle market at this time, and the John Griffiths company performed well in 1896. However, late that year, SF became seriously ill with rheumatic fever, which the press generally attributed to overwork, and was out of action for three weeks. He had to miss the shareholders' meeting of the John Griffiths company held in Dublin in December 1896, but Du Cros stood in for him and paid tribute to the work he had done. However, the success of the company was short-lived as the cycle boom of 1896 began to fade. When, in February 1898, the Humber company cancelled its agency agreement, the John Griffiths company was forced into liquidation.[87] Humber had been going through its own financial difficulties at the time following a fire at its factory in 1896 and its transition from making cycles to making cars, so it would seem the loss of the agency was no fault of SF.

Harvey Du Cros pioneered manufacture of pneumatic tyres and employed SF from 1893. *The Wheelman (9 January 1897)*

Shortly after his recovery from rheumatic fever, SF spent Christmas at Cornbury Park. On 9 January 1897 the *Irish Field* carried the following report:

> On Christmas Day [SF] was the hero of a most exciting fight with flames at Cornbury Mansion, the country seat of Mr. Harvey Du Cros. As usual, the Du Cros family were holding their Christmas reunion, all the members of the family being assembled, together with a few chosen friends as guests. Most of the party were out riding in the

> park when it was noticed that the woodwork behind one of the fireplaces was in flames, and the ancient mansion was in immediate danger of destruction by fire. Edge, however, at once took in the situation, rushed off for Arthur Du Cros and several wet blankets, and by the aid of a ladder he and Arthur were soon in the blazing planks fighting the flames like trained firemen. Never was a more exciting scene witnessed. All the old racing power and training came back to the two crack cyclists, and they fought the flames as they had often fought out a punishing finish in their racing days. Then Fred Du Cros arrived on the scene, and helped the two in their now winning fight. The flames were soon conquered, and by the time Mr. Du Cros and party arrived back they had nothing to do but listen to tales of 'how we saved the house'. Needless to say, the health of the fire-conquering trio was drunk with great éclat at dinner that night. Congratulations to S.F. Edge on his recovery, and to Mr. Du Cros on the escape of Cornbury from loss.

There had always been some rivalry between SF and Harvey Du Cros's six sons. Duncan says that SF was treated 'as a specially favoured protégé' by the father and was a regular house guest at Cornbury Park.[88] It must be of significance that in *Wheels of Fortune*, a history of the Dunlop company written by one of Harvey Du Cros's sons, Sir Arthur Du Cros, SF is described simply as a 'departmental manager', and that only in a photo caption. With the collapse of the John Griffiths Cycle Corporation, SF returned to the Dunlop company only to find that the work he had been doing previously was now being done by Du Cros's sons, and so he left the company early in 1899.[89] For a few months he devoted his energies to the Sunlight Incandescent Gas Mantle Company, but still kept closely in touch with the developing motor industry.

SF had meanwhile been briefly connected with, and a director of, the Paris Singer company in Clapham in 1898.[90] This was his first involvement with motor car manufacture, albeit abortive. Singer's company was planning to produce a car with a two-cylinder, 4½hp engine, although up to that point it had been making gas engine-driven dynamos. At least one car was made and a detailed description of it was published in *The Automotor Journal* of 16 June 1900, but there is no record of any car having been sold, and the company was wound up by the end of 1900.

As already recounted, before he left Du Cros's employment, SF had been able to purchase, from Lawson, the 6hp Panhard et Levassor known as 'No 8', which had finished second in the Paris–Marseille race of 1896, and which had taken part in the London-to-Brighton drive later the same year.[91] When purchased by SF, it had solid tyres, tiller steering and 'hot-tube' ignition. SF was convinced that there must be a British engineer who could build a car at least as good as 'No 8', so he started to look around. It was Walter Munn, a racing cyclist with whom he had remained in close contact, who suggested that SF contact Montague Napier, a fellow member of the Bath Road Club with whom SF was already acquainted.[92]

Montague Napier was the grandson of David Napier, the founder of D. Napier & Son. The firm had built its reputation making coin-weighing

➢ Harvey Du Cros lived at Cornbury Park, Oxfordshire, where SF was a frequent house guest. *Author's collection*

machines and printing presses but had declined in later years under the management of Montague's father, James, who died in 1895, following which Montague acquired the business from his father's estate. Munn told SF of Montague Napier's skills as a precision engineer and his interest in the motor industry as a means of revitalising his family's business.

SF wrote to Napier and within a few days was visiting the factory in Lambeth. The company was still making coin-weighing machines but Napier had also had a go at making an internal combustion engine for a car. When shown this twin-cylinder water-cooled horizontal engine, SF was unimpressed, and told Napier as much, although he recognised that Napier was 'an engineer of uncommon skill'. SF suggested it would be better to start by trying to improve on cars that were already successful, and for this purpose asked Napier to make modifications to the steering of 'No 8'. This was done to SF's satisfaction, SF describing the difference in driving as 'extraordinary', and he wrote to *The Autocar* recommending all owners of cars with tiller steering to have them converted to wheel steering. SF then asked Napier to make further modifications, to the cooling system and the lubricators.

As SF gave him more and more tasks, Napier's interest in motor cars gradually increased, and he soon asked SF if he could build him a complete engine for 'No. 8'. This was to be a twin-cylinder vertical engine that would differ significantly from the Panhard unit in having electric-spark ignition rather than hot-tube ignition, which Napier refused to contemplate.[93] When the engine had been completed and installed, SF found it, and its new ignition, to be a significant improvement, and became convinced that Napier had all the skills necessary to embark on manufacture of entire cars. Over the next few months, SF persuaded Napier to start production of cars on the basis that he, SF, would purchase all of them. Hence SF in effect became Montague Napier's salesman in a similar way to Charles Rolls becoming Henry Royce's salesman just a few years later, although SF never persuaded Napier to brand his cars as 'Edge-Napiers'.

This is Panhard 'New No 5' with Charles Jarrott at the wheel, accompanied by SF. Like 'No 8', it had been fitted with a steering wheel, pneumatic tyres and electric ignition by Montague Napier. *Royal Automobile Club*

By October 1899, Harvey Du Cros was now heeding SF's earlier advice that the future lay with motor cars, not cycles. SF persuaded him to put up the capital for a new partnership that would operate from Du Cros's premises at 14 Regent Street, London. Thus an announcement was made that a firm to be known as the Motor Vehicle Co would shortly enter the motor trade offering cars made by D. Napier & Son, the new company having contracted to take the entire output of Napier cars for a 'term of years' (although it was to be 1900 before the first Napier made its appearance). Bodies were to be built by Mulliner of Northampton. The new firm also acquired the English agencies for Gladiator and Clément-Panhard cars. It initially employed, in addition to SF, a secretary, a typist, two clerks and two mechanics.[94]

Around the same time, SF, Jarrott and Duncan formed the De Dion-Bouton British & Colonial Syndicate Limited with capital of £10,000 and premises also at 14 Regent Street. SF was Managing Director with Jarrott as Manager.[95] The headquarters of this company soon moved to Brook Street and later to 10 Great Marlborough Street to separate it from SF's other agencies (Gladiators continued to be sold alongside Napiers at 14 Regent Street). This situation, where SF was the sole agent in Britain for competing makes, was to lead to conflicts.

The first order by the Motor Vehicle Company was for three two-cylinder and three four-cylinder Napiers, and one or two Gladiators and Clément-Panhards. The agreement with Napier included a commitment to supply 396 cars by the end of 1904.[96] The price was to be negotiated between SF and Napier, with SF then free to set his own price for sale to the public.

Meanwhile, in November 1899, SF entered his Napier-engined Panhard in a 100-mile trial from London to Oxford and back, organised by the Automobile Club of Great Britain and Ireland. The car performed well, climbing Red Hill, on the Oxford Road, at 11½mph, and Dashwood Hill at 9mph.

A few weeks before this, on 5 October 1899, SF was on his way to an Automobile Club meeting in Whitehall, probably driving 'No 8', valued at £830, when a 'light cart shot out... at a very rapid pace, and [SF's] car could not avoid it'. He had to spend £42 on repairs and sued the owner of the cart for damages. The owner put in a counter-claim for damages to his cart, claiming that SF was 'travelling at a furious rate'. A jury ruled in favour of the cart owner and SF had to pay £15 damages, plus a further £15 to a man who had sustained injuries from being thrown out of the cart.[97]

On 13 November 1899, Lawson's Motor Car Club organised a repeat of the Tour to Brighton that had taken place in November 1896 to celebrate the passing of the Locomotives on Highways Act. SF, in his Napier-powered Panhard 'No 8', was one of the entrants to set off from the Metropole Hotel in London, led by Jarrott in his Panhard. Of the 104 starters, 95 reached Brighton in time for a banquet at the Hotel Metropole, with SF amongst the leaders.

SF was already beginning to realise that the best way to promote sales of the new Napier cars would be to prove that they were equal to those of longer-established foreign manufacturers by entering them in long-distance races on the continent. First, however, it made sense to test the cars on home ground.

1900

As cars were still a rare sight on the roads of Britain, the Automobile Club decided that a major trial covering a large part of the country would increase public awareness at the same time as demonstrating the practicability and reliability of this new form of road transport. The Thousand Mile Trial was planned for the spring of 1900 and most of the work of organising it fell on the broad shoulders of the Secretary of the Automobile Club, Claude Johnson, who went on to become Managing Director of Rolls-Royce Ltd.

SF saw this ambitious event as an excellent opportunity to introduce the Napier car to the public. With the trial due to start on 23 April, Napier's small factory in Lambeth had to work flat out for three months to produce its first car in time. Prior to its manufacture, this car had already been sold to Mr Edward Kennard JP, who was a keen hunter and owned an estate at Market Harborough, Leicestershire. His wife, Mary, was a novelist but also a skilled mechanic. When SF visited them shortly before the trial, he was surprised to find Mrs Kennard in the stable yard in mechanic's overalls busy repairing punctured tyres (the couple already owned a De Dion tricycle and a small Benz).[98] SF had gone to ask whether it would be possible for him to drive the Napier in the trial and he was surprised how readily its owner agreed. Mr Kennard even asked to be allowed to ride as a passenger, to which SF acquiesced, although there was only going to be a temporary two-seater body fitted.

The car was not an exact copy of the Panhard and was fitted with a 9hp engine, complete with electric ignition of course. It left the Napier

◄ To publicise Napier, SF competed in the Thousand Mile Trial of 1900 with a car that had just been sold to Edward Kennard. Here, his wife Mary repairs a puncture with young St John Nixon and Charles Jarrott. *Clive Boothman collection*

factory only five days before the start of the trial and was put through a rigorous programme of testing, which it came through without showing any particular weakness.[99] For reasons lost in the mists of time, the car was christened 'Sir Charles', probably by Mrs Kennard.

At that time there was a 14-year-old assistant, St John Nixon, helping out at 14 Regent Street. His parents had been living in Belvedere Road when the Edges arrived from New South Wales and became good friends with the family. St John's father, Alfred Nixon, had been a long-distance tricycle rider, holding the Land's End to John O'Groats tricycle record for many years.[100] St John was already racing tricycles and motor tricycles quite successfully and, despite his young age, had already been fined for exceeding the speed limit of 12mph on the public roads. He looked after 'No 8' for SF and went almost everywhere with him in the car. SF decided to take the lad with him on the Thousand Mile Trial, throughout which he had to sit on the floorboards, with his feet on the step, since the two seats were already occupied by SF and Edward Kennard.

The Trial started from Hyde Park Corner at 7.00am, Nixon having spent the night at SF's flat in Bloomsbury, and they reached Bristol that evening. SF's cousin, Cecil Edge, was also participating, as a passenger on an Ariel quadricycle driven by J.W. Stocks, as were the Hon. Charles Rolls (driving a Panhard), the Hon. John Scott-Montagu (later Lord Montagu of Beaulieu), Alfred Harmsworth (later Lord Northcliffe) and Herbert Austin (later Lord Austin), amongst other motoring pioneers. The only lady entrant was Mrs Louise Bazalgette,

Competitors in the Thousand Mile Trial assembled beforehand in the Royal Agricultural Hall in Islington, London. *Author's collection (photo by Argent Archer)*

Mrs Louise Bazalgette with her 3hp Benz was the one lady entrant on the Thousand Mile Trial. *Author's collection (photo by Argent Archer)*

although Mrs Kennard followed the proceedings with her chauffeur in a De Dion.

Charles Jarrott, with Harvey Du Cros Junior riding as his mechanic, drove 'No 8' with the Napier engine but had to drop out on the first day due to 'gear-box trouble'.[101] One of the competitors, a Mr Mann driving a Marshall, did not reach Bristol until 11.30pm that first day, with one or two cars arriving after midnight.

In *My Motoring Reminiscences*, SF was at pains to point out the harsh conditions that the competitors encountered. Whilst these days it is easy to cover 1,000 miles within 24 hours in air-conditioned comfort, it has to be appreciated that the crews on this run were utterly unprotected from the elements. Furthermore, most of the roads were unsealed, so they often found themselves driving through clouds of fog-like dust or encountering thick mud. The cars did not carry spare wheels, so when a puncture occurred, which happened frequently, the tyre had to be removed and the puncture repaired by the roadside. There were no dynamos fitted to the engines, so cars with electric ignition required replacement batteries from time to time. Lighting was generally by candles, with paraffin lamps considered a luxury. Engines frequently overheated, and starting them (by cranking) was often difficult. Gear-changing was also tricky and braking unreliable. When going up a hill near Peebles, SF missed a gear-change and his Napier began to roll backwards. In the words of St John Nixon, 'Edward Kennard got his foot under a certain part of my anatomy, ballooned me out on to the road and jumped for life.' But SF stuck at the wheel and managed to steer the car backwards until the bottom of the hill was reached.[102]

The second night was spent in Manchester, the route having passed through Birmingham, Matlock, Buxton, and Macclesfield. Subsequent nights were spent in Kendal, Carlisle and Edinburgh, before turning back towards London on 4 May, via Newcastle, Leeds, Sheffield and Nottingham. Of the 65 cars that had started on 23 April, 35 reached London on 12 May.[103] One-day exhibitions had been organised in the major cities passed through, with proceeds being donated to the Transvaal War Fund, the Boer War in South Africa (1899–1902) then being at its height.

'Sir Charles' completed the distance, although not without minor breakdowns. Between Birmingham and Manchester, the engine's speed governor broke, after which Nixon had to control the engine speed with a wire gripped in his hand.[104] In Manchester, the aluminium carburettor broke in two and Montague Napier had to travel from the factory by train and repair it with copper wire and Plaster of Paris.[105] Then in St Albans, shortly before reaching London, the forward-and-reverse lever jammed. While SF removed the top of the gearbox, Nixon was sent to a blacksmith's shop to borrow a crowbar with which to free the gears.

After the finish, the surviving cars were driven to Crystal Palace, where the awards were presented. Since the event was a trial and not a race (the speed limit of 12mph could not be exceeded on public roads) there was not a winner as such, but Charles Rolls was awarded the Gold Medal for 'the most meritorious performance, irrespective of class'. The Napier came first in its class (for privately owned vehicles selling for between £300 and £500) and was awarded a medal by the Automobile Club de France for the second-best performance overall.[106] The Thousand Mile Trial

clearly achieved its objective of demonstrating to the British public the potential of the motor car, which it did far more effectively than the original Emancipation Run of four years earlier.

The first four-cylinder Napier was delivered not long after the end of the Thousand Mile Trial.[107] This car became the subject of a bet between SF and a certain Mr Otter. The latter wagered £50 that no car could ascend Porlock Hill in Somerset, which had a gradient of mainly one in six, but on some corners was one in four.[108] The condition was that Mr Otter would accompany the car on a horse and that the Napier should carry one passenger. In the event, SF was accompanied by his friend, F.T. Bidlake, and a mechanic, and left Mr Otter and his horse far behind as the Napier stormed up the hill.

SF subsequently entered this car in the Paris–Toulouse race held in July 1900. He and

▲ SF repairs a puncture during the Thousand Mile Trial. Looking on is Mary Kennard, who was following the Napier in her own car, and at the back is St John Nixon *Motoring Picture Library, National Motor Museum*

▼ The Motor Power Co., Ltd. had an agreement with Napier to sell all the cars it could produce. *The Autocar (14 July 1900)*

Napier Motors and Cars

8 BRAKE HORSE-POWER MINIMUM GUARANTEED.

ENGINES CAN BE DELIVERED RAPIDLY.

Definite dates of delivery given for Cars by arrangement.

THE MOTOR POWER CO., LTD.,

14, REGENT STREET, LONDON, S.W.

Sole Directors: HARVEY DU CROS and S. F. EDGE.

James Gordon Bennett Jnr, proprietor of the *New York Herald*, offered a trophy for an annual motor race, the first of which was organised by the Automobile Club de France in 1900. *The Autocar (6 July 1903)*

Montague Napier were already thinking of entering the Gordon Bennett race in 1901 and felt that useful experience could be gained by competing in this earlier event. SF was pleased that he was able to persuade the young Charles Rolls, well before his involvement with Rolls-Royce, to be his mechanic.[109] This was the first time a British-built car had been entered in an international race. However, on their way to the start at 3am, a pipe connecting the water jackets cracked and they had to seek the services of a local blacksmith, arriving at the start 45 minutes late. The car performed well for the first 40 kilometres, after which the engine started to lose power, running on three cylinders only.[110] The pair soon abandoned the race and made their way back to Paris. SF realised that a very different vehicle would be required if he were to compete successfully in the Gordon Bennett race, and Napier agreed to build such a car.

James Gordon Bennett Jnr was a wealthy American, proprietor of the *New York Herald*, founded by his father, who offered a trophy in an attempt to encourage other countries to compete with the dominant French manufacturers. The first race was organised by the Automobile Club de France and was held in June 1900, not long after the Thousand Mile Trial. One of the rules was that every part of a competing car should be manufactured in the country in which the car was built, and it was recognised at an early stage that British-made tyres were not as dependable as those made in France. SF did not enter this 1900 Gordon Bennett race, although it is likely that he went to watch it because he described it in some detail in *My Motoring Reminiscences*.[111] Five cars started: three French Panhards driven by René de Knyff, Fernand Charron and Léonce Girardot; a Belgian Snoeck-Bolide driven by Camille Jenatzy; and an American Winton driven by Alexander Winton. The contest was run between Paris and Lyons, a distance of 354 miles, and saw many accidents. Only two cars finished, both Panhards, and Charron was declared the winner at an average speed of 38.6mph.[112]

In July 1900, SF entered a 16hp, four-cylinder Napier in a hill-climbing contest organised by the English Motor Club at Tilburstow Hill, just south of Godstone, Surrey.[113] The Napier was described as a racing car, with a sales price of £1,300. He had also entered a 6hp De Dion tricycle, driven by the young St John Nixon, and a 2¾hp Ariel tricycle. Jarrott was competing on a 6hp De Dion tricycle and G.H. Smith was there on an Empress 2¾hp tricycle, amongst others. There were only two other cars (as opposed to motor tricycles) competing and SF achieved fastest time, climbing the hill at a speed of 18.39mph.[114]

In November 1900, SF watched a trial at Crystal Palace in which two Decauville cars were entered, one of which completed 1,000 kilometres non-stop, while the other covered 1,000 miles in 48 hours. SF described, with great sympathy for the drivers, the monotony of driving around this small track of three laps to the mile in freezing conditions, but perhaps this gave him the idea for his 24-hour record to be described later.[115]

SF relates an anecdote of an event that took place in the winter of 1900. On a 'perishingly cold' day he drove to Brighton, with Nixon and his sister as passengers. On the return journey, at night, they passed a group of 'country yokels', one of whom picked up a large piece of ice and threw it at SF, hitting him on the head. SF leapt off the car and, throwing off his heavy clothes as he ran, chased after the culprit, eventually catching him cowering behind a haystack. SF decided to make him take off his clothes — jacket, waistcoat and trousers — and asked his name. Driving off with the clothes, he met another group of 'yokels' a few miles down the road, stopped, and asked if they knew Bill Giles. When they confirmed that they did, SF threw the clothes at them, asking them to return them, and drove off with no further explanation.[116]

Jarrott told of a similar incident. He was driving a voiturette with two friends as passengers and J.W. Stocks was driving a quadricycle with SF as passenger. On an open country road, Jarrott passed a horse-drawn trap travelling in the opposite direction, the driver of which deliberately lashed out at Jarrott with his whip. Jarrott turned the car around and saw the driver of the trap also lash out at Stocks and SF. Both cars pursued and overtook the trap, the driver of which was given a good beating, while his passenger ran off into the fields.[117]

1901

Just a few months after the Bill Giles incident, in March 1901, SF was being driven in a car to Brighton when it passed through a crude speed trap set up by the police. A measured distance had been marked out on the road and the car's passing was timed with a stopwatch. From this, the police calculated the car's speed at 22mph at a time when the speed limit was 12mph. The police were unable to stop the car but must have recognised SF, so he was charged on two counts: failing to stop when asked to do so by two police officers and exceeding the speed limit. SF had to hire a prominent lawyer, Staplee Firth, who was able to convince the magistrate that SF was not the driver, and SF was awarded £5 in costs.[118]

At this time, SF and Eleanor were still living at 7 Tavistock Chambers, Bloomsbury, with Jarrott as their lodger.[119] Built in 1888, Tavistock Chambers still stands today, close to the British Museum.

It was at around this time that SF first became interested in motor boats, and had a boat made for him by Saunders and fitted with one of the early 16hp four-cylinder Napier engines. The boat was moored at Southampton, and whenever he had the opportunity, SF would drive there from London, take the boat across to Cowes, and spend the weekend there with friends.[120]

The Paris–Bordeaux Race, 1901

As a French team had won the first Gordon Bennett race in June 1900, it fell to France, under the rules, to organise the following year's event. The Automobile Club de France duly decided that it should be run concurrently with a race from Paris to Bordeaux, in May 1901.

Napier had planned to enter four cars, but in the end only one was ready in time. SF described the car, seemingly sarcastically, as 'being built by Napier, solely on his own ideas of what a successful racing car should be'.[121] It was rated as 50hp, could carry 14 gallons of water and 50 gallons of petrol, and, according to SF, weighed a massive 3¼ tons. Earlier, in April 1901, SF had written one of his many letters to *The Autocar* stating:

> Mr. Napier and I are spending a great deal of time and money to try and make Napier motor carriages that will bring back to us the Gordon Bennett Cup from abroad. We shall build carriages not only for this year's race, but immediately these carriages are on the road, fresh ones will be put in hand for next year's race and for the Nice race. But we do not want our friends to applaud us before we have done something to applaud. We are spending the money and doing the work, and if we succeed, we shall only be too pleased for every Englishman to take credit of an English car winning the great automobile race of the world, whether it be this year or five years hence.[122]

To qualify for the Gordon Bennett Trophy, the cars had to be 'entirely constructed and all their parts manufactured in the country which such cars represent'.[123] SF had suspected at an early stage that they would not be able to find tyres in Britain that could cope with such a heavy car. There were limited opportunities to road test the car in England, given the 12mph speed limit, but the tyres gave so much trouble when driving the car to Paris for the start of the race that SF and Montague Napier, who was riding as mechanic, decided to fit French tyres.[124] Thus, they could compete only in the 'open' Paris–Bordeaux race and not for the Gordon Bennett Trophy. In the event, only three cars competed in the Gordon Bennett race, all French: two Panhards and a Mors.

In the open race, SF was fourth to be flagged off (after the three Gordon Bennett competitors), at 4.15am on 9 May 1901, with cars leaving at two-minute intervals. At Chartres, SF was lying fifth but by the time he reached Tours he had fallen back to seventh. There they met Charles Jarrott and Harvey Du Cros Junior, who had driven from England in a Panhard to watch the race. SF's cousin, Cecil Edge, was also there as 'crew' and fed SF with sponge cake, while H.O. Duncan was there as a reporter for *The Autocar*.[125] Jarrott described Montague Napier as not being 'in that robust state of health which made starting a huge

➢ In 1901, SF raced the 50hp Napier in two major continental events, Paris–Bordeaux and Paris–Berlin, within a few weeks of each other. He is pictured in Paris a few days before the start of the race to Berlin. *The World on Wheels*

engine like that fitted to the Napier a pleasure' and had to assist him in restarting it.[126] The engine was fitted with a huge lever to start it, in place of the usual crank handle, and it still took the robust Jarrott 20 minutes of tugging on it before the engine eventually roared into life.

Not long after, SF had to retire with a worn-out clutch. As SF and Napier sat in the stranded car, SF told Napier that there was no point going to the expense of producing a huge car capable of speed if it were impossible to utilise that speed.

The pair had had a narrow escape in the race when approaching an unexpected turning at some speed. SF tried to declutch but found that an oil can had become wedged beneath the pedal. He did get round the corner, but on two wheels. Montague Napier never took part in a race again!

Only one car completed the Gordon Bennett race, a Panhard driven by Léonce Girardot, while Henri Fournier won the open race in a Mors.

The Paris-Berlin Race, 1901

SF competed again a month later in the Paris–Berlin race, which took place between 27 and 29 June 1901, in the same 50hp car that he had driven in the Paris–Bordeaux race. This time Jarrott also took part in a Panhard owned by Harvey Du Cros, and Charles Rolls drove a Mors. They started from Champigny, just outside Paris. SF started some time after Jarrott and caught up with him within about 80 kilometres, being timed at 69mph over a flying kilometre on this stretch. When Jarrott had to turn round to pick up his mechanic, Smits, who had been thrown out of the car on a sharp corner, SF was able to pass him![127] However, soon after that, when overtaking another car in a cloud of dust, SF hit a wall and broke one of the

Napier's springs, so had to pull out without even completing the first stage.[128]

From Sedan, where his race had ended just before he reached the Belgian border, SF wrote the following to Montague Napier. The letter is reproduced verbatim since it provides a good picture of the challenges and risks a racing driver (and his mechanic) had to face:

> The car went excellently and, prior to my puncture, I overhauled several who had started in front of me, not counting Panhards — about five, I think, including Jarrott, who had started half an hour before I left. Then my troubles began.
>
> I punctured when going at top speed. My cover ran down the road in front of me and my air tube went to roost in a tree. Before I could pull up I had run some distance on the rim with the result that it was badly dented. We took 34 minutes to bodge it sufficiently to take the cover at all. After this I had no less than four nails through the cover (all the same cover) near side back, and all different nails. We patched all, however, and went on serenely with very few cars in front. In fact, as I write four hours later, they are passing through fast.
>
> Have just heard that G. Hourgières on a Mors has been killed on the frontier — ran into a wall around the corner [this turned out to be a false alarm — Hourgières survived]. Can quite believe it, as, although the corners were well marked and the whole

SF and the 50hp Napier attract a crowd during the Paris–Berlin race. Charles Rolls, another competitor, is standing close to SF, wearing a beret. *Clive Boothman collection*

thing splendidly organised, many parts are bad for racing — up and down mountains around right-angled corners, etc. We did not suffer very much from these obliquities as, being so fast on the straight, we could afford to go reasonably around the bends, although after our tyre-bowling episode we had to be careful as the cover was only held in the rim in places.

Our great disaster, however, occurred just outside here. We overtook a car, passed it in the dust and struck the wall of a bridge. I broke my back spring, which I am trying to get repaired. Have just been told that Fournier ran over a man at Rheims and that the latter is dead. I can quite believe it, as the people stood in the road in solid blocks while we approached them at 70 miles per hour and divided before us as a London crowd divides before the Lord Mayor's Show. It was really quite 'off'! I found Jarrott at one place face to face with a wall. Do not quite know why, but there seemed no harm done, so did not stay to enquire what he was bowing to. Shall hear later.[129]

▲ Dashwood Hill near High Wycombe was the scene of one of SF's two hillclimb class wins achieved with the 50hp Napier in the summer of 1901. *Clive Boothman collection*

The race was again won by Henri Fournier on a Mors at an average speed of 44.1mph over 687 miles. Jarrott came in 10th on his Panhard at an average speed of 36.1mph, and Rolls finished 29th.[130]

In between these two continental races, SF entered the 50hp car in two hill-climbing contests, to which it was more suited. The car performed well at both events, at Tilburstow Hill on 6 June and Dashwood Hill on 6 July, winning its class. It climbed Tilburstow at 38mph,[131] compared with the 18mph he had achieved in the 12hp Napier a year earlier.

SF was back in France in November, when the 50hp Napier won its class at the Gaillon hill climb in a time of 1 minute 3 seconds, beating the nearest competitor, a 40hp Panhard, by 10 seconds.[132] The French manufacturers were beginning to realise they had to take British competitors seriously.

Before the end of the year the 50hp car was scrapped and the engine put into a boat.[133] A lighter car was going to be needed for 1902.

The 'Glidden Tour'

Before we leave 1901, mention should be made of the 'Glidden Tour', which provides an example of SF's success as a salesman, and the lengths to which he would go to ensure customer satisfaction. Charles Glidden was an American who, having made his fortune from a telephone and telegraph business, retired in 1901 at the age of 43.[134]

On 9 July 1901 he took delivery of a 16hp Napier. He was planning a round-the-world tour, and while still in America had been impressed by reports of the first Napier car's performance in the Thousand Mile Trial. By August he was driving it in France when the engine started losing power. SF wasted no time sending a mechanic out to France with the necessary spares to repair the engine.[135]

Satisfied by the service received, Glidden ordered a second Napier, and this time SF convinced one of his employees, Charles Thomas, to ride with Glidden as he continued his world tour. Thomas had only just returned from a year in India where he had delivered a Napier to the Maharajah of Balrampur, staying on to teach the owner and many of his retinue to drive, so SF had to use all his powers to persuade Thomas to set off again.[136]

The 1902 Napier was replaced in 1903 with a more powerful 24hp model and over a five-year period (1901–06) Glidden and his wife travelled around the world, covering over 46,000 miles in Napiers in 39 different countries including Australia, Canada, China, India, Japan, Sweden and the United States. Part of this distance in Canada and the United States was covered on railway tracks, the Napier having been fitted with specially made flanged steel wheels. Thomas rode with them most of the time, returning home only for occasional short breaks, during one of which he got married.

SF made maximum use of the publicity gained from this tour, which Glidden was reporting on directly to the *Boston Globe*, and on 10 September 1906 a luncheon was given in Glidden's honour by SF and Montague Napier at the Café Royal in London.[137]

The achievements of the 'Glidden Tour' were highlighted in a sales brochure issued by S.F. Edge, Ltd in 1911.
Author's collection

46,000 Miles Twice Round the World in a Napier Car.

The Best Possible Proof of Suitability for the Colonies and Abroad.

The longest Reliability Record ever Established

Not over the smooth main roads of Europe, but over the roughest tracks in all parts of the world, and many thousands of miles away from the factory.

Mr. Glidden in India.

Mr. Glidden in Burmah.

Reproduction of Letter and Certificate from Mr. C. J. Glidden.

[COPY.]

S. F. EDGE, Limited,
14 New Burlington Street,
London, England.

HOTEL SOMERSET,
BOSTON, MASS.

Gentlemen,

Having completed my tour of the world with the Motor Car, started from London in 1901, I cannot close this great incident in my life without highly commending the wonderful performance of the Napier Car.

The journey covered the better part of eight years of travel, on which I was accompanied by Mrs. Glidden.

The Napier was transported unpacked on twenty-six steamers.

To make the drive of 46,528 miles in 39 countries, I have motored 377 days, twice encircling the Globe, crossing the Arctic Circle in Sweden, and reaching the most southerly road in the world in New Zealand.

Changing the wheels to steel rimmed wheels suitable to run upon the rails, I drove my Napier from Minneapolis to Vancouver and Chicago to Mexico over the following railway lines :

Road.	Miles.
Soo & Canadian Pacific	1,803
Rock Island	3,300
Fort Worth & Denver	82
International Great Northern	837
National Lines of Mexico	753
Total ...	6,775

The miles driven in each country are as follows :

	Countries	Miles		Countries	Miles
1	Afridis	41	21	Holland	435
2	Annam (crossed frontier)		22	Hongkong ..	170
			23	Ireland	1,510
3	Australia	2,109	24	India	4,345
4	Austria	627	25	Italy	1,253
5	Bavaria	295	26	Japan	1,122
6	Belgium	160	27	Java	1,250
7	Bohemia	315	28	Mexico	753
8	Burmah	509	29	Monaco	35
9	Canada	1,251	30	New Zealand ...	1,145
10	Ceylon	1,334	31	Scotland	1,458
11	China	308	32	Spain	30
12	Cochin China ...	652	33	Straits Settlements	303
13	Denmark ...	306	34	Swat	21
14	Egypt	640	35	Sweden	1,540
15	England	3,976	36	Switzerland ...	1,097
16	Fiji	200	37	Syria	797
17	France	5,495	38	United States ...	7,977
18	Germany ...	1,546	39	Wales	549
19	Greece	944			
20	Hawaii	30		Total ...	46,528

Miles not included in the above would bring the total up to 50,000 of which the Car in your Garage has performed the last 40,000. On this remarkable drive over mountains, through jungles, rivers, and for many miles on roads simply staked out, no accidents have occurred nor has there been over one hour's delay on the road.

The Napier daily carried safely its heavy load of passengers and baggage to the intended place of rest for the night.

Very truly yours,
(Signed) CHARLES J. GLIDDEN.

CHAPTER 6

THE GORDON BENNETT VICTORY 1902

In 1902 the race for the Gordon Bennett Trophy was again to be run simultaneously with a longer event, this time from Paris to Vienna. It would take place over four days, from 26 to 29 June 1902, and the route would pass through Basle, Zürich, Bregenz, Innsbruck and Salzburg, with the Gordon Bennett race ending at Innsbruck, 387 miles from Paris. The regulations for 1902 imposed a weight limit for the cars of 1,000kg.

It was already clear to SF from the problems encountered when racing the 50hp Napier that a successful car would need to be designed around the capabilities of the tyres, which, for the Gordon Bennett races, still had to be British-made. Montague Napier gave this a lot of thought, with SF's involvement, and designed a new car for the 1902 race. This was to have a shaft driving the rear axle in place of the sprockets and chains of the 1901 car, and the whole car, with its four-cylinder engine of 6½ litres, weighed in at just 933kg.[138]

Unfortunately, the new car was not ready until 19 June, just seven days before the start of the race, leaving very little time for testing and fixing any faults.[139] The car was booked on a boat from Folkestone to Boulogne leaving at 11.30am on 24 June, and the mechanics at the Lambeth factory worked through the night getting it ready for the team to depart before it was light. This time SF's cousin, Cecil Edge, was to ride as mechanic, but Napier also came with them to Paris. The three of them travelled on the car together with numerous spare tyres, spare parts and tools.[140]

As they neared Folkestone, they encountered their first problem. On investigation they found one of the cylinder heads had cracked and water was pouring into the engine.[141] Napier was certain that there was no spare cylinder head at the factory and booked himself straight into a hotel. SF, however, managed to telephone the factory and discovered that there was one. Two mechanics were sent with the spare on the first train, the car was hoisted onto the deck of the boat, and the mechanics succeeded in replacing the cracked cylinder head before they reached Boulogne.

Wisely Napier asked one of the mechanics to accompany them to Paris (quite where he sat is not clear). Before they even got to Paris, they came to a halt again: this time it turned out the second gear pinion had bent teeth, apparently due to failure to case-harden it before fitting.[142] They drove into Paris using first and third gears only and parked in a stable. While SF and his cousin got some rest, Napier and his mechanic removed the offending gear, took it to the factory of SF's friend, Clément, straightened up the teeth and case-hardened it. This took them the whole night, and SF had little time to get to the weighing-in station. Having passed the scrutineering, SF was on his way to the weighbridge when Napier ran up to him and told him that when rebuilding the gearbox they had left out a spacer, such that it would be possible to engage two gears simultaneously.[143] So a second night had to be spent in the stable while the gearbox was stripped down and rebuilt. The race was due to start at 3am and they only just had time to pick up some food, which they could eat on the way. Within minutes of reaching the starting point they were off.[144]

Only four cars were competing for the Gordon Bennett Trophy, and they started first. SF's Napier was the only British car amongst the starters, lined up against the French team of three: René de Knyff on a Panhard, Henri Fournier on a Mors, and Léonce Girardot (winner of the 1900 race) on a CGV.[145] Two Wolseleys were meant to make up the British team of three but only one (driven by Herbert Austin) made it to the starting line, and that very late.[146] In the open race, Charles Jarrott was the only British driver, competing in a Panhard.

To SF's surprise, after so many problems, the car went well and kept up a good speed for

A new 40hp Napier was built for SF's attempt to win the Gordon Bennett Trophy of 1902 and was rather lighter than the 50hp version that he had campaigned the previous year. *Clive Boothman collection*

200 miles, but at that point one of the rear tyres punctured. This was not unexpected and they got to work replacing the inner tube (they were not carrying a spare wheel, so had to remove the cover and fit a spare tube) but then to their horror they could not get the tyre pump to do its job. Their only chance was to stop the next competitor to see if they could borrow a pump, but they were concerned that no competitor would want to be delayed in that way. They were in luck, since the next car along, which SF flagged down, was a Mercédès driven by Count Louis Zborowski who, rather than waiting for them to pump up the tyre, just gave them the pump. SF described Zborowski as the 'Prince of good sportsmen'.[147]

After just over six hours, they reached the first 'neutralised zone' (resting place) at Belfort, where they were able to get their first proper sleep since leaving Lambeth two days earlier. Of the Gordon Bennett competitors, de Knyff was ahead (4 hours 18 minutes) and first overall in the open race, but Girardot had dropped out early as had Fournier a bit later when a gear-shaft broke in his Mors. At this point SF was 11th overall.

Motor racing then was a very different sport from the Grand Prix racing of modern times. There were no support cars (Montague Napier had to travel to Paris in the passenger seat of the racing car, with Cecil Edge crouched on the floor) and no pit crews, although SF had made some

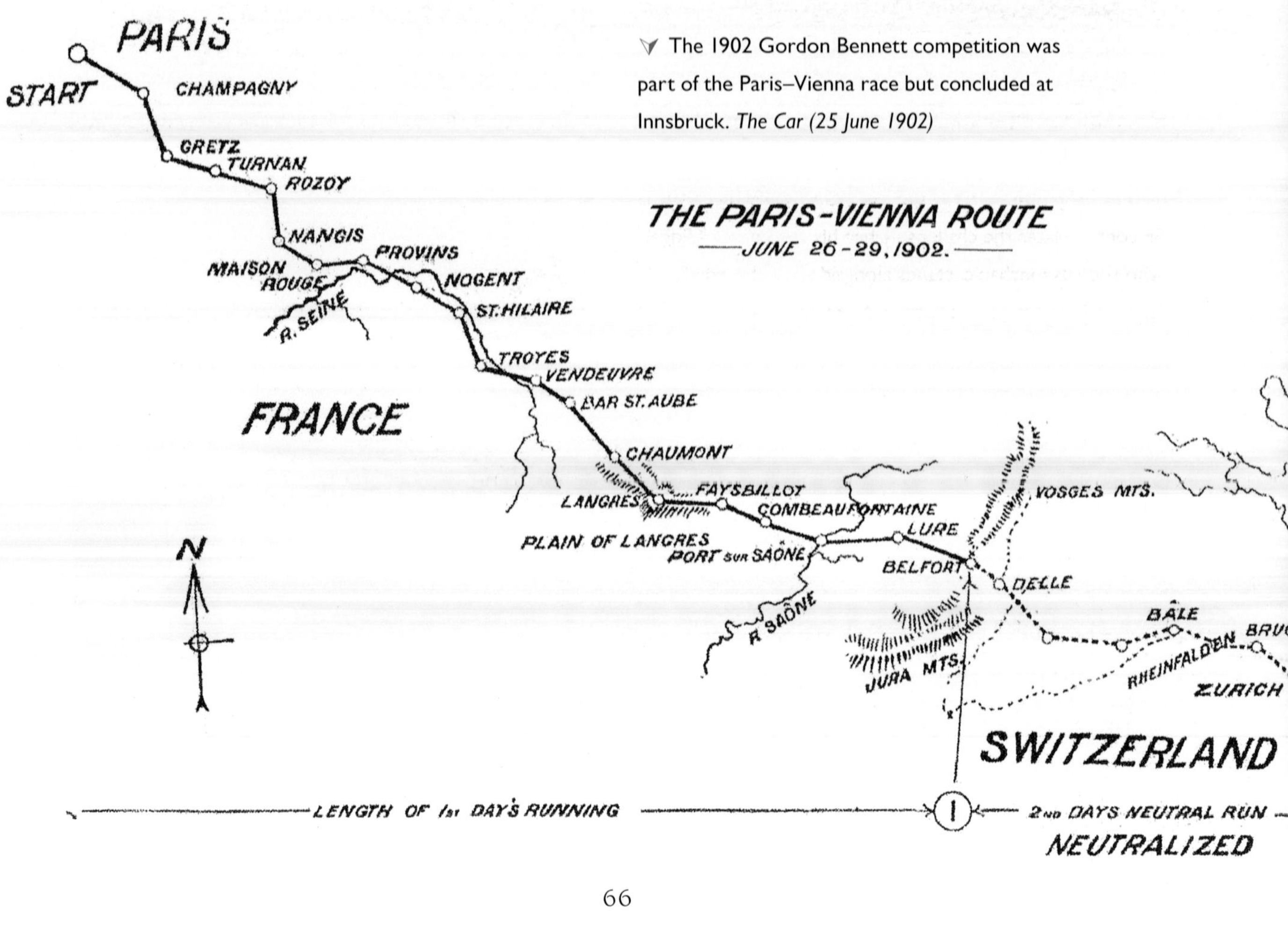

The 1902 Gordon Bennett competition was part of the Paris–Vienna race but concluded at Innsbruck. *The Car (25 June 1902)*

Just before the start of the 1902 Gordon Bennett race, SF contemplates the challenge while his cousin Cecil Edge, who rode as mechanic, stands alongside. The bearded figure behind the car is probably Montague Napier.
Motoring Picture Library, National Motor Museum

arrangements for spare tyres to be delivered along the route. Other than that, they had to do their own navigation, buy their own food along the way, and carry out their own repairs. Strange as it seems today, no prior arrangements had been made for hotel accommodation in Belfort. The Edges found that all hotels were fully booked, and after a lengthy search, were eventually accommodated in an attic over a shop in which 'a large number of hams were in process of curing'.[148] They had no alarm clock so had to tip a local policeman to wake them up at an early hour by throwing stones at their window.[149]

They woke to find all four tyres of the Napier flat, so had to fit new inner tubes before starting. The next stage, to Bregenz in Austria, was 'neutral' (non-competitive), and they again had a trouble-free run, driving all the way in top gear.[150] SF now knew that Fournier and Girardot had dropped out but realised that his only chance of winning was if de Knyff's car broke down and the Napier somehow reached Innsbruck. Their confidence was on the up, but little did they know what was in store for them. Ahead lay the Arlberg pass in Austria. SF was less worried about the long climb up than he was about the descent since the brakes on the Napier had been steadily deteriorating. He was also still worried about whether the repaired second gear would hold out.

In Bregenz they were again left to their own devices: neither of them could speak German, there was no support team and no assistance from the race organisers, so they had again to wander around the town looking, unsuccessfully, for a hotel with a bath, which they were desperately keen to have. They had to settle for a room with a washbasin. They met Jarrott, who was having great trouble with his Panhard, the frame of which had broken. Jarrott and his mechanic, George Du Cros, managed to buy some steel bolts and an auger but could not buy any wood, so they spent the night breaking up their bedroom furniture and drilling it ready to be used to strengthen the frame of their car.[151]

The next morning SF and Cecil again found all tyres flat.[152] After replacing the inner tubes they set off for the Arlberg pass. On the way up, on the winding road cut into the side of the mountain, they passed several competing cars that had broken down.[153] On the way down the brakes turned out to be useless and SF frequently had to change down into first gear to slow the car. Every 50 yards or so there was a flat stretch of road to allow horses to rest on the way up, and SF described the descent as resembling 'coming down a flight of stairs'.[154] SF was worried that this would break the frame of the Napier. Partway down they passed an abandoned Panhard but could not make out whose car it was. At the bottom they stopped to check whether anything was broken and were horrified to find that 'the whole back part of the body had vanished'.[155] All their tools, spare parts and spare inner tubes were lost. While pondering over this they were passed by Jarrott and George Du Cros, who gave them the good news that the broken-down Panhard they had passed on the descent was de Knyff's, so all they had to do to win the Trophy was to reach Innsbruck, 30 miles away.

They found that they still had spare outer tyres (covers) although the spare inner tubes were lost. SF decided that, as there was no longer any time pressure, it would be worth fitting the new covers to protect the inner tubes and give them the best

▲ SF waves to onlookers after his victory with Cecil Edge in the 1902 Gordon Bennett race. *Motoring Picture Library, National Motor Museum*

chance of lasting through to Innsbruck. The problem was that they had no jack and no tyre levers. They had to pull the covers off the rims with their bare hands while rolling the car forward a bit at a time as they could not lift the wheel off the ground. The same process was followed as they put the new covers on. Their hands were 'torn to pieces and were bleeding when the work was done', and SF later described the struggle as 'the greatest and most dramatic' in his 40-odd years of motoring.[156] But it was worth it since they then motored on without incident to Innsbruck, where they were given a great reception.

Later, however, attempts were made to disqualify SF on the grounds that he had received assistance from some French peasants along the way. Accounts vary, and there may even have been more than one incident. Duncan, writing sometime after the event but apparently quoting SF, records: '...we flew off the road into a field. We got down from the car and drove off some people who wished to push it up a bank. We found that no damage had been sustained except that the water tank had had its connections broken. We wired these up as well as we could and got along happily again.'[157]

The Motor, in an article on 'lucky escapes' in March 1930, told a different story, although the

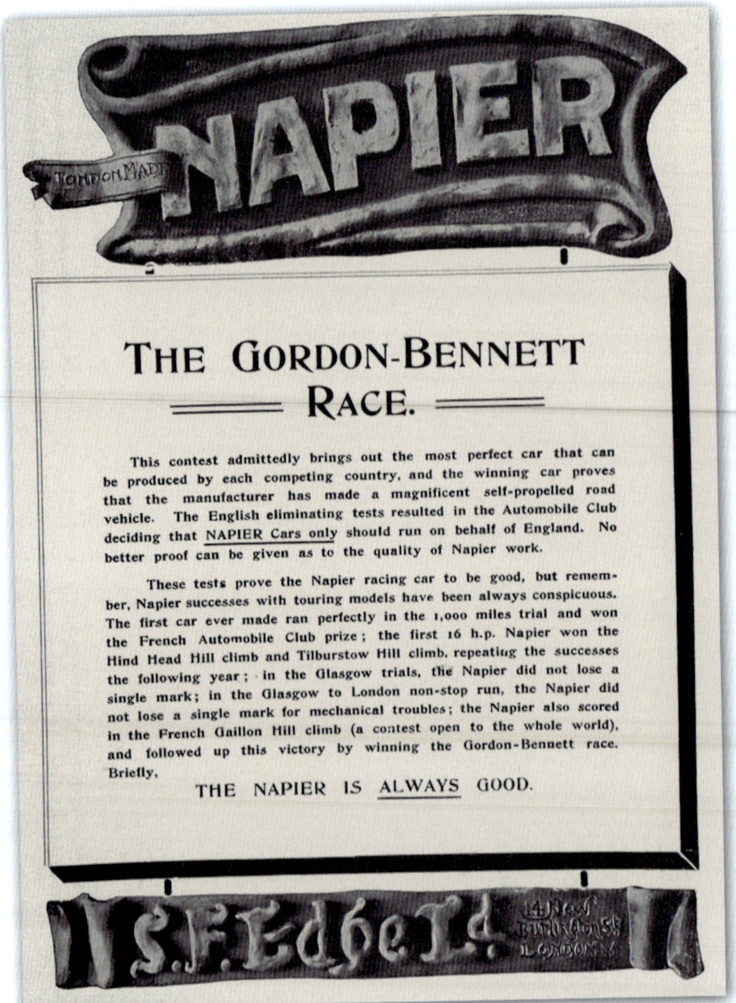

This published illustration was captioned: 'S.F. Edge, who brought the Gordon Bennett Cup to this country.' *Author's collection*

SF issued an advertisement with particularly eye-catching graphics after the Gordon Bennett victory. *gracesguide.co.uk*

source was not disclosed. In this account, not long after leaving Bregenz, SF had been driving at about 60–65 mph when, on rounding a corner, he found railway crossing gates blocking the road. He braked hard but ended up running down an embankment of some 40 feet and landing in a lot of bushes. These broke the fall to such an extent that he was able to get back quickly onto the road.[158]

Other accounts claim that he was assisted, either by 30 Austrian soldiers or by 30 French peasants. SF does not give much away in *My Motoring Reminiscences*, simply saying of the complaint 'we were supposed to have run into a river and to have been pulled out by forty peasants',[159] without confirming or denying whether this was the case. It is possible that he did get some help in getting the car back onto the road, but it seems those protesting were equally unclear as to the facts, and after discussion the Gordon Bennett Trophy was awarded to Britain, helped by the fact that the Napier had been the only car to finish. The trophy was won by the Automobile Club of Great Britain and Ireland (ACGBI), not by SF or Napier.

Having reached Innsbruck, SF pressed on through Salzburg to Vienna, now able to obtain and fit some French inner tubes since the Gordon Bennett regulations no longer applied. They did this by bluff, fooling a French tyre depot that they were part of the French team. It did not work at the first depot but they tried again at the next one they came to — and were successful.[160] They reached Vienna after a total of 19 hours 16 minutes, excluding the 'neutral' Belfort-Bregenz stretch, corresponding to an average speed of 31.9mph. In the open race, the Napier was placed eighth out of 23 finishers in the 'heavy cars' class, and 15th out of 80 finishers overall.[161] It was the only British car to reach Vienna, Herbert Austin's Wolseley having failed to get beyond Belfort. The rest were mainly French, but with three Mercédès from Germany. The overall winner, surprisingly, was a 'light' car — a 16hp Renault driven by Marcel Renault. The winner of the 'heavy' car class was Henri Farman in a 70hp Panhard.

The winning of the Gordon Bennett Trophy by Britain may seem like a hollow victory, with just one finisher from only four competing cars, but it carried great significance. It put Britain on the map as a serious manufacturer of motor vehicles, which otherwise had been the preserve of the French, it gave Napier excellent publicity, and it made SF a national celebrity. Furthermore, since the regulations required that 'The Race shall be run in the country of the holding Club', the ACGBI was now charged with running the 1903 race in its own territory, thus introducing road racing to the British Isles.

It was voiced at the time that if de Knyff had reached the end instead of SF, it might have spelt the end of the Gordon Bennett races, with the French appearing invincible. As it was, the result was a severe blow to the French, who had been becoming complacent.

The race even introduced a new exclamation to the English language: 'Gordon Bennett', an expression indicating great surprise or amazement.

SF did not race again in 1902 but, as evidence that he was enthusiastic about all sorts of transport, whether on land or water or in the air, he made his maiden ascent in a balloon, setting off from Berners Elms, rising to 35,000 feet and landing at Codington, near Bicester.[162]

▼ A replica of the Gordon Bennett Trophy was commissioned by SF and is now held by The Veteran Car Club of Great Britain. *The Veteran Car Club of Great Britain*

CHAPTER 7

RACING ON LAND AND SEA

1903 TO 1906

As the British team had won the 1902 Gordon Bennett race, the 1903 event was to be organised by the Automobile Club of Great Britain and Ireland (ACGBI). Up to that point, there had been great opposition to racing on public roads in England, but the Club was determined to find a way of organising a race, even if it meant an Act of Parliament had to be passed. From the Irish came the suggestion that it could be held in one of the many sparsely

Looking chauffeur-like, SF prepares to drive a 12hp Napier in 1903. *The Veteran Car Club of Great Britain*

populated areas of that country, so the search for a suitable course began.[163] It was thought more appropriate to have a closed circuit, albeit of public roads, rather than holding a 'city-to-city' race, and eventually a figure-of-eight circuit centred on Athy, about 50 miles from Dublin, was chosen. Irish MPs were enthusiastic about the idea, and a Bill was passed through parliament on 24 March 1903.[164]

The cars making up the three-car British team were to be determined by competition, so Eliminating Trials were organised. Montague Napier had agreed to build four racing cars, three of which were similar to the previous year's winner, and a fourth with slightly more power. The Star Manufacturing Company Ltd of Wolverhampton also wanted to take part in these trials, and it ended up that one of its cars, of 80hp, would compete against three Napiers to determine the trio that would make up the British team. The trials comprised three events: a flying kilometre and a standing mile took place on the Duke of Portland's Welbeck estate in Nottinghamshire and there was a hillclimb up Dashwood Hill near High Wycombe. There was no official permit for the run up Dashwood Hill, so the location was kept secret until the morning of the contest, and the trial (which was completed by 4.30am) was held before the police were aware of it.[165]

Pictured in 1903, SF's faithful companion *Bully* takes charge of 'his' Napier and weighs up whether to risk 'sampling the legs' of two policemen. *The Veteran Car Club of Great Britain*

It was the cars that were competing for a place in the team, not the drivers. It had already been decided that SF and Jarrott would drive in the race itself, and they both decided to be spectators during the trials. The three Napiers were driven by the Hon Charles Rolls and Jack Stocks on the 45hp racing cars, and Mark Mayhew, driving his own 35hp car, with the Star being driven by Joseph Lisle, son of the founder of that company.[166] The Star did not perform well, coming last in each of the trials, and Stocks, being fastest, was chosen to drive the third Napier in the main race.

Between the trials and the race at Athy, the infamous, and tragic, Paris–Madrid race took place, starting on 24 May. As the Napier factory was fully committed to preparing its cars for the

Gordon Bennett race, it did not enter this one. Jarrott was to drive a 45hp De Dietrich, and SF decided to go and spectate, albeit with one of the racing Napiers.[167] The first leg was from Paris to Bordeaux, a route that he and Jarrott had followed in the 1899 race. In SF's words, at the start 'disorder and chaos reigned supreme',[168] and along the route spectators were blocking the way. Not long after the start a spectator crossing the road was killed. Later, Leslie Porter, driving a 45hp Wolseley, lost control of the car when negotiating a level crossing.[169] The car overturned and the poor mechanic struck a wall, rebounded, and was then crushed under the car, dying instantly. The mechanic's name was Nixon, and SF was relieved to learn sometime later that it was not his young friend St John Nixon.[170] Many more accidents followed, several resulting in fatalities of drivers, mechanics or spectators. Marcel Renault, winner of the previous year's Paris–Vienna race, drove into a tree and killed himself. His brother, Louis, was also racing and did not learn of Marcel's death until he reached Bordeaux. SF followed the route at a safe distance but passed horrifying wrecks all along the way. Fernand Gabriel, driving a Mors, arrived first in Bordeaux, and Jarrott came in third. Mayhew, on his Napier, had had a lucky escape when the steering failed and he missed a tree by inches.[171]

While the surviving drivers were discussing in Bordeaux whether they wanted to continue, an edict came from the French government

▼ Before the 1903 Gordon Bennett race, candidates for the three-car British team took part in Eliminating Trials. Among those taking a break here, alongside a private road on the Welbeck estate in Nottinghamshire, is Jack Stocks (left), who was selected to drive one of the Napiers after performing best in the trials. Besides SF (with his back to the car wheel), the group also includes (from left) Roger Fuller (reclined and turned to the camera), Mark Mayhew, Charles Jarrott and Clifford Earp. *Clive Boothman collection*

➢ The 1903 Gordon Bennett course, in Ireland, was centred on Athy and made alternate use of two loops heading westwards and eastwards from a common stretch that included Athy itself. *The Autocar (27 June 1903)*

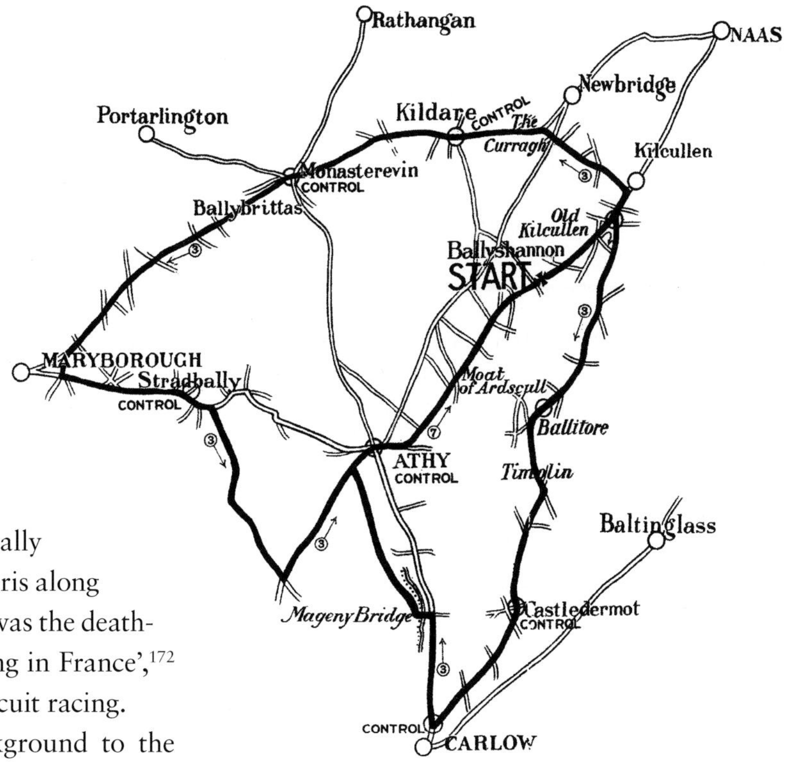

forbidding all further racing on French territory. The cars had to be towed to the railway station and put on a train back to Paris. SF had great difficulty convincing the officials that he was not a competitor, but eventually he was allowed to drive back to Paris along the same route. In his words 'this was the death-knell of long-distance motor racing in France',[172] and marked the move towards circuit racing.

Such was the immediate background to the Gordon Bennett race to be held in Ireland on 2 July 1903. It was fortunate that the Act had already been passed allowing it to be held in Ireland, and the use of a figure-of-eight circuit would make it slightly easier to police. The two loops were of 40 and 51⅞ miles, and three full laps and one of the longer loop only were to be completed, making a total distance of 327½ miles.[173]

The race was to start at Ballyshannon with a straight run of nearly two miles in front of a grandstand. Then the cars would turn right into the shorter of the two loops, heading down to a control at Castle Dermot, and back to the start via Athy. This time round they would turn left into the longer loop, taking them through Kildare and turning left before Maryborough to bring them back to Athy.[174]

The three Napier drivers spent some time practising at the track before the race, during which they ran over some chickens. They always paid for any birds they killed, but then SF noticed that more and more chickens found their way onto the road, and the price started to go up.[175] This time they were joined by a team of mechanics from the factory to help them service the cars.

SF decided to drive the most powerful of the four cars built, rated at 80hp, while Jarrott and Stocks would drive two of the 45hp cars. The French team was to comprise René de Knyff and Henri Farman on 70hp Panhards, and Fernand Gabriel on an 80hp Mors. Germany entered three Mercédès cars, driven by Camille Jenatzy, Baron Pierre de Caters, and Foxhall P. Keene, while America entered two Wintons, one of them driven by Alexander Winton himself, and

▲ The Napier team before the 1903 Gordon Bennett race, with Jack Stocks (left), Charles Jarrott (centre) and SF (right), all in 45hp cars. *Motoring Picture Library, National Motor Museum*

▼ Another view of SF in a Napier before the 1903 Gordon Bennett race. *Motoring Picture Library, National Motor Museum*

SF's Napier, the 80hp version he finally selected for the 1903 Gordon Bennett race, passes through a control. *Motoring Picture Library, National Motor Museum*

a Peerless to be driven by Louis Mooers.[176] At the weigh-in, the Panhards were over the limit of 1,000kg and various parts had to be removed to bring the weight down. The Daimler Motoren Gesellschaft, makers of the Mercédès cars, had suffered a devastating fire at its factory just three weeks before the race when all three of its 90hp entries were destroyed. The company had to borrow three 60hp cars from its customers to enter in the race.[177]

Lisle on the Star and Cummings on a Wolseley were given the honour of being the course cars, and each drove a loop before the start of the race to make sure the route was clear. SF, as the previous year's winner, was first away at 7am and set up the fastest time for the shorter loop, but at the end of the first full lap, Jenatzy was ahead.

Soon after that, SF's British-made tyres began to let him down again. One rear tyre came off altogether and the rim was then damaged.[178] He kept going but was steadily losing more and more time to the race leaders. He was last of the five finishers, coming in two hours after Gabriel in a Mors in fifth place, but SF was subsequently disqualified for having been push-started after a control (a fact he chose not to mention in *My Motoring Reminiscences*).

Stocks did not even complete one full lap, colliding with a barrier and smashing a front wheel. Jarrott, who was accompanied by a young mechanic named Cecil Bianchi,[viii] had a near-fatal accident on the second lap when his steering gear broke. The car turned over and Bianchi, who had been held onto the car by a strap around his arm, became trapped underneath it. Jarrott, although he had broken his collarbone, made a super-human effort to lift the car. Even then, Bianchi could not get out from under it until some bystanders came to hold the car up while Jarrott got underneath, cut the strap and dragged him out.[179] Then, apparently, both of them fainted and the bystanders, thinking they were dead, covered them with white sheets.

The winner was Jenatzy in a Mercédès, followed by the three French cars. The award for most popular driver, if there had been one, would have gone to de Caters, a non-finisher in a Mercédès, who not only stopped to check that Jarrott and Bianchi were not too seriously injured in their accident, but stopped again at the grandstand to pass on the news to the officials and friends of Jarrott.[180]

In *Ten Years of Motors and Motor Racing*, Jarrott had this to say of SF's performance in this race:

> I was thrilled as I lay in my bed after my accident in that race to hear the story of Edge's passage by the grand-stand on the first round. I knew the physical strength necessary to keep one's car on the road at that spot, and I also knew the difficulty of steering the car which Edge was driving, and I realised that he had thrown all caution and care to the winds, and that come what might he had decided not to be beaten if devilment and courage in driving could count. And such a spirit I admire.[181]

SF was well aware of the money Napier had spent preparing the team for the Irish race but was determined that the company should still try to win back the Gordon Bennett Trophy in 1904. However, he agreed with Napier that it would not build new cars, but would compete with those that had raced in Ireland.

After the race, SF briefly devoted his time to boats, maybe wanting to forget about cars for a while. A steel-hulled boat, named simply *Napier*, had been fitted with the 50hp engine from the 1901 Paris–Bordeaux race and this was entered for, and won, the Harmsworth Trophy, held in Queenstown Harbour, County Cork, shortly after the race at Athy. The boat was steered by 21-year-old Miss Dorothy Levitt, who had been employed as a secretary at S.F. Edge, Limited since 1902, initially on a temporary basis. She came to SF's attention possibly because of her good looks (she was described as having long legs and eyes like pools) and sense of adventure, and quickly became his private secretary. SF had encountered a French female racing driver in the Paris–Berlin race of 1901, Camille du Gast, and realised there was good publicity to be had for Napier with a lady driver. SF arranged for Miss Levitt to be taught to drive, and it turned out she had a natural ability. She was also sent to France for a few months in 1902/3 to learn more about the motor industry.

They only just had time to get from Queenstown to Edge Hill in Warwickshire to take part in the

viii SF was again accompanied by his cousin, Cecil, as mechanic, and Arthur MacDonald rode with Stocks.

➤ Dorothy Levitt at Cowes in August 1903 in *Napier*, which was powered by the 50hp engine that had been used by SF in the Paris–Bordeaux race two years earlier. *Clive Boothman collection*

Sun Rise Hill Climb on 25 July 1903. This time Miss Levitt rode as passenger in SF's car.

On 7 August 1903, *Napier* took part in the West Cowes Regatta, again steered by Dorothy Levitt with SF looking after the engine.[182] There were three other competitors, and *Napier* won by nearly three minutes.

On 3 October 1903 the pair were in Southport for the Speed Trials. Dorothy Levitt made her motor racing début with a 12hp Gladiator (SF was also agent for these cars), and won her class. SF was competing on the 45hp Napier and won a 'silver bowl' but not the main race.

Development of the Six-Cylinder Engine

For some time, SF had been giving much thought to the idea of a six-cylinder engine. Unlike Montague Napier, he was not a trained engineer, but that did not stop him telling Napier what he wanted. In *My Motoring Reminiscences*, SF acknowledged that he was not 'the first man to produce a six-cylinder engine',[183] failing to mention that Montague Napier designed and manufactured it, SF having only come up with the idea. He also observed that eight-cylinder engines had already been built, but felt that this configuration was too long, and that a six-cylinder engine represented a happy medium.[184] He did, however, claim, justifiably, that Napier's six-cylinder engine was the first successful one.

SF discussed his ideas with Montague Napier early in 1903. Napier resisted at first but eventually gave in.[185] Right from the start, when the engine was first run on a test bench, it seemed to meet all SF's expectations, and he could not wait to take a car out on a test run. When that day came, with Arthur MacDonald as his mechanic, he drove out from the Lambeth factory and headed straight for Tilburstow Hill.[186] SF was immediately impressed by both the smoothness and the silence of the engine. Until, that is, a certain speed was reached, when a periodic vibration set in. Nevertheless, the car stormed up Tilburstow Hill in top gear, and SF was confident that the vibration problem could be overcome. The prototype engine was a 30hp one, but they decided that the first production model should be of 18hp.[187]

The new model was launched at a dinner held on 16 October 1903 at the Trocadero Restaurant near Piccadilly. The guest of honour was Earl Russell,[ix] who gave a toast to 'success to the English Automobile Industry'. He paid tribute to SF who 'with Mr Napier had done so much from every point of view to place the English automobile abreast of all its competitors by building and driving a car whose name was second to none and was all English.' It seems that the vibration problem with the prototype must have been overcome since in his speech SF said: 'The chief features of the new car will be its absolute quietness at all speeds and its entire freedom from engine vibration or road shock. The good points of the engine are obtained mainly by perfect balancing...'.[188]

Much scepticism was voiced about the six-cylinder engine, the main concern being the increased number of moving parts. Critics included SF's friend, Jarrott, whom SF describes as being 'particularly bitter against it'.[189] The criticism was unjustified, as evidenced by the subsequent popularity and success of six-cylinder engines. Rolls-Royce, for example, introduced its own six-cylinder 30hp car in 1905, followed by the highly regarded Silver Ghost in 1906, by which time 12 other British companies were making six-cylinder cars.[190] Appendix 3 sets out some of the correspondence on this subject from the pages of *The Autocar* in late 1906. SF understood yet again that the best way to demonstrate the quality of the new engine would be by success in trials and races.

SF ended the 1903 season competing successfully in a hill climb organised by the Nottingham Automobile Club at Kettleby.[191] And in December he was a guest at the Annual Dinner of the Norfolk Automobile and Launch Club, at which he gave a speech on 'The Past, Present, and Future of Motor Cars and Motor Launches'.[192]

1904

Napier had bought four acres of land in Acton in 1903 and that winter the factory was moved there from the cramped premises in Lambeth. Montague Napier had now been joined (from 1901) by Arthur Rowledge, who had played a key role in the development of the six-cylinder engine. Under Napier's supervision, Rowledge now set to work designing a racing car for 1904.

The 1903 Gordon Bennett Trophy having been won by Germany, the 1904 race was to be held in that country. A road circuit of 79½ miles based on Homburg was identified and a date of 17 June set. The race would be over four laps of the circuit, with a total distance of 318 miles. Despite their failure in Ireland, Napier and SF agreed that they should enter again, mainly out of patriotism and disdain for the chances of any other British car winning.

The British team was again to be selected by holding Eliminating Trials, which took place from 10 to 12 May. Racing on roads in England was still prohibited but the ACGBI managed to

ix Frank Russell, the second Earl

Chevalier René de Knyff (centre) with Charles Jarrott (left) and SF during the Eliminating Trials in the Isle of Man. *Grand Prix Library/Maurice-Louis Branger*

SF poses with riding mechanic Arthur MacDonald at the Isle of Man Eliminating Trials before the 1904 Gordon Bennett race. *The Automotor Journal (21 May 1904)*

In Douglas, SF sets off for one of the tests for the 1904 Eliminating Trials. *Motoring Picture Library, National Motor Museum*

get a bill passed in the House of Keys in the Isle of Man that allowed the Eliminating Trials to be held there. The Napier company entered three cars, all 1903 four-cylinder models: SF would be driving the 80hp car, with Clifford Earp (a Napier employee) driving a 55hp car and J.W. Stocks a 40hp car. Mark Mayhew and John Hargreaves also entered their Napiers as private owners. They would be competing against three Wolseleys, one of which would be driven by Jarrott, and three Darracqs, which were built in Glasgow although of French design.[193]

The first day included tests of speed, acceleration and accuracy of stopping, during which SF generally put in the best performance. Two of the Darracqs dropped out at this point. On the second day a hill climb was held and on the third day a speed trial along Douglas Promenade, in both of which SF was again fastest. While returning from the second run, the brakes on Earp's Napier jammed, and he skidded into a wall, badly damaging the car, and the third run was abandoned. The judges announced that evening that the British team would comprise one Napier (SF's) and two Wolseleys, saying that Earp would have been in second place but for his accident. SF submitted a formal protest to the Secretary of the Automobile Club on 16 May asking him to 'bring before your committee my very strong protest of such a judgement as being absolutely unfair, and against the best interests of Great Britain winning the Gordon Bennett race',[194] but his protest was rejected.

Interest in the race had increased significantly since 1902, when only four cars had competed. In addition to the British team, this time there were teams entered by Germany, France, Austria, Belgium and Italy. SF chose Arthur MacDonald as his mechanic, and they travelled together on the 80hp Napier via Rotterdam to Homburg.[195] They were able to do several practice runs around the circuit before the race, but on one of them 'a sudden snap was heard as though someone had broken off the neck of a soda-water bottle'.[196] It turned out to be a broken crankshaft. They immediately sent a telegram to the factory asking for a new crankshaft to be sent out and had to hire a horse to tow the car to Weilmünster. SF had tried, unsuccessfully, to phone through to Homburg, but their long absence was noticed and a search party, comprising Jarrott and Browning (the Dunlop agent), was sent out, half expecting to find dead bodies by the roadside. From Weilmünster, SF and MacDonald were able to travel by omnibus towards Homburg and Jarrott and Browning sped past it without realising that SF was inside.[197] The pair finally reached Homburg at 10pm, by which time a telegram had already arrived confirming the despatch not just of a new crankshaft, but also two spare cars and three mechanics. One of these cars, being driven by Earp, had the new six-cylinder engine.

It turned out there was little damage to the 80hp car other than a clean break in the crankshaft, so MacDonald set to work fitting the new crankshaft as soon as it arrived.[198] To pass the time, SF asked if he could ride around the course as passenger on other cars, but all of them seemed to break down for one reason or another. The repairs to his car were completed in time for more practice laps before the weighing-in on 16 June. The six-cylinder car driven by Earp had arrived by this time, but SF felt the repaired four-cylinder car would be more reliable. As he

➢ Somewhere in Germany during the 1904 Gordon Bennett race, SF embarks on another leg of the route. *Getty Images/ Ullstein Bild*

➢ Another view of SF and Arthur Macdonald competing in the 1904 Gordon Bennett race in Germany. *Grand Prix Library/Maurice-Louis Branger*

This portrait of SF appeared in *The Tatler* in 1904. *Author's collection*

was pushing his car onto the weighing machine, petrol leaking from the car behind, driven by Friedrich Franz Opel, caught fire, and SF was lucky to be able to quickly push his car forward, away from the ensuing blaze.[199]

The race itself was started at 7am the following day by the German Emperor, Kaiser Wilhelm II. Jenatzy set off first, on time, with SF next in line. At the end of the first lap, SF was in third place, with an average speed of 51mph, Léon Théry having moved into second place. A puncture on the second lap slowed him, but on the third lap he was only five seconds slower than Jenatzy. Then, early into the fourth lap, mechanical failure struck again and SF was out of the race.[200] Théry ended up taking first place for France, on a Richard-Brasier, with Jenatzy on a Mercédès coming in 10 minutes behind. The Wolseleys driven by Sidney Girling and Charles Jarrott finished 9th and 12th respectively.[201]

It had been a frustrating time for SF, with the lack of success in both 1903 and 1904, and the ignominy of Napiers being beaten by Wolseleys. He was particularly upset, however, by the way his protest after the Eliminating Trials had been treated by the ACGBI. His business commitments also made it difficult to devote so much time to being an amateur racing driver. So he decided that the race in Germany would be his last, although he would continue to take part in speed trials and hill climbs in England.[202]

As in 1903, he again turned to sport on water. In April 1904 he entered a new boat, *Napier Minor*, built by Saunders with a 73hp Napier engine, in an event in Monaco, but was forced to withdraw when the boat nearly caught fire.[203] On 27 June he entered *Napier Minor* in a race in Kiel Harbour, at which King Edward and the Kaiser were to be present, but this was cancelled due to bad weather. SF believed that *Napier Minor* would have coped well with the rough seas, so he made a run over the whole course to demonstrate this, in the hope that it would persuade the organisers to rescind their decision, but this was not to be. His protest had been addressed to the Kaiser, as president of the organising club, and that same afternoon, SF received a call from the Kaiser, who apologised for the cancellation, explaining that no-one else was prepared to race, and expressed the hope that SF would take a sporting view and withdraw his protest. SF duly did so. The main race, for the Kaiser Cup, was, however, held the following

➢ SF also turned his hand to racing on water in 1904 and used *Napier Minor*, which had a 73hp engine, in various events, including a Calais–Dover cross-channel race. *The Motor Boat (25 November 1904)*

➢ SF also competed with *Napier II* — fitted with two 75hp Napier engines — in a variety of events, including the International Harmsworth Trophy race of 1904. *The Motor Boat (25 November 1904)*

day despite continuing bad weather, and *Napier Minor* won against two German boats, which failed to finish due to the rough seas.

On 26 and 27 July, a reliability trial was organised on Southampton Water that was to last 10 hours on each of two consecutive days. For this, SF entered another new boat, the twin-engine *Napier II*, which had been designed and built by Yarrow, as well as *Napier Minor.* SF was steering *Napier Minor*, which 'was by far the most successful boat on the first day'.[204] On the second day the weather was much worse, and there was a problem with the ignition coil, but *Napier Minor* still managed to complete 123.89 sea miles in 9 hours 33 minutes 28 seconds. It was awarded the Gold Medal in its class.

The International Harmsworth Trophy race was then held in the Solent on 30 July 1904. For this, SF entered *Napier II. Napier Minor* was also entered, although SF does not record who was piloting it. In the first heat, against an American boat, SF got a bad start, but the American boat then ran into problems of its own and SF won.[205] *Napier Minor* also won its heat, and in the fourth heat, *Napier II* and *Napier Minor* had to race against each other. The more powerful boat, *Napier II*, won, but had damaged its hull and started to leak, so SF steered *Napier Minor* in the final, against a French boat. This time SF got off to a better start than his competitor and held the lead all the way through. However, SF was again to be disappointed. He had consulted the officials over the substitution of *Napier Minor* for *Napier II*, and no objection had been raised. *Napier Minor* was clearly the slower of the two boats. Only after it had beaten the French boat

At the Bexhill Speed Trials, cars competed two at a time on this strip of coast road. SF's 20hp Napier is one of the cars seen neck and neck in the distance at the 1904 event. *Author's collection (photo by Argent Archer)*

was a protest made, and the cup was awarded to France.[206]

On 8 August he was back in *Napier Minor* again for the Calais–Dover cross-channel race organised by the Automobile Club de France. There were several classes, and *Napier Minor* was in the 'Racers' class (the fastest), in which the main competitor was a boat named *Mercédès IV*. In the event, *Mercédès IV* reached Dover first, in just over one hour, with *Napier Minor* five minutes behind.[207] On reaching Dover, the Mercédès went to the wrong side of the pier and could have been disqualified. SF declined to issue a protest as in his view it had demonstrated that it was the faster boat, so the Mercédès was awarded first prize. In *My Motoring Reminiscences*, SF compares this sporting gesture on his part with that of the French team in the International Harmsworth Trophy. This also became a talking point in the press at the time.

Edmund Dangerfield, now proprietor of *The Motor*, had chartered a cross-channel steamer, the *Queen*, thinking he and his guests could watch the start in Calais, then overtake the competitors and watch the finish at Dover. They were disappointed, having failed to grasp the power of internal combustion engines.[208]

SF also took part, in *Napier II*, in the second race for the Gaston Menier Cup, which was held in Trouville in August 1904. It was very much the same crowd involved in motorboat racing as in motor racing, and the cup was won by Henri Fournier, winner of the Paris–Bordeaux race in 1901. *Napier II* was not running well and came in last.[209]

SF was back in Southampton in *Napier Minor* in September 1904 when he had the opportunity to come to the aid of a damsel in distress. A passenger in an ocean liner, the *Orinoco*, realised, just as the boat was about to leave, that her jewel case had been left in her hotel room. It was sent for, but the liner had already set off by the time the jewel case reached the quayside. SF chivalrously offered the services of *Napier Minor*, which set off with the jewel case in chase of the liner. When they caught up, the jewel case was hauled on board, amid cheers from the passengers.[210] In contemporary reports the lady passenger was anonymous, but 'Cives', who reported on an interview with SF in the *Daily*

Report of 16 November 1907, suggested that it was Eleanor, although with no indication of where she was heading.

Amid all this activity on water, SF had found time to attend the Bexhill Automobile Meeting between 1 and 3 August. Speed trials had first been held at Bexhill in 1902 on a private track owned by Earl de la Warr. A local resident had obtained an injunction preventing the holding of a similar event in 1903, but it was allowed in 1904. SF competed in a 20hp Napier, with Eleanor as passenger. Stocks was there in a De Dion, Cecil Edge in a Gladiator, and Jarrott in a De Dietrich, amongst many other well-known names. The overall winner was A. Guinness in a 60hp Mercédès, but SF won his class, for cars costing between £750 and £1,000,[211] and was awarded a magnificent trophy.

1905

SF stuck to his decision not to enter any more motor races. The Acton racing department had a busy year, however, and SF must have been closely involved behind the scenes. Napier entered the 1905 Gordon Bennett race — the last to be held — in the Auvergne on 5 July, and Clifford Earp came in a creditable ninth on a 90hp car, behind Charles Rolls on a Wolseley.[212] SF's cousin, Cecil, had been one of the Napier drivers in the Eliminating Trials. One of the objections that led to the demise of the Gordon Bennett races was the limit of three cars per country, which did not give enough of the ever-growing number of manufacturers the chance to take part.

Early in the year Arthur MacDonald recorded a speed of 104.65mph in the new six-cylinder racing car at the Florida Speed Week in Daytona. Clifford Earp also successfully campaigned the same car, winning the Château-Thierry hill climb in October 1905, and the Dourdan speed trials a few days later.[213]

On 7 June 1905, SF was back at the old stomping ground of his youth, Crystal Palace, for a Motor versus Horse Safety Demonstration. One of the 90hp Gordon Bennett racers took part along with a De Dion and a Mercédès. The mighty Napier was pitted against a single-horse 'trotting sulky' to test which could pull up in the shortest distance from a speed of 12mph. The Napier won easily with a distance of 26 feet 6 inches compared with the horse-drawn carriage's 53 feet.

Meanwhile, SF maintained his interest in racing motorboats, although again he was reluctant to be the competitor. He was one of several members of the Automobile Club, including Lionel de Rothschild and John Scott-Montagu, who founded The Motor Yacht Club in May 1905 (it became the Royal Motor Yacht Club in 1910). A derelict paddle steamer, the *Enchantress*, was purchased and converted in record time to become a floating clubhouse, which included 25 'sleeping cabins', moored at Netley in Southampton Water.[214]

The British Motor Boat Club also held its inaugural meeting in May 1905, on the Thames at Kingston. Seaton Edge, SF's younger brother, who had returned from Australia, was one of the founding members. The two clubs eventually merged in 1933.

More boats had been built that were fitted with the latest Napier engines, and carried names that could easily be confused: *Napier*; *Napier I* to *Napier IV*; *Napier Minor* and *Napier Major*. One

Dorothy Levitt was SF's personal assistant at this time and is pictured in an 8hp De Dion-Bouton before the Scottish Reliability Trial of May 1905. The other car is a 12hp De Dion-Bouton driven by Jack Stocks, who had been one of the Napier drivers in the 1903 Gordon Bennett race. *Author's collection (photo by Argent Archer)*

such boat was owned by Lord Howard de Walden, and another by Lionel de Rothschild and the Hon John Scott-Montagu jointly. Both boats were entered in the third International Harmsworth Trophy race held in the Bay of Arcachon, France, in September 1905. De Rothschild's boat was to be steered by Seaton Edge, while Scott-Montagu handled the other boat.[215] The race boiled down to a competition between the two Napier-powered craft, with Scott-Montagu winning the Trophy for Britain.

The Brighton Speed Trials, which have survived to this day, were held for the first time in July 1905 and lasted four days. On the final day, Ladies' Day, Dorothy Levitt set the best time in an 80hp Napier. *Author's collection*

In August 1905, SF had the unusual experience of reading of his own death. The *Berliner Tageblatt*, a German newspaper, published the following paragraph on 10 August:

> The well-known motor racer, Edge, who won the Gordon Bennett Trophy race in 1899 [*sic*] has been killed in a motor accident. They have telegraphed us from London that the motor races at Brighton were marred by a serious accident. The motor racer, Brown, was going for a trial spin with Edge. When the car was trying to pass a pedestrian, it over-turned, and Edge was killed while Brown was injured.[216]

While it was true that Brown had had an accident while out for a 'trial spin' and was badly injured, neither SF nor anyone else was in the car, and SF did not hear of the accident until some time later.

SF never forgot his friends in the Anerley Bicycle Club. On 7 October 1905, he chaired a meeting of the club's older members over tea, at which he suggested an Old Boy's Cup, and made a 'handsome donation' towards the purchase of a trophy.[217]

1906

On 24 February 1906, a dinner was held at the Grand Hotel in London at which SF announced that his company (the sole agent for Napier cars) would be giving a three-year guarantee with every six-cylinder car sold. Montague Napier was absent through illness, requiring 'a lengthened change of scene',[218] and during his speech SF paid tribute to Napier, 'to whom British automobilism owed more than could well be imagined'.[219] SF reported that the value of British motor cars manufactured in a month, amounting to £468,000 in January 1906, for the first time exceeded that of imported cars, which were valued at £317,000 in the same period. Furthermore, he estimated that the value of cars manufactured in Britain in the whole of 1906 could reach £6,000,000. He also mentioned that orders totalling £294,000 had already been received for Napier cars to be delivered in 1907.[220]

Lord Montagu, as he now was, following the death of his father in November 1905, entered his boat, *Napier*, for a race in Monaco in April 1906, but he became ill and instead Seaton Edge raced it.[221] The event saw a close fight between Montagu's boat and one owned by the racing driver Baron Pierre de Caters, but Seaton in *Napier* pulled ahead on the final straight to claim the win.

Lord Montagu was back in charge of his boat, now called the *Yarrow Napier* (although built by Saunders), for the International Harmsworth Trophy held in Southampton on 9 August 1906, and led from start to finish.[222]

Meanwhile, in July 1906, *Napier Major*, a sea-going 45ft motor cruiser fitted with a 24hp Napier marine engine and owned by SF, had won the A.J. Wilson Challenge Cup. The boat went on to win the cup again in 1907 in a race from Gravesend to Cowes and SF was able to retain the cup having won it two years in succession.

By the end of 1906, the Brooklands circuit was under construction, and SF's focus moved away from motorboats and back towards motor cars. One of the last major competitions he entered before the opening of Brooklands was a two-day meeting at Bexhill organised by the Crystal Palace Automobile Club in May 1907. The Napier team was out in force, with SF, Cecil, Sidney Smith, Henry Tryon, Frank Cundy and Dorothy Levitt all competing in 40hp, 60hp and 80hp cars. On the first day, SF set a new record for the track at 73.77mph. In the final event, for four-seat cars costing over £700, Cecil Edge in an 80hp car won 'by a bonnet's length' against Smith in a 60hp example.[223]

The pages shown overleaf appeared in a sales brochure issued by S.F. Edge, Ltd in 1911. The first page catalogues Napier's numerous competition successes on water; the second page shows two Yarrow-built Motor Torpedo Boats with Napier engines. *Author's collection*

Achievements of Napier Marine Motors

RECORDS of continual successes are the best possible guarantee of the design and efficiency of Napier Boats.

A Napier Boat finished first in the race for the Harmsworth Trophy in 1903, and the following years, 1904, 1905, 1906.

The British Admiralty officially recognised the superiority of the Napier design by using a fast Napier Boat for scouting in connection with the Naval Manœuvres.

In 1904 a Napier Boat carried off the Kaiser's Cup at Kiel and finished first in the Harmsworth International Trophy once more. Other prizes and medals won by the Napier Boats during that season totalled 30.

In 1905 the Napier Boats again won the principal Marine events of the year. "Napier II" started in 15 races and finished in 12. "Napier" started in 17 races and finished first in 5 and second in 9.

During the 1906 season the Napier Boats again proved their reliability and speed in trials and races, beginning in Monaco, where in April of that year "Yarrow-Napier" won the two 50-kilometre races, beating the fastest foreign boats. The continuous successes of Napier Boats in subsequent years are shown below.

Napier Marine Trophies and Successes.

Cowes Cup.—Won by Napier.

Harmsworth Cup.—Won at Queenstown.

Trouville—1 Mile Race.

Gaston Menier Cup.

Royal Victoria Regatta.—First.

Captain Orr Ewing's Cup.

Kaiser Cup.—At Kiel.

Motor Boat Reliability Trial.—Gold Medal.

Cross Channel Race (Calais to Dover).—"Napier Minor" Second.

British International Cup.—Finished First.

Portsmouth Regatta.—"Napier Minor" won Challenge Cup and First Prize from scratch.

Monaco **100 Kilometre Scratch Race.**—Won by "Napier II." "Napier" Second.

Ocean-going Voyage of "Napier Major."—**London to Shetland Isles and Back.**

Race.—**Boulogne to Folkestone and Back.**—"Napier II." First.

Entente Cordiale Cup.—At Cowes.

British International Cup.—At Arcachon.

Deutsch Cup.—At Arcachon.

Reliability Trials.—2 Gold Medals.

Motorist and Traveller Challenge Cup.—At Burnham.

Flying Mile Championship, Gold Medal.

Eliminating Race for British International Cup.

Simon Cup.—At Kiel.

Daimler Cup.—At Kiel.

44-knot Race.—At Cowes.

Handicap Race.—At Burnham.

Handicap Race.—At Burnham.

British International Cup.

Reliability Trials.—Gold Medal.

A. J. Wilson Trophy.

Liverpool Bay Cup.

British Motor Boat Club Cup.—At Liverpool.

Entente Cordiale Cup.

Motoring Illustrated Cup.

Motor Boat Cup.—Sea Mile Record.

Van de Stegen Cup.—Ostend.

British Motor Boat Club.—London to Cowes,

Dover to Ostend Race.

50-kilometre Scratch Race.—At Monaco.

50-kilometre Handicap.—At Monaco.

Flying Mile Championship.—At Burnham.

Cruisers' Race.—At Burnham.

London to Cowes Race.—Won A. J. Wilson Challenge Cup outright. B.M.B.C. Silver Cup and Gold Medal.

Dover.—Race for Cabin Cruisers.—Silver Cup.

Dover.—Race for Cabin Cruisers.—Silver Cup.

Cowes.—Race for Cabin Cruisers.—Silver Cup.

Race Round the Isle of Wight.—Rhinefield Challenge Cup and B.M.B.C. Gold Medal.

Race from Southampton to Weymouth.—Rothschild Cup.

Weymouth Race for Cabin Cruisers.—Lieut. Rhodes Cup.

Southampton Race for Cabin Cruisers.

Gravesend Handicap Race for Boats exceeding 10 knots.

Lowestoft.—Brooke Challenge Trophy.

Lowestoft Town Cup.

London to Cowes Race for Sea-going Cruisers winning S. F. Edge Challenge Cup and Miniature, also B.M.B.C. Trophy for first boat to finish the Race.

Ramsgate Cabin Cruisers' Race.—Commodore's Cup.

Ramsgate under 10 knots B.M.B.C. Cup.

Dover.—Dover to Ostend Race for Sea-going Cruisers' B.M.B.C. Cup.

Cowes Cabin Cruisers' Race B.M.B.C. Cup.

Cowes—not exceeding 10 knots Race B.M.B.C. Cup.

Cowes.—Race Round the Isle of Wight.—Rhinefield Challenge Cup.

Burnham Cabin Cruisers' Race B.M.B.C. Cup. Also 11 Second and 6 Third Prizes.

H.M.B.C. Ramsgate Cup.—Cabin Cruisers' Race for the Ramsgate Borough Cup—"Napier Major" First.

Southampton not exceeding 8 knots M.Y.C. Cup.

M.Y.C. Open M.M.A. Race.—"Lucinha" (Napier) First.

M.Y.C. Handicap Race for Boats over 15 knots.—"Lucinha" (Napier) First.

M.Y.C. Restricted Racing Cruiser Class—"Lucinha" (Napier) First.

B.M.B.C. London to Southampton Sea-going Cruisers' Race.—"Napier Major" won B.M.B.C. Cup for first boat in (fastest time).

Cowes B.M.B.C., M.M.A. Cabin Cruisers' Race—"Napier Major" First.

B.M.B.C., M.M.A. Race.—"Lucinha" (Napier) First.

M.Y.C. Restricted Racing Cruiser Class.—"Lucinha" (Napier) First.

B.M.B.C. Meeting at Burnham-on-Crouch.

M.M.A. Race for A. J. Wilson Challenge Cup.—"Lucinha" (Napier) First.

Handicap for Boats exceeding 12 knots.—"Lucinha" (Napier) First.

6½-8 Metre International Racing Cruiser Class.—"Lucinha" (Napier) First.

Pernambuco (Brazil) **Open Championship** won by "Napier IV."

Ramsgate Town Cup won by "Napier Major."

Vice Commodore's Cup won by "Napier Major."

Royal Temple Yacht Club Cup won by "Napier Major."

London to Cowes Race for S. F. Edge Challenge Cup won by "Napier Major."

Cowes B.M.B.C., M.M.A. Cabin Cruisers' Race.—"Napier Major" First.

B. M. B. C., M. M. A. Silver Cup.—"Napier Major" First.

B. M. B. C., M. M. A. Silver Cup.—"Napier Major" First.

Royal Cowes Town Regatta Cup.—"Napier Major" First.

Rhinefield Challenge Cup for Isle of Wight Race.—"Napier Major" First.

A Fast Yarrow-Napier Torpedo Boat.

Napier Marine Motors.

IN yet another branch Napier Motors have led the way, and that is in Naval work. The Yarrow-Napier Motor Torpedo Boat No. 1176 has demonstrated the possibilities of the adoption of internal-combustion motors where speed is a consideration and saving of weight and increased radius of action are necessary. The latest type of Yarrow-Napier Torpedo craft, which has been put into practical use for Naval purposes is 100ft. long, with a beam of 13ft. 6in. The whole turtle and upper decks are built of light steel plate. The motors consist of 6-cylinder engines designed by Messrs. Napier and constructed by Messrs. Yarrow, which develop 600 h.p., driving four propellers. This boat has been specially designed for coast defence.

THE Yarrow-Napier is 60ft. long, and is designed as a torpedo boat. She is fitted with three sets of engines, driving triple screws, and has attained a speed of over 26 knots, and when fully equipped for service of 24½ knots. The speed of a steamboat of this size would only be 18 knots, with a much reduced radius of action and larger crew.

After their Majesties the late King and the Queen Mother of England and the King and Queen of Spain had been for a trial trip in her and expressed their appreciation of her speed and the ease with which she was manipulated, the Yarrow-Napier was purchased by the British Admiralty, who have rechristened her "Mercury II," and she has now been attached to the submarine flotilla.

Noiseless Napier Marine Motors are noted for smoothness and steadiness in running, absolute silence and absence of all vibration. These qualities coupled with reliability, for which all Napier productions are unsurpassed, particularly fit the Napier Marine Motor for use in Gentlemen's Yachts and Cruising Launches of all dimensions.

We are prepared to quote for Napier Engines alone or for completely equipped Motor Vessels of any size.

CHAPTER 8
BROOKLANDS
1907 TO 1908

Up to this point, 1906, motor racing had never taken place in mainland Britain, and the motor industry had no facility for testing motor vehicles. The legal speed limit on British roads was 20mph, and Acts of Parliament had been required for the 1903 Gordon Bennett race in Ireland and the 1904 Eliminating Trials in the Isle of Man. Furthermore, such races on large circuits using public roads did not provide good spectator sport.

The idea of a closed, purpose-built, motor racing track had first been suggested by a young gentleman by the name of Oswald Massingberd-Mundy in 1903, when the Automobile Club of Great Britain and Ireland had been trying to work out how to stage the 1903 Gordon Bennett race. Massingberd-Mundy had already identified available land in Riddlesdown, near Purley, south of London, including Purley Bury House, which could become the Clubhouse and race headquarters. The ACGBI had been sufficiently interested to arrange for a delegation to visit the site and had invited SF to join it as an expert,[224] not just because of his recognised skill and experience as a racing driver, but also because of his intimate knowledge of the area gained during his cycling exploits with the Anerley Bicycle Club. SF gave his approval and Massingberd-Mundy started drawing up detailed plans and negotiating a lease of the site. However, for reasons that are not clear, although probably related to difficulty in raising sufficient finance, the track was never built.

SF was therefore very interested when he received a letter in 1906 from one Ernst de Rodakowski, an Amsterdam-born Austrian who became a British citizen in 1903. Rodakowski told him of new plans to build a motor track on the outskirts of London and invited him to a dinner at which it would be discussed.[225] There SF learnt that Hugh Locke King, a keen motorist with a large estate near Weybridge, Surrey, was willing to construct a track on his land. Locke King was eager to get as much advice as possible, especially from those who had taken part in motor racing on the continent. There was much discussion over the optimal length of such a circuit. Jarrott, who was also consulted, was in favour of as long a distance as possible, to enable high speeds to be attainable, while SF felt spectators would enjoy it more if it was made as short as possible. In the event, a track of 2.75 miles was built, which was probably closer to SF's way of thinking than to Jarrott's.

Even at this early stage, before a decision had been made to go ahead with the construction, SF informed the meeting that he would like to book the track for the first available opportunity, for an attempt to drive, single-handed, at 60mph for 24 hours.[226] SF was aware of only one similar attempt, in America in 1905, when two drivers, Charlie Merz and W.F. 'Jap' Clemens, achieved an average of 45.6mph over 24 hours.[227]

After extensive consultations, by the autumn of 1906 the decision was taken to proceed with construction as quickly as possible. Colonel Holden, RA, at one-time Chairman of the competitions committee of the Automobile Club, was put in charge of the design of the track. The cost of construction was to be borne from Locke King's pocket, and an early estimate for the cost of laying the track, building three bridges and erecting eight miles of fencing was £22,004.[228] But this was for a flat track, and Holden insisted that the curves would have to be banked so that high speeds — as much as 90mph — could be maintained. By November 1906 the estimate had been increased to £43,000, and by December to £60,750. The final cost, once the track had been opened, has been estimated at £150,000. This left Locke King near bankrupt and a sick man. At the opening of the track, he had to be driven by his wife Ethel, who had more or less taken over the running of the family's affairs. SF followed the progress with interest and made several visits to the site during construction.

The track, although not quite complete, was opened on 17 June, with the first race meeting to be held on 6 July. However, SF was allowed to book the track for 28 June for his 24-hour record. For the attempt, he chose a 60hp touring model,

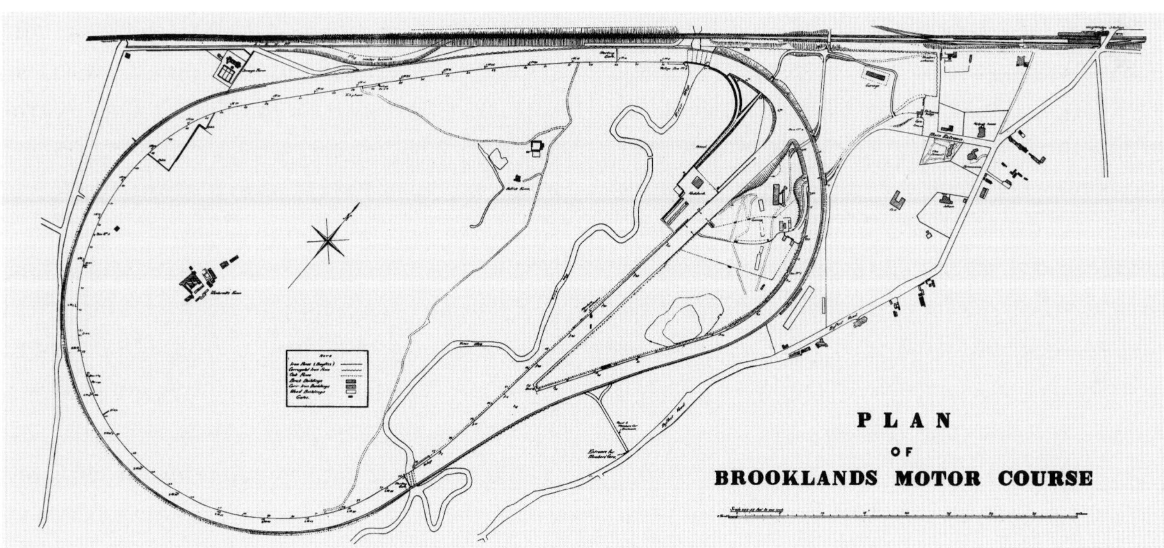

A plan of Brooklands motor course dating from 1907, the year of its construction. *Brooklands Museum Trust*

◄ In this paddock scene at Brooklands before the start of SF's 24-hour record run, Montague Napier (in raincoat) is talking to Ethel Locke King while Hugh Locke King (right) turns his attention elsewhere; the man with his back to the camera is probably Colonel Holden, who was in charge of the track's design. *Brooklands Museum Trust*

with minimal bodywork, a very large petrol tank behind the two seats, and a special windscreen, built to his own design. To 'break the monotony', he was to be accompanied by two other Napiers, each with two drivers, who were all testers at the Napier works.[229] The three cars were each painted a different colour: SF's was green while the other two were red and white. SF was conscious that much time could be lost in changing tyres, so the car was fitted with Rudge-Whitworth detachable wheels carrying Dunlop tyres, and a quick-lifting jack was designed. At the last minute, SF realised that the track needed to be lit since the new white surface made it difficult to navigate using only the cars' acetylene headlamps. So some 350 lanterns had to be procured and placed at ten-yard intervals around the inside edge of the course.[230]

Jarrott again seemed to have a difference of opinion with SF. He had told *The Autocar* reporters in January 1907: 'Really, I don't think sixty miles per hour for twenty-four hours on end without stopping is possible, or anything like it. Only men in perfect condition and young [SF was now 39], could hope to approach it. There is also the question of tyres, which I think will be a problem, and I feel sure they will use up very quickly when in use at that speed continued for so great a length of time.'[231]

SF was certainly aware that success would depend as much on his personal endurance as that of the car, and he went through a rigorous training regime prior to the attempt. This included a cold bath each morning, a swim in the lake at his 'country place'[x] in Frensham when possible, a spin on a bicycle, and long walks. He also indulged in fishing: 'A restful out-of-door occupation, which tends to put one in a perfect state of health', and 'Angling trains one to keep the muscles in good

x Uplands, Tilford, Surrey.

SF gets ready for the rigours of driving his 60hp Napier round Brooklands for 24 hours. The car is fitted with massive acetylene headlamps and a special windscreen of Edge's own design. *Brooklands Museum Trust*

SF's green Napier (left) was accompanied on the 24-hour run by two other Napiers — one painted red, the other white — in order to help 'break the monotony'. All three cars averaged over 60mph during the 24 hours. *Brooklands Museum Trust*

condition for sitting still'. He further claimed to be 'an absolute teetotaller and a non-smoker', although some have said that at other times he enjoyed the occasional glass of light claret.[232]

The attempt started at 6pm on Friday, 28 June 1907, and SF had a 'splendid sleep during the day', declaring later that 'I felt very fit, as never before in my life'.[233] SF was accompanied at the trackside by Eleanor, and Montague Napier and his wife were also present, together with a whole team of mechanics. SF's mechanic was his chauffeur, Joseph Blackburn, who insisted on riding with him for the whole 24 hours despite SF's intention that other mechanics would relieve him. Jarrott seems to have overcome his earlier scepticism and was now an enthusiastic supporter, described by *The Autocar* as 'confident that Edge would succeed'.[234]

During one brief rest for SF while his Napier was being refuelled and fitted with replacement tyres, one of Montague Napier's nieces presented him with her doll. *Brooklands Museum Trust*

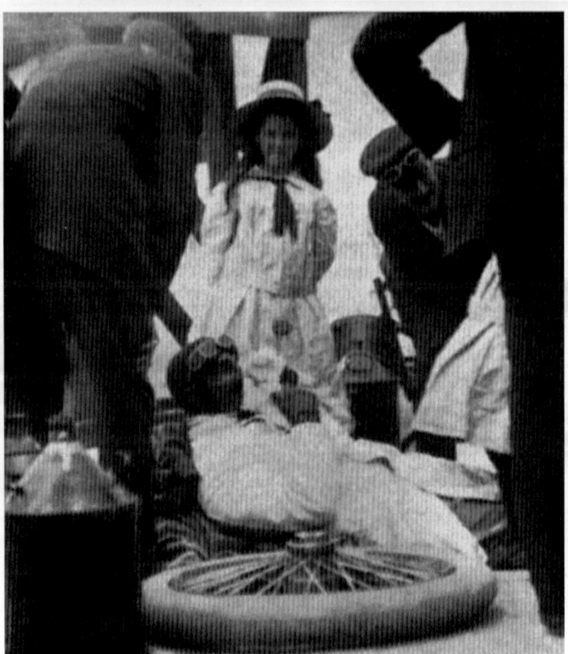

The Trial was observed by the Royal Automobile Club, as the Automobile Club of Great Britain and Ireland was now known. In charge of the timekeepers was A.V. Ebblewhite, who continued to be the permanent timekeeper and handicapper at Brooklands until its closure in 1939.

The Napier covered 70 miles in the first hour, and the first stop was for water at 8.10pm. At that point the lanterns were lit all around the track, and SF pressed on through the night. At 350 miles came the first stop for a change of tyres, which the team carried out very efficiently, being well-rehearsed. However, occasionally tyres would come off the rims while the car was out on the circuit, but the wheels were strong enough for SF to be able to continue driving at 60mph round to the 'depot' for a new wheel to be fitted. 'The car ran like the proverbial clock and never caused me a moment's anxiety'.[235] The greatest distance run in any single hour was over 72 miles, in the 14th hour, and the slowest was the 23rd hour, when 61 miles were covered.

The track, which was not fully finished at this time, was already giving trouble, with holes appearing that had to be filled with gravel as the cars continued circulating. On the penultimate lap, as a result of vibration caused by the rough track, the specially designed windscreen broke, and the glass struck both SF and Blackburn full in the face, but fortunately neither of them were cut.[236] They had been lucky with the weather until towards the end of the run, but as they pulled up at the end, the heavens opened.

▲ Frederick Gordon Crosby captured this night scene of SF's Napier on its way to a 24-hour distance record of 1,581 miles 1,310 yards at an average speed of 65mph. *The Autocar*

The total distance covered in 24 hours was 1,581 miles 1,310 yards, giving an average speed of 65 miles 1,594 yards per hour, comfortably above SF's goal of 60mph. The red and white 'support' cars also completed the 24 hours at an average of over 60mph, but each had more than one driver. SF changed clothes once because the night was cold, but the following day was warm. He took no food during the stops but was fed bananas by Blackburn while driving. During the 24 hours a total of 24 tyres had to be changed on his car. While tyres were being changed, he would lie down for a few moments, which he found refreshing. The last tyre change, made close to the end of the run, was timed at 31 seconds from the moment the car stopped to when it moved off.[237] This was not quite up to modern Formula 1 standards but very impressive nevertheless, and a far cry from the 1902 Gordon Bennett race when SF and his cousin were left to their own devices and had to change tyres with no jack! After the run ended, SF drove himself to the White Lion Hotel in Cobham where he 'slept like the proverbial top the night through'.[238]

The event had been a tremendous success, providing excellent publicity for the Napier concern, which by now was employing 1,200 people at Acton, and giving SF a further boost to his reputation as a successful, and heroic, sportsman.

This British 24-hour record stood for 18 years until beaten by Thomas Gillett driving an AC at Montlhéry, another banked high-speed track near Paris. Weybridge residents had been quick to complain about the noise during the night of SF's attempt, and no more 24-hour events were permitted at Brooklands. As a record on British soil, SF's solo achievement still stands.

The official opening of Brooklands took place on 6 July 1907. Although SF did not race, he set up and managed a team of five Napiers, to be driven by Henry Tryon, Sidney Smith, Cecil Edge and Frank Newton. The cars included a 90hp model, known as *Samson*, with a tubular radiator running down each side of the engine compartment.

The opening meeting was not a success from an organisational point of view but provided more good publicity for Napier. A crowd of 13,500 attended and 500 cars entered the grounds. Tryon won the Marcel Renault Memorial Trophy, Clifford Earp, now driving for a rival concern, Iris, coming second. Smith was less successful, forgetting to put the car in gear before attempting to start his race![239] Newton was competing for the Byfleet Cup, and his race was declared a dead heat with Jarrott driving a De Dietrich. Jarrott lodged a protest, but it was disallowed. SF immediately challenged Jarrott to a race for £1,000 between his Napiers and any cars Jarrott could put up, but the challenge was declined.[240] Cecil Edge competed for the Montagu Cup but had to retire with fluid leaking from his car, the Cup being won by John Hutton on a Mercédès.

The Napier racing team was back at Brooklands for the August Bank Holiday meeting on 5 August 1907. Newton won the International Plate, and the Belgian Plate was a 1–2 victory for Napier, Tryon winning by 100 yards from Cecil Edge. Browning then won the Oatlands Selling Plate on a 38.4hp Napier. The names of the trophies are reminiscent of horse racing, and indeed to

◄ To celebrate the successful 24-hour record, a dinner was held for the employees and various friends of the firms S.F. Edge, Limited and D. Napier & Son. Gold stopwatches were presented to the drivers of the other two Napiers that took part, and to Joseph Blackburn, who rode the whole distance with Edge. Closest to the camera, the man with the moustache is believed to be Joseph Blackburn, while SF is standing alone at the far side of the room. *Brooklands Museum Trust*

begin with all the arrangements followed horse racing practice. Initially, the drivers had to wear different coloured shirts so that they could be identified, like jockeys, and many of the races were 'handicap' ones. However, Ebblewhite was quick to insist that the cars be identified by numbers painted on them, instead of by the colour of the drivers' clothes.

In that first season, 1907, the Napier team scored six wins, one tie, one second and two third places, and collected prize money totalling £1,678.[241]

SF privately booked Brooklands for 2 January 1908, for an attempt to recapture the 50-mile flying start record. Tryon, driving a 60hp Napier, successfully established a new record at 79.44mph. As he continued in pursuit of the 100-mile record, a burst tyre caused a wheel to lock up, the car spun around three times, and Tryon was thrown out. He was lucky to suffer no more than bruising, and he was up and about within a few days.[242] Jarrott then went out on a four-cylinder De Dietrich on 5 February and pushed the record up to 83.11mph. SF could not stand for that, so Newton was sent back with the same 60hp car, and was able to achieve 85.41mph before going on to set new records for 100 miles and 150 miles, and for one and two hours, the last two of which had been set by SF the previous year.[243]

The first meeting of 1908 was held on 18 April. There was a race for 90hp cars in which Newton's Napier slipped down the banking towards Dario Resta's Mercédès on the last lap. The two cars touched momentarily, and spokes went flying, but Newton was able to regain control and pull clear, going on to win the race. Resta lodged a protest, but it was not upheld.[244]

The Napiers that raced in the opening meeting at Brooklands included *Samson*, in which SF is seen. The car had a tubular radiator on each side of its 90hp six-cylinder engine. *Brooklands Museum Trust*

In August 1908, a race of 100 miles was run. It was marred by a fatal accident, when Charles Lane hit a parapet of the bridge in his Mercédès. The mechanic, William Burke, was thrown out and died soon after. One of the Napiers also crashed following a tyre burst, but without fatalities. Newton, in a 60hp Napier, won the race at 98.5mph.[245]

Another race for 90hp cars was run in June 1908, and this time Newton in *Samson* was pitched against a giant chain-drive FIAT of 89.5hp, driven by Felice Nazzaro. In practice on Saturday Newton stripped a gear on the Napier. The car was returned to the factory and the mechanics worked all through Sunday making a new gear, with Newton driving the big car from Acton to Brooklands at 4.00am on the Monday morning ready for the race that day.[246] The race was to be of nine laps but Newton, having led from the start, had to retire on the third lap with a 'fired big-end bearing', leaving Nazzaro to drive on alone and win the race at 94.75mph.[247]

In the middle of the racing season came the sad news that SF's cousin, Cecil, passed away on 27 July 1908 at the tender age of 28. A successful racing driver in his own right, he had accompanied SF on the 1902 and 1903 Gordon Bennett races and played a leading part behind the scenes during the 24-hour drive at Brooklands. He was an employee of SF and had driven non-stop for 1,107 miles in an 18hp Napier in 1904. He was also the driver of the Napier that made a Brighton–London–Edinburgh run in top gear in October 1905, and in May 1907 he had won a gold medal for his performance in a 40hp Napier in the Frome hill climb. *The Autocar* reported that he had been suffering for some months with a chest complaint, but that at Brooklands on 8 June he looked 'almost robust'.[248] Elsewhere his death was attributed to 'consumption', a term commonly used to describe tuberculosis. He must have been sorely missed by SF.

SF (with back to camera) talks to Ernst de Rodakowski, general manager of Brooklands, in August 1908. *Brooklands Museum Trust*

Disturbed by the accidents that had occurred at Brooklands, especially by the death of Burke and, possibly, by the death of his cousin, who had played a key role in managing the racing team, SF wrote the following letter that *The Times* published on 23 September 1908:

> Sir,
> The views which have been so well expressed in your columns with regard to dangerous motor racing have interested and impressed me greatly.
>
> I feel that you will realize that the question is a very serious one for the manufacturer.
>
> There can be no doubt that the rapid development of the automobile has in the past been very largely due to racing, and the public undoubtedly then took a great interest in it, but your recent utterances have developed the fact that there is now an immense volume

➢ Dorothy Levitt on a 26hp racing Napier at Brooklands in 1908. However, the Brooklands Automobile Racing Club barred women from racing. *Motoring Picture Library, National Motor Museum*

of public feeling against dangerous racing, and that there is a general idea that the automobile is developed and established so sufficiently that racing demonstrations of an extreme type are no longer necessary.

As one who has been responsible for most of the racing in this country, I think it may perhaps be my duty in deference to public feeling to be the first manufacturer to publicly announce my intention of withdrawing Napier cars from all dangerous competitions.

In making this announcement I hope the public will accept my assurance that my sole object in automobile racing in the past was to demonstrate the ability of a British manufacturer to hold his own in this high type of engineering against any one in this world, not withstanding the long start our faulty legislation gave our foreign competitors in this great industry.

I feel that that object has now been achieved, and that the British motor-car now leads in type, design, and workmanship.

As I have said, this matter is a serious one for the manufacturer; and it is possible that abstention from racing contests may, as some think, react upon my firm. I must therefore qualify this declaration of my withdrawal from abnormal contests by claiming liberty to lead the fray again if I have mistaken the trend of public feeling.

I would add that my decision in relation to racing will involve no relaxation in every possible scientific effort towards the refinement and development of the British motor-car.

Yours truly,
S.F. EDGE. 14, New Burlington Street, W., Sept. 22.

Another factor in reaching this decision may well have been the financial difficulties his company was experiencing following the slump in sales resulting from the 'Panic of 1907' as described in the next chapter.

SF now focused all his attention on his various business activities.

CHAPTER 9

BACK TO BUSINESS

1902 TO 1912

We must now turn back to 1902 to follow SF's business activities from where we left off in Chapter 5. SF was a director and shareholder in various companies, but it should be made clear that he was never a director in the Napier company, initially called D. Napier & Son, although he liked to give the impression that he was. His relationship with D. Napier & Son was always as the sole agent for sales of cars. Confusion arises because he was agent for several other makes as well as Napier (Panhard et Levassor, Aster, Gladiator, Clément and De Dion-Bouton), through companies that frequently changed their names, most of which were run along with, it seems, some companies he did not own, from 14 Regent Street, London. By mid-1902, SF had moved his offices and showrooms to 14 New Burlington Street, a lane off Regent Street.

SF does not touch much on his business activities in *My Motoring Reminiscences*, and we have H.O. Duncan to thank for throwing some light on them in *The World on Wheels*, published in 1926.

We saw in Chapter 5 that SF was involved in the formation, in 1899, of the Motor Vehicle Company and the De Dion-Bouton British and Colonial Syndicate Ltd. Harvey Du Cros was the main investor in the former, with the latter being formed by SF, Charles Jarrott and Duncan. It was the Motor Vehicle Company that entered into an agreement with Napier to sell all the cars it could produce, but soon after that the business was incorporated as the Motor Power Co., Ltd. The De Dion-Bouton company was the sole agent in Britain for the products of the French company of that name. Also, the Dunlop Motor Company had been formed in 1897 with a capital of £25,000 and with SF, Jarrott and Harry Lawson as directors. The name of this company was changed to The Dion Dunlop Motor Company, in 1899. The names are misleading, because this company had nothing to do with the manufacture or sale of tyres, which was the preserve of Harvey Du Cros's Dunlop Pneumatic Tyre Co, incorporated in 1896. That company's main operations were in Coventry, but it also had offices at 14 Regent Street. The Dion Dunlop Motor Company's main revenue was licence fees collected from the British Motor Company and De Dion-Bouton.[249] Harry Tempest Vane, who later rose to a high position in the Napier company, was appointed Secretary of this company in April 1904, and was probably already Secretary of the Motor Power Co., Ltd.

The French manufacturer, De Dion-Bouton et Compagnie, had been founded in 1883 by Compte (Count) Albert de Dion, Georges Bouton and Charles Trépardoux, based in Puteaux, a suburb of Paris. By the start of the 20th century, it was the largest motor manufacturer in the world. While Panhard, Daimler and Napier made 'heavy' cars, De Dion-Bouton made light cars but also sold its small one-cylinder engines to as many as 150 other manufacturers around the world for use in motor tricycles and light cars. In 1900, De Dion-Bouton sold an estimated 400 cars and 3,200 engines.[250] So the British agency was of some value.

In Chapter 3 we came across Harry Lawson as the organiser of the International Motor Exhibition in 1896, and the owner of the British Motor Syndicate, formed in 1895. Lawson's objective had been to buy up as many patents as possible, and to charge licence fees to motor manufacturers for the use of these patents. This was the subject of much litigation. In 1897 the company changed its name to the British Motor Company Ltd, but by 1898 it was bankrupt. A reconstruction scheme resulted in the remaining assets being taken over by the newly created British Motor Traction Company Ltd in September 1900. SF held nearly all the mortgage debentures over a large proportion of the assets of this company, which included all the patents that had been purchased for enormous sums by

For his advertising of Napier cars, SF emphasised his company's name and presented testimonials from satisfied customers, as in this 1902 example. *gracesguide.co.uk*

Lawson,[251] and he was appointed as a director of the company.

Thus, at the start of 1902, SF was in control of, or had substantial interests in:

- The Motor Power Company, Ltd
- The De Dion-Bouton British and Colonial Syndicate Ltd
- The Dion Dunlop Motor Company
- The British Motor Traction Company Ltd.

He was also listed as a Director of the Ariel Cycle Co., Ltd.

In 1902, a new company called S.F. Edge, Limited was formed, which took over the business of the Motor Power Company, still acting as agents for Gladiator cars as well as Napiers. It seems that the Du Cros family still had a controlling financial interest in the new company, and it is not clear why they allowed SF, ever the self-publicist, to name it after himself, but maybe this was in recognition of the fact that SF was running the show, and the Du Cros family were 'sleeping partners'.

On 12 December 1902, the Ivel Agricultural Motors Limited was formed by Dan Albone. The company was named after a river that ran through Biggleswade, Bedfordshire, the town where Albone was born in 1860 and where his parents ran a pub. He was another racing cyclist (founder member of the North Road Cycling

▲ The Marquis Albert de Dion was a co-founder of De Dion-Bouton, which was the world's largest motor manufacturer at the time when SF began his collaboration with Napier. *The World on Wheels*

➤ A 1901 De Dion-Bouton *vis-à-vis* of the type sold by the De Dion-Bouton British and Colonial Syndicate Ltd. *Author's collection (photo by Argent Archer)*

Club in 1886) and had invented and patented a petrol-powered general-purpose agricultural vehicle — what would now be called a farm tractor, although the term did not come into use until later — which would go on to replace the much heavier steam-driven traction engines. The Marquis of Granby, John Scott-Montagu, SF, Charles Jarrott and Dorothy Levitt (SF's personal secretary at the time) were appointed directors of this company.[252]

The British Motor Traction Company continued to be the subject of much litigation as it tried to collect royalties from most manufacturers, including foreign companies such as De Dion-Bouton and Mercédès. An example of the sort of patents it held was one for the 'float-feed carburettor', which many motor manufacturers used. Under the terms of the patent, anyone importing a foreign car fitted with a float-feed carburettor was expected to pay a royalty of 10%, based not on the cost of the carburettor but on the cost of the complete chassis!

Duncan had this to say in *The World on Wheels*:

> It is certain that if a small royalty on a reasonable basis had been asked, it would have been paid to avoid trouble and litigation; but those who only wished to earn big dividends followed quite the wrong policy. Perhaps it was better for the trade that this was so; otherwise the patent question would have been involved in paying endless royalties that would have led to the formation of a number of 'octopus' companies or syndicates to collect the spoil, much to the detriment of business.[253]

Motoring pioneers come in all sizes: The Marquis Albert de Dion (left) talks to Georges Bouton. *The World on Wheels*

SF also had a conflict of interest being the representative of the French De Dion-Bouton company and thus earning sales commissions as well as claiming royalties from the French company. At the same time he was selling Napier and Gladiator cars in direct competition with De Dion-Bouton.

Duncan again:

> Considerable friction arose with the French manufacturers and Edge over the patent matter, more so when the latter officially notified De Dion-Bouton of his title as

The Napier works at Acton circa 1904: in the foreground are two of the new six-cylinder chassis. *The Veteran Car Club of Great Britain*

The grinding bay in one of the workshops at Acton. *The Autocar (17 November 1906)*

> sole owner of the English patents. It was difficult to reconcile the situation with Edge as managing director of De Dion-Bouton Ltd [the British agent] and the propaganda carried on by him at the time for the English-made Napier car. The position was a strange one and the old Puteaux firm — especially the Marquis de Dion — could not understand it or see any way out of the difficulty.[254]

Early cases were upheld in favour of the British Motor Traction Company, but it lost a major case brought by Charles Friswell on behalf of the Motor Trades Protection Society, and eventually the company was wound up. SF was, however, given the opportunity (in 1907) to buy some of the 'master patents', including those for De Dion and Mercédès.

He explained the situation to Montague Napier and, with the understanding that they would divide any profit that might eventually be made equally between them, Napier put up £1,000 in cash.

SF's and Napier's businesses thrived over the five years from 1902 as sales of Napier cars grew. The Napier factory expanded significantly after moving to Acton in 1903, and large Napier cars were selling well to wealthy individuals[xi] throughout the empire, especially in India and the Middle East. The profit made by D. Napier & Son in 1901 was £19,[xii] and in 1904 was £18,117,[255] when about 500 men were employed,[256] and the workforce had grown to 1,000 by 1906.[257] During this period, the phrase 'the best car in the world' referred to Napier, although by 1907 Rolls-Royce was referring to its Silver Ghost as the 'best six-cylinder car in the world'. SF meanwhile bought the entire production of vehicles from Napier at agreed prices and was free to market them at whatever price he felt he could get. In May 1900 he was paying £400 for an 8–9hp car and selling it for £500.[258]

The De Dion-Bouton company was also doing well, with healthy sales of cars and engines, and Duncan records that it was paying dividends of £2,000 in 1901–02, rising steadily to £5,000 in 1905–06.[259] By this time the Dion Dunlop Motor Company Ltd had faded from the scene, and the business was probably transferred to the De Dion-Bouton company in 1906.

In October 1905, it was announced that S.F. Edge, Limited would be selling an 18hp Regent car, SF explaining that the aim was to 'meet the demands of clients who require a less costly car than the Napier'.[260] A very detailed technical description was given, but nothing was said about the manufacturer, although it is likely the cars were imported from Germany. They were still listed as being for sale, at £400 (chassis only), in 1906, when an equivalent 18hp Napier was selling for £600.[261] Thereafter, nothing further is heard of them, and it seems likely that very few, if any, were sold.

---

xi A sales catalogue issued in 1911, for example, listed numerous public figures as customers, including the Duke of Norfolk, Duke of Bedford, Lord Montagu, Rt Hon H.H. Asquith, Rt Hon A.J. Balfour, Colonel Mark Mayhew, Lionel de Rothschild, H.M. The Queen of Siam, The Nizam of Hyderabad, and many others.

xii A note on the value of the pound: as a very approximate guide, based on a retail price index, between 1900–12, £1 was worth about £120 today; between 1920–29, £1 was worth about £50 today.

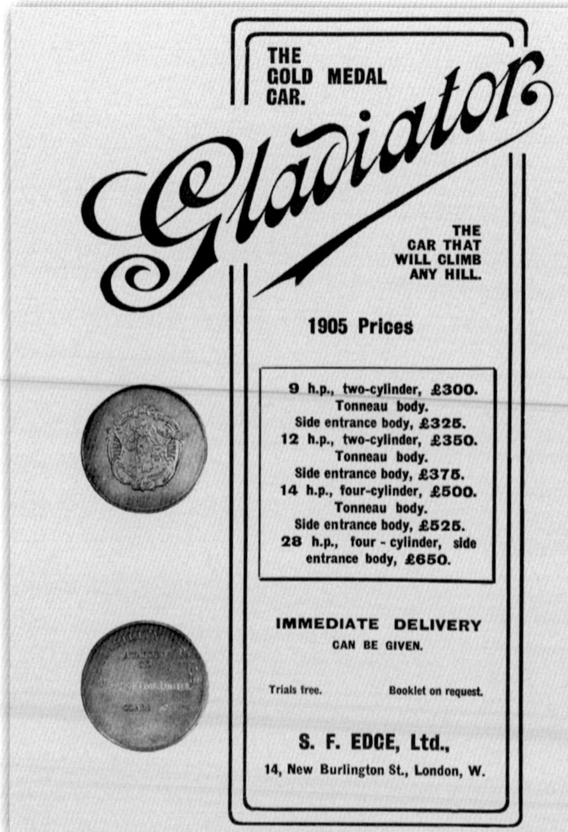

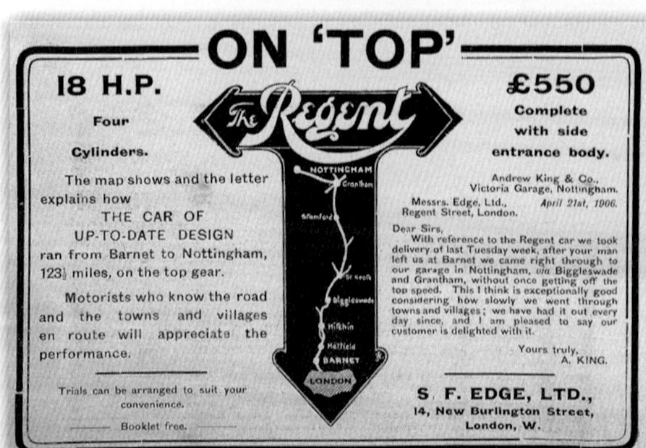

▲ SF sold makes of car other than Napier: a significant one was Gladiator of France; the Regent, which is thought to have been built in Germany, was short-lived. *gracesguide.co.uk*

During 1906 a company called Hertford Street Motor Hiring Co was formed to take over the hiring department of S.F. Edge, Limited. It was incorporated as a limited company in 1910 and the company's business was the hiring out of Napier carriages to the high and mighty of London, including the Master of the King's Horse for His Majesty's guests at the Coronation of George V in June 1911. This company operated in conjunction with the Electromobile Company, Ltd, which had been founded in 1902 and whose business was described as the building, maintaining, charging and storing of battery-powered cars.[262]

SF was a director, and probably shareholder, in both these companies, which together operated from large premises at 7 Hertford Street, Mayfair, London. Hertford Street had been a fashionable residential street, but some properties were converted for commercial use around this time. The two companies occupied a garage covering over one and a half acres bordered by Carrington Street and Brick Street.[263] Built on the site of the Mayfair ducking pond, the massive concrete structure, 300ft long and 80ft wide, comprised a basement, ground floor and first floor, with a flat roof onto which cars could be driven for washing. In 1907 the Electromobile Company described it as 'the World's Greatest Garage'. By 1914 the two companies had merged and were together employing nearly 200 drivers and mechanics. SF must have maintained a financial interest in these companies since he used 7 Hertford Street as his London office address at least until 1927, and may even have had a '*pied-à-terre*' there.

SF must have been doing well for himself because by 1906 he had been able to buy a 'country estate' at Uplands, Tilford, near Farnham.

S.F. Edge, Ltd sold no fewer than eight Napiers to the Nizam of Hyderabad in 1906. Two of them are shown. *The Autocar (8 December 1906)*

SF was a director of the Electromobile Company, which manufactured, maintained and garaged electric cars at 7 Hertford Street, Mayfair, where the flat roof could be used for washing and parking cars. *The Auto (9 March 1912)*

Lawrence Stocks, son of Jack Stocks, recalled weekends spent there with his parents as house guests between 1907 and 1909 and described it as a perfect place for shooting and trout fishing in the private ponds.[264] One Christmas Eve SF staged a firework display on the frozen surface of the nearby Frensham Great Pond. SF was no doubt trying to recreate the weekends he used to spend with the Du Cros family at Cornbury Park. Regular guests at Tilford were a friend of SF, the actor Bransby Williams (1870–1961) with his wife and their four children, who also holidayed with SF in Selsey. Williams was famous for his impersonations, and probably entertained SF's guests on these weekend retreats.

FLOTATIONS

In 1907 SF decided to realise some of his assets by floating new companies. 'Floating' involved incorporating a new company and inviting the public to buy shares in that company, which would then buy the assets and goodwill of an existing company, thus often enabling the owners of the existing company to realise a part of their investments. SF did this for both S.F. Edge, Limited and De Dion-Bouton, Limited, floating S.F. Edge (1907), Limited and De Dion-Bouton (1907), Limited as the new companies, which then bought the assets of the respective predecessors.

Before the flotation of S.F. Edge, Limited, SF held 19,888 (49.72%) of the 40,000 shares issued by the company. The new company, S.F. Edge (1907), Limited, was formed with a capital of £275,000, The business of the old company was to be acquired by the new company for £200,000, which included £93,000 of goodwill, the consideration being in the form of 200,000 ordinary shares of £1 each in the new company issued to the owners of the old company. A further 75,000 shares were being offered to the public in the prospectus issued at the end of July 1907.[265] The Directors of the new company were SF, as Chairman and Managing Director, The Hon Dudley Massey Pigott Carleton, William Du Cros, The Hon Derek William George Keppel, and Montague Napier, and the Secretary was H.T. Vane. The prospectus disclosed the sales of S.F. Edge, Limited as having been (for years ending in February):

1901 £18,229
1902 £41,090
1903 £94,260
1904 £201,963
1905 £210,203
1906 £236,143
1907 £333,117

Gross profits for the four years ending 31 December 1906 were £163,681. The prospectus declared that the business of the company was 'Dealing in Napier Motor Cars' and confirmed that the new company would inherit the right to purchase the 'whole output' of the Napier factory until at least 1921. References were made to a licence sold to an Italian company to manufacture Italian cars of Napier design[xiii] and to negotiations being underway for a similar arrangement in the USA.

At a shareholders' meeting held in November 1907, SF reported that 63,058 of the 75,000 shares offered to the public had been taken up, giving a total of 263,058, but less than 25,000 of the new shares had been subscribed for by the public, the remainder being bought by SF, Du Cros and companies related to them.[266] Of the total, it appears SF held only 96,666 shares (37%), with the Du Cros family holding slightly more. Montague Napier held 1,000 shares in his own name at this point. SF told the meeting that the company was specialising in 'the six-cylinder principle' with the hope of getting the highest class of motor trade in Britain and abroad.

The prospectus for De Dion-Bouton (1907), Limited had been issued slightly earlier, in March 1907, with 185,000 shares of £1 each being offered to the public. The Directors of this company were SF as Chairman, Jack Stocks as Managing Director, H.O. Duncan as Managing Director in France, S. Van den Bergh, W. Scott-Leefe and Arthur Phillips. The Secretary was Walter Munn, the man who had reintroduced SF to Montague Napier in 1899.

The flotation was not without some drama. The prospectus initially claimed that the company held the rights to manufacture De Dion-Bouton cars in England. When the Marquis de Dion saw this, by chance, he was furious and threatened legal action. Duncan had to act as intermediary, and SF had to back down, signing an agreement that gave the French firm the sole right to manufacture in England. The public response to the offering was small and the Underwriters, the Prudential Trust Corporation, had to buy £165,000 of the £185,000 of shares on offer.[267] *Motor Finance* subsequently reported: 'Mr. S.F. Edge... was unable to reply to our criticisms or explain the various unintelligible and misleading paragraphs in the prospectus.'[268] SF continued for a time as Chairman of the new company at a salary of £1,750 per annum, but the relationship with the Marquis de Dion got so bad that eventually SF was persuaded to step down in exchange for a payment of £4,000 or £5,000.[269]

Duncan estimated that SF 'pocketed' nearly £50,000 from the sale of the assets of De Dion-Bouton Limited.[270] Included in these assets were

xiii *The Autocar* of 7 September 1907 carried a photograph of two fine-looking Napiers on the Grand St Bernard pass in the Alps that had been built by the San Giorgio Company. Arthur MacDonald, SF's riding mechanic in the 1904 Gordon Bennett race, had been sent to Italy to supervise the construction. The business had been wound up by 1909, however.

the patents bought from Lawson with the £1,000 advanced by Montague Napier, as mentioned above, and Napier was 'undoubtedly astonished' when SF handed over part of the £50,000 received. Overall, Duncan estimated that SF netted some £250,000 out of the two flotations[271], but this is clearly overstated, and in reality the flotations were a financial failure.

At the time of the flotation of S.F. Edge (1907), Limited agreements were in place whereby SF would receive a salary of £2,000 per annum and a commission of 5% of the profits, and this agreement was to remain in place for 21 years.[272]

The Panic of 1907

The flotation of S.F. Edge (1907), Limited took place shortly after SF's 24-hour record at Brooklands. The timing was fortunate, not just because of the publicity generated by his record-breaking run, for the last quarter of 1907 witnessed the first global financial crisis of the century. Known as the 'Panic of 1907' or the 'Knickerbocker Crisis' (named after the Knickerbocker Trust, the largest of the US financial institutions to collapse), it had many similarities to the global financial crisis of 100 years later. In mid-October 1907 prices on the New York Stock Exchange fell by 50% from their peak of the previous year, sparking a recession exceeded only by the Great Depression that followed the Stock Market crash of 1929.

Sales of Napiers plummeted: in 1907 the factory turned out 299 cars, but in 1908 they produced only 187 cars and 11 taxis.[273] As a consequence, the accounts of S.F. Edge (1907), Limited for the 15 months ended 30 September 1908 reported a net loss of £48,834. SF used the old trick of holding the Annual General Meeting on 31 December 1908 to limit the number of shareholders attending, but even so, it was a source of embarrassment to him: so much so that the report to the shareholders for the year ended 30 September 1909 stated: 'To compensate for this loss, Mr S.F. Edge proposes to consent to the cancellation of 48,834 shares held by him in the company.'[274] Thus SF bore the entire loss for 1907–08 himself, despite the fact that he was still in partnership with Harvey Du Cros, and this reduced his interest in the company to less than 23%.

The balance sheet at 30 September 1908, as reported in *The Automobile Owner and Steam and Electric Car Review* of January 1910, included on the assets side:

Sundry debtors	£20,732
Bills receivable	£5,847
Deposit with D. Napier & Son	£34,600
Stock in hand	£101,001
Total	£162,180

This gives an insight into the problem the company was facing. The agreement with D. Napier & Son had been 'to purchase the entire output of Napier cars' although at some point this had been modified by adding 'up to £120,000 per annum'. This was not a problem as long as demand remained high, but the company was now in a position where it could not sell all that Napier produced. Hence the high value of stock at £101,001, which probably represented more than 300 vehicles.[275] Put another way, if their annual purchases were limited to £120,000, the last ten months of purchases (£100,000) were unsold at

the year-end. The contract with D. Napier & Son, which had been the principal asset of S.F. Edge, Limited at the time of the flotation, had now become onerous.

This could explain the decision taken at an Extraordinary General Meeting held in the second quarter of 1909 to cancel the arrangement between S.F. Edge (1907), Limited and DNS and the subsequent announcement that Napier cars would be sold by the company only until the end of 1910. This was the sole activity of the company, so effectively it was announcing its winding up.

The minutes of DNS record that a 'settlement agreement' between 'Messrs Du Cros and S.F. Edge of one part and M.S. Napier and D. Napier & Son of the other part' had been approved on 19 July 1909, and this was followed by the purchase by DNS of 100,000 shares in S.F. Edge (1907), Limited, for an undisclosed sum, on 30 November 1909.[276] It was reported that the greater part, if not all, of these shares had belonged to the Du Cros family. In January 1910, of the 216,724 shares in S.F. Edge (1907), Limited in issue, 109,000 (just over 50%) were held by DNS, 47,832 were held by SF, with only 500 held by Harvey Du Cros. The balance of 59,392 was held by other companies, including the Scott and Clipper Tyre Company and the Regent Carriage Company (a coachbuilding firm in which Harvey Du Cros had an interest).[277]

Shortly before these share transactions took place, SF had travelled to the United States, arriving in New York on board the Cunard liner *Lusitania* on 13 August 1909.[xiv] The purpose of

This caricature of SF was published in *The Automotor Journal* in 1909. *The Automotor Journal (24 April 1909)*

his visit was probably to learn more about the motor industry and its market, but it is likely that he also needed to visit the Napier Motor Company of America that had been set up to assemble cars from parts shipped from Acton. There had been an ongoing debate about the need for tariff reform (America had a 45% 'protective' tariff on imported vehicles) and how difficult it was for British car manufacturers to export to the United States, so this would have been an attempt to overcome the problem. The American

xiv The *Lusitania* was sunk by a German submarine in May 1915, with the loss of 1,197 lives.

company, situated in Jamaica Plains, Boston, was in financial difficulties early in 1909 and eventually closed its doors in 1912.[278]

On his return to London, SF was interviewed by *The Autocar*,[279] and when asked whether American cars were 'equal to a Napier or a Rolls-Royce', he singled out the Pierce-Arrow as being 'in every way first-class'. He also commented on drivers being much more disciplined than they were in Britain, but the 'street surfaces in New York were a disgrace to a great city'.

Sales had started to pick up in 1909: having produced only 187 cars and 11 taxis in 1908, DNS produced 366 cars and 556 taxis in 1909; 617 cars and 562 taxis in 1910; and 801 cars and 135 taxis in 1911.[280] S.F. Edge (1907), Limited reported a net profit of £4,078 for the year ended 30 September 1909. The profit for the year 1909–10 was £17,000, for the year 1910–11 was £11,611, and for 1911–12 was £54,822.[281] The production of taxis, starting in 1908 although short-lived, was a significant step, reflecting Napier's belief in the need for diversification into what he called 'business vehicles'. A significant customer for taxis was W. & G. Du Cros, run by two sons of Harvey Du Cros, William and George. SF, however, was not happy with this as he felt that it damaged the image of Napiers as 'the best cars in the world'. The sale of taxis was clearly less profitable for S.F. Edge (1907), Limited.

As early as 9 February 1910, the DNS Board approved the sale of all of their 109,000 shares (including the 100,000 shares they had purchased in November 1909) to SF,[282] again for an undisclosed sum, although elsewhere it was reported that SF paid £110,000 for these shares. It would seem that the agreement whereby S.F. Edge (1907), Limited (which in 1910 changed its name back to S.F. Edge, Limited) would buy the entire output of Napier cars had continued uninterrupted during this period, despite the resolution to terminate it, but this was not acknowledged in the minutes until 28 October 1910 when 'a trading agreement between D. Napier & Son Ltd of the one part and Messrs S.F. Edge Ltd of the other part, to come into force for a period of four years commencing 31 Oct 1910' was approved. Then on 18 September 1911 this agreement was extended 'for a further term of three years'.

The net loser in these transactions seems to have been the Du Cros family, who previously held a controlling interest in S.F. Edge (1907), Limited, but whose shares were effectively transferred to SF, with the collaboration of D. Napier & Son. One has to speculate whether this was an elaborate plan by SF, and possibly Montague Napier, to take over control from the Du Cros family, by convincing them that the business was going to close, and thus they should sell their shares at a reduced price. However, it is also possible that Harvey Du Cros, concerned by the losses made in 1907 and not optimistic about the future, was looking for a way to exit the business. This is ironic in the light of the events of 1912, as we shall see shortly.

The relationship between SF and his one-time mentor and sponsor, Harvey Du Cros, was clearly not good at this time, and in July 1911 SF took Harvey to court, suing for 'one half of the profits of the Panhard and Levassor Motor Agency, Gladiator Motor Agency, and Panhard Repair Works'. There was also the Clément

agency, from which SF claimed 3% of the total amount of purchases from the French company. It was explained to the Court that, following the formation of the Motor Power Company in February 1900, SF suggested to Du Cros that they also take on the Panhard et Levassor and the Gladiator agency. The Panhard company, however, 'would not allow Mr. Edge to be associated with the agency, and suggested that it should be conducted by Mr. Du Cros'. Du Cros agreed to run the Panhard agency in his name from 14 Regent Street, while the Napier and Gladiator business was to be carried on by SF from 14 New Burlington Street, with Du Cros agreeing to pay half of the profits from the Panhard agency to SF, which he did to begin with.[283]

The Panhard balance sheet of May 1906 was the last that SF had been allowed to see, and he had received no payments after that.[284] When SF asked Harvey Du Cros for a copy of a subsequent balance sheet, Du Cros took great offence, writing:

> The Panhard business and your business are on an entirely different footing. You are not entitled to have the one treated as the other. I will never send you the Panhard balance sheets. You are not a shareholder. There has been a gift of profits, but the agency belongs to me absolutely. You have now brought matters to a position that you have been aiming at for some time. I prefer your open enmity to your covert opposition.

The Court had earlier been shown a letter to SF written by Du Cros in December 1895 in which he had expressed a very different sentiment:

> I should like to tell you how greatly I appreciate the support you have always given me. I lay awake a long time this morning, and came to the conclusion that there is no one I feel disposed to depend on more than yourself. I have unlimited confidence in you, and a very great regard for you.[285]

The Court was then told that Harvey Du Cros had been trying to get out of these arrangements for some time, and in 1905 devised a scheme whereby all Panhard cars would be sold at a loss to two of his sons, William and George, who would then benefit from the profits of the business (the implication being that his actions were fraudulent). Harvey argued that the half-share of the profits had been a 'gift' by him to SF 'of his own free will in appreciation of past services and part of a sentimental, honorable, agreement between them'.

Just two days later this was reported as having been settled out of court, with payment of a 'sum which would give him [SF] substantial satisfaction for the claim for damages', and 'with charges of fraud being withdrawn'.

The Hutton car

Another attempt at diversification during the slump in sales in 1908 had been the building of the Hutton car. The regulations for the 1908 Tourist Trophy race on the Isle of Man stipulated that only four-cylinder cars could compete, with a maximum cylinder bore of four inches (hence the race became known as 'the four-inch race'). SF, having been so active in promoting the six-

cylinder Napiers (see Appendix 3), did not want to contemplate the idea of a four-cylinder Napier winning a race. An agreement was therefore reached with John Hutton, a successful motor racer who already had his own car company, under which the Napier factory would build cars for him to enter in the Tourist Trophy, with the car being branded as a Hutton. The cars that resulted, however, were so similar to Napiers, including the iconic radiators, that the idea of badge-engineering them as Huttons was pointless. A contract to build 360 cars for Hutton between 1908 and 1911 was entered into,[286] but Hutton's business went into receivership soon after and the contract was cancelled.[287] Only three Huttons were built, all entered in the Tourist Trophy race. Two of them (one driven by Hutton) crashed during the race but the third, driven by William Watson, won.

FLYING MACHINES

The first decade of the 20th century also saw the development of manned flight. The Wright brothers, Wilbur and Orville, had made their first flight in a powered, heavier-than-air machine in South Carolina in December 1903. In 1909, Louis Blériot made the first flight across the English Channel, and by 1910 aircraft were already being built in Britain by the British and Colonial Aeroplane Company (later to be called Bristol) and A.V. Roe, amongst others.

As early as 1901, SF was offering a 'Napier Flying Machine' for £950, but this was a steerable balloon fitted with an engine, and there is no record of any being sold.[288] At the time of the Motor Show in November 1909, SF wrote:

> I think you may be perfectly certain within a reasonable period that good, sound flying machines will come forth from the Napier factory, but when they do they will be machines of a type which I shall have first used myself thoroughly, and they will not be sold until they are sufficiently safe for us not to run the risk of losing our customers.

In May 1910, it was reported that SF was 'devoting not a little of his time to aviation' and that he had already made several successful flights.[289]

SF usually showed great foresight in anticipating future developments in transportation, seeing the potential of first the pneumatic tyre, then the motor car. However, he seemed to underestimate the speed at which powered flight would become safe and reliable, although he recognised that 'really long flights will be possible'. In an article in February 1910, he suggested that an 'airway' be built between Purley and Brighton. This would be a clear path, something like a grass runway that would connect the two places, above which aeroplanes could fly, 'open on certain days of the week to aeronauts, who would, of course, pay a fee for the privilege of using it'. The benefit, he suggested, would be that 'if he does not succeed in actually flying the whole distance, he will be able to finish his journey on wheels.'[290] He claimed that if there was such an airway, he could sell 'a hundred aeroplanes tomorrow'.[291] He had discussed the possibility of Napier building aircraft, that 'could be bought for £300 or £400', but that the company would not do so unless they were safe, and that he would test them himself.

The death of his friend the Hon. Charles Rolls on 12 July 1910 at the age of 32, must have been

a great shock to SF. Rolls, while effectively having been the Sales and Marketing Director of Rolls-Royce Limited until his resignation in 1909, enjoyed flying in balloons as a sport, making over 170 ascents, and was a pioneer aviator. He had successfully made a non-stop two-way flight across the Channel on 2 June 1910 and was demonstrating his Wright Flyer at a display at Bournemouth when the tail of the plane broke off, and he plunged to his death. SF attended his funeral at Llangattock Church in Wales on 18 July.

SF made other prophecies in a speech to the National Society of Chauffeurs on 16 March 1910. Talking about motoring 50 years' hence, he predicted that roads would be paved with artificial rubber so that cars could be run with iron tyres,[292] that the price of a car would be £50, and that the number of chauffeurs would be counted in millions.[293]

In 1910, SF bought Gallops Homestead, on the South Downs in East Sussex, and began a new phase of his life as a 'gentleman farmer'. These photographs show it in 1950, as advertised for sale, and include the clock tower built for SF. *Michael Cooke collection*

BECOMING A COUNTRY GENTLEMAN

Less than three years after he bought his house at Tilford, SF moved to Stock Farm, Churt, on the other side of Farnham, which included several thousand acres of land suitable for pheasant shooting. Then in 1910 he purchased Gallops Homestead on the South Downs near Ditchling, in East Sussex. Shortly afterwards, in 1911, he purchased two neighbouring farms, Blackbrook Farm in Westmeston and Malt House Farm in Streat. Together these came to some 15,000 acres of land comprising ten different farms, presumably tenanted,[294] with SF as the 'gentleman farmer', and one wonders whether he was already planning for his retirement from the motor industry.

Gallops Homestead, designed by the architect C.H.B. Quennell, had been built at a cost of £2,200 as a weekend retreat for a resident of London, with five bedrooms, a thatched roof, a coach house and staff quarters.[295] SF expanded it after he bought it, doubling its size, probably still using Quennell as the architect. The stables were

extended and converted to garages, and SF had a large clock tower built. The house still stands today, recently renovated, but much as SF knew it.

The year 1911 was relatively uneventful, although busy, for SF, now that he had withdrawn his team from racing, and with the economy having recovered from the 1907 slump. Perhaps he was absorbed in settling into Gallops Homestead. However, he found time to help set up a coachbuilding company, the Cunard Motor & Carriage Co. Ltd, which established itself in Putney and quickly, with SF as Chairman and Harry Vane as one of the directors, became the primary supplier of bodies for Napier cars.[296] During the year he was also able to sell a 15hp Napier Landaulette for over £600 to none other than Winston Churchill. The Churchills were on holiday in Scotland at the time, so Napier provided one of its engineers to drive the car to meet the Churchills there and then act as their chauffeur. Soon after, Churchill was appointed First Lord of the Admiralty by Prime Minister Asquith. SF was to meet Churchill again in less pleasant circumstances in 1917.

South Africa

Early in 1912, SF was off to South Africa accompanied by Charles Jarrott, who had also retired from motor racing and was now associated with Crossley, the long-established engineering firm in Manchester. They sailed together on the *Walmer Castle* from Southampton, returning in April. SF was keen to sell Napiers throughout the then British Empire, and he cited the objective of his visit as being 'to discover by practice, observation, and enquiry what was, or what would form, a really suitable motor car for use in that country'.[297] He took an 'Extra strong' 15hp Colonial Napier with him, and while there drove over 3,000 miles in it. The Royal Automobile Club of South Africa hosted a dinner for them at the Mount Nelson Hotel in Cape Town on 8 February 1912.

In a lengthy interview, conducted at his Gallops Homestead and published in *The Autocar* of 13 April 1912, he detailed how, starting in Cape Town, he put his car on a train to Kimberley, then drove to Johannesburg, where the Mayor and members of the Johannesburg Automobile Club drove out to meet them, and escort them into the city. He then put the car on a train to Bulawayo, from where they drove to Mafeking. Subsequently they made a trip to the Victoria Falls on the Zambezi. While praising the beauty of the scenery, and the hospitality of the South Africans they met, he complained about the lack of road signs and the scarcity of petrol supplies. It was common to find gates across the roads that had to be opened and closed, and he counted 160 such gates in the 250 miles between Mossel Bay and Cape Town. He concluded that there was a good market not just for cars of the right design, but also for commercial vehicles and motorcycles, adding that he learnt much about how British cars should be modified to suit the local conditions.[298]

This trip was clearly dedicated to the promotion of sales of Napier cars, with no hint of doubts about the future, yet SF's life was about to change dramatically before the year was out.

➢ The illustrations on the following seven pages show the cover and various inside pages from an 86-page sales brochure issued by S.F. Edge, Ltd in 1911. *Author's collection*

THE NAPIER BOOK

1911 – 1912

Being a clear and concise statement of fact about the Noiseless Napier, told in an interesting and simple manner

S. F. EDGE LTD.

Telephones: 8926, 8927 8928 and 8929 Gerrard.

Telegrams & Cables: "Nitrifier, London." Cable Codes: Liebers, Western Union and A.B.C. (5th Edition).

14 New Burlington St., London, W

Napier Works, Acton Vale, London

Two-seated Doctor's Coupe (closed).

15 h.p. Noiseless Napier Doctor's Coupé.

THIS car has been produced to meet the requirements of Doctors and other Professional Gentlemen having use for a small four cylinder car which can be used open or shut, which will climb anything in the way of a hill, having a good turn of speed if rapid journeys are necessary. It is constructed to seat two persons comfortably, and, if desired, an extra seat folding down into the fishtail can be fitted. The body can be entirely open or closed as required, the glass windscreen remains a fixture, its lines having been designed to give the car a most symmetrical appearance.

15 h.p. Standard Chassis (8 ft. 10 in. Wheelbase) and Body. (Code Word **HADDOCK**)
15 h.p. de Luxe Chassis (9 ft. 10 in. Wheelbase) and Body. (Code Word **SKATE**)
Lamps to choice extra.

Two-seated Doctor's Coupe (open).

For Specification of Chassis see Page 25.

65 h.p. 6-Cylinder Noiseless Napier Torpedo.

THIS is the type of car which won the Dewar Trophy in 1910 for the best performance of any car during the season under Royal Automobile Club supervision. This Trophy was awarded for a run on a 65 h.p. Noiseless Napier Car, fully loaded, from London to Edinburgh and back on top speed without a single change of gear. The petrol consumption was 19·35 miles per gallon. After the road portion of the trial the car was driven on Brooklands track where it attained a speed of 76·042 miles per hour.

45 h.p. Chassis, Body, Double Screen and Winding Hood. (Code Word **WHITEBAIT**)
65 h.p. Chassis, Body, Double Screen and Winding Hood. (Code Word **BASS**)
Detachable Wire Wheels if required, and Lamps to choice extra.
Extras if required: Interior Footrest and Tool Receptacle. Tool Box on step.
Spare Wire Wheel Brackets. Single screen shown, but Double Screen is recommended.

For Specifications of Chassis see Pages 27 and 28.

30 h.p. 6-Cylinder Noiseless Napier Landaulette.

THIS carriage is specially suitable for those who require a car for travelling rapidly and comfortably, with good luggage carrying capacity and whilst combining all the necessary appearance of a smart Town Carriage, can be opened sufficiently for country touring to allow the occupants the pleasure of an almost open car when the weather conditions are suitable. Its ample speed and ability to easily negotiate hills make it a luxurious car in every sense of the word. This car seats 7 persons.

30 h.p. Chassis and Body. (Code Word **MINNOW**)
Lamps and Horn to choice extra.

Landaulette Bodies, suitable for 30 h.p. Chassis, can be supplied, to seat four persons inside and two outside (including the driver), with Canopy and Glass Screen.

For Specification of Chassis see page 26.

Napier Commercial Vehicles.

A Group of Napier Lorries used by the British Military Authorities for Transport of Baggage and Stores.

Full Particulars and Specifications of Delivery Vans, Luggage Lorries, Cabs, etc., together with details of Cost of Running, will be supplied on application.

Extract from the "Daily Telegraph," September 21st, 1909.

"ONE of the features of to-day's fighting near Tadpole Bridge was the excellent service rendered by a Maxim mounted on a motor carriage. The carriage is driven by a 6-cylinder Napier Engine, and acted with one of our cavalry regiments—I may not mention which—throughout the day. The Irish Guards made a desperate effort to capture the precious weapon, and a company of mounted infantry galloped hard to seize it ; but the trusty motor outdistanced the fleetest horseman and the fierce Irishry alike, and, taking up a fresh position, peppered them until they had hastily to seek cover to escape from its projectiles. The battle will be renewed with the dawn tomorrow."

Part of the fleet of Napier Motor Cabs operated by the Coupé Co. in public service. A similar fleet of Napier Cars, well equipped, is also operated by the same company, for private hire. There are also many hundreds of Napier Cabs running in London marked "W. & G.," "Gamage Bell," etc.

These are but a few of the many hundreds of NAPIER CABS running in London. These Cabs have now run over eight million miles.

65 h.p. 6-Cylinder Noiseless Napier
90 h.p. 6-Cylinder Noiseless Napier

Specification of 65 h.p. Noiseless Napier 6-Cylinder Motor Chassis.

PRINCIPAL DIMENSIONS AND DETAILS.—**65 h.p.**—**Bore,** 5in. (127m/m). **Stroke,** 5in. (127m/m). **No. of Cylinders,** 6. **Transmission,** live axle. **No. of Speeds,** 3. **Frame,** pressed steel. **Road Gauge,** 4ft. 8in. (1m422). **Wheel Base,** 11ft. 2in. (3m404). **Length behind Dash,** 8ft. 2¼in. (2m496). **Width of Frame,** 32in. (813). **Extreme Width,** 5ft. 6in. (1m6·74). **Front Tyres,** 880 by 120 m/m. **Back Tyres,** 895 by 135 m/m. **Gear Box. Bearings,** Ball. **Engine Bearings,** Plain. **Petrol Feed,** Pressure. **Lubrication,** Forced. **Ignition,** Napier Synchronised (Battery and Coil), also H.T. Magneto.

MOTOR.—Napier 6-cylinder engine, cylinders arranged in pairs. The camshaft and all gearing entirely enclosed in aluminium oil-retaining case. Inlet and exhaust valves operated from one camshaft, and interchangeable. Special Napier patent controllable carburettor, controlled by accelerator pedal and actuated by a lever on steering wheel.

IGNITION (Synchronised and H.T. Magneto).—Advance and retard provided for both ignitions operated from steering wheel.

TRANSMISSION GEAR.—Three speeds forward and a reverse. The drive on the top speed direct. The driving surfaces of the clutch have metal to metal contact (no leather used), the surfaces being kept lubricated, to give a smooth, silent, and gentle engagement, the clutch is devoid of end thrust when engaged.

WATER CIRCULATION.—By rotary pump, actuated by positive drive and relatively slow running. Radiator with induced draught system of cooling fitted.

SMOKELESS LUBRICATION.—By the Napier automatic forced feed system to all parts necessary, operated by a pump, driven from the camshaft, which forces the oil through a strainer from a well to all the various engine bearings, whence it returns to the well. A pressure gauge on the dashboard. Screw-down grease cups to all parts where required.

BRAKES.—Two independent sets of powerful metal to metal brakes, one operated by the driver's foot, the other operated by hand, of internal expanding type, either brake sufficiently powerful to prevent the car running backwards or forwards.

FRAME.—Of steel channel section, the central portion of deep section. All road springs very long and flexible to ensure easy riding. Transverse spring at back.

SPRINGS.—Long and Flexible to give easy riding, and of ample strength to withstand the strains of rough roads.

LIVE AXLE.—Chainless drive, being by means of cardan shaft to the live axle of special Napier design and construction.

ROAD WHEELS.—Artillery pattern, with oak spokes and steel bosses.

TYRES.—Plain to all four wheels, 880 by 120m/m front, 895 by 135m/m rear.

STEERING.—By wheel, every part adjustable for wear. All levers and rods with their ends of solid steel forgings, all joints thoroughly secure.

PETROL TANK.—Fitted at the rear end of the frame, the supply to the carburettor by means of mechanically operated air pump.

BEARINGS.—Of ample dimensions. Ball-bearing thrusts fitted wherever necessary. Ball-bearings to all road wheels.

DASHBOARD.—Made of wood ; or if of solid aluminium extra if specified and agreed on at time of order.

FINISH.—Brass or Nickel to parts such as Radiator, Hub Caps, Sectors and Levers on Steering Wheel, Grip of Brake Lever, and Pressure Pump.

LAMP BRACKETS.—Two brackets for side lamps, fitted to dashboard. One tail lamp bracket and number plate combined.

TOOLS AND ACCESSORIES.—Our quotation includes the following tools and spare parts: Two double-ended Spanners, one Adjustable Spanner, one Screw-driver, one Oil Feeder, one Hub Key, one Accumulator, one Valve Cap Spanner, one Box Spanner, Spare Nuts, Bolts, and Pins, assortment of Split Pins, one Interrupter Plug, one Induction Pipe Spanner, one Carburetter Cap, One Instruction Book.

GUARANTEE.—In the event of a purchase being made according to this Specification, we will give the owner our special printed form of guarantee extending over three years from date of delivery.

TERMS.—One-Third Deposit payable with Order, remaining Two-Thirds when Car or Chassis is ready for delivery, according to whichever is offered.

DELIVERY.—At 14 New Burlington Street, London, W., free.

OPTIONAL EXTRAS.—

One Pair Head Lamp Brackets, Nickel or Brass Plated, extra. Head Lamp Brackets included free if Head Lamps purchased from us.

A few Owners of 59·99 h.p. 6-Cylinder Noiseless Napiers.

Duke of Bedford
Duke of Fife
Marquis St. Mars
Earl of Berkeley
Earl of Lonsdale
Viscount Curzon
Lord Devenport
Lord Farquhar
Lord Revelstoke
Sir Herbert Ashman
Sir George Mayrick
Sir John Miller
Sir Malcolm M'Eachern
Sir George Pilkington
Sir Marcus Samuel
Rt. Hon. A. J. Balfour
Colonel Mark Mayhew
Major Shewell
Captain D. Watt

Captain Watson Cameron
Lieut. J. B. Waterlow
Mrs. L. M. Barker
Christopher Bird, Esq.
Stephen Cliff, Esq.
H. B. Money-Coutts, Esq.
W. R. Fasey, Esq.
Harvey du Cross, Esq.
F. Baring-Gould, Esq.
C. E. Galbraith, Esq.
H. S. Higginbottom, Esq.
H. Livesay, Esq.
Mrs. L. Walker Munro
Marshall O. Roberts, Esq.
Hon. Chas. N. Rothschild
Leopold de Rothschild, Esq.
Lionel de Rothschild, Esq.
Arthur Sassoon, Esq.
H. O. N. Shaw, Esq.

Franklin Thomasson, Esq.
J. White Todd, Esq.
J. Alexander-Todd, Esq.
G. S. Topham, Esq.
A. M. Vestey, Esq.

A few Owners of 59·99 h.p. 6-Cylinder Noiseless Napiers abroad.

H. H. The Maharajah of Idar, India
Sir Montague Allan, Canada
General Spitzer, U.S.A.
Captain French, Vancouver
E. R. Rathbone Bacon, Esq., N. York
Edson Bradley, Esq., U.S.A.
F. C. Brandauer, Esq., Munich
W. Campbell Clarke, Esq., U.S.A.

T. A. Comber, Esq., Brazil
F. Wellman, Esq., U.S.A.
Geo. Marshall Allen, U.S.A.
Snr. Lagos, Argentine
M. Henri de Malglaive, Algiers

A few Owners of 90 h.p. 6 Cylinder Noiseless Napiers.

Earl of Lonsdale
Captain Hamilton
Stuart de la Rue, Esq.
C. A. Cain, Esq.
Lionel de Rothschild, Esq.
C. A. Walker, Esq.
H. E. Count Alexis of Santa Eulalia
J. C. Eaton, Esq., Canada
T. L. Kan, Esq., Java
T. D. Morison, Esq.

SUBSTANTIAL EVIDENCE
THE NAPIER IS
THE PROVED BEST CAR
B.M.B.C. Cup, Ramsgate
Aston Hill Climb, 1908
House of Commons Challenge Cup
Southport Cup Flying Kilometer
Inter Club Oakamore Hill Climb
Brooklands Automobile Racing Club, Private Stakes
British Motor Boat Club
One Mile, Napier First
"Daily Mail" Challenge Cup
"Won by Napier Major"
Blackpool Cup
Minneapolis Trophy
S. F. Edge Challenge Trophy for London to Cowes race
Wilson Challenge Trophy
The Tourist Trophy.
The Dewar Trophy
The Montagu Cup
Lowestoft Town Cup
International Challenge Cup at Portmarnock
Essex County A. C. Cup
Van der Slegen Ostend Trophy
Gordon Bennett Trophy
Blackpool Cup Fastest Flying Kilometer
Liverpool Bay Cup.
5 Mile Heavyweight Championship, Florida
Bexhill Cup
Kaiser Cup
Earl De La Warr's Cup, Bexhill
Motoring Illustrated Challenge Cup
The O'Gorman Trophy
British Motor Boat Club Prize for first boat to finish in London to Cowes race
Millar Trophy
Liverpool Bay Cup
Thomas Trophy
Wilson Challenge Cup.
British Motor Boat Club Cup
B.M.B.C. Commodore's Cup
Entente Cordiale Cup.
Midland Automobile Club.

CHAPTER 10

TRANSITION

In *My Motoring Reminiscences*, SF records: 'In the early autumn [of 1912], I decided to sell out my interests in S.F. Edge Limited to Montague Napier. I took this step for various reasons. My life had been a very strenuous one in raising the Napier car to the standing it then enjoyed. It ranked second to none in the world, and its reputation had been won on the hard field of competition. The love of the country which was innate in me and the wish to follow some other occupation of a less exacting nature had become stronger as the years passed. Farming in one form or another seemed to be both a healthy and enjoyable life for any man who had indulged in a whirlwind of commerce almost from his boyhood.'[299]

It is quite possible that he was suffering from 'burn-out', and he refers to 'at least one breakdown in health due to overwork'.[300] He does not, however, touch on his personal circumstances. Furthermore, at some point, likely to be between 1908 and 1910, he and his wife Eleanor separated.

In their cycling days, when she accompanied SF on many trips, Eleanor had done much to promote the cause of cycling by women, and she was mentioned in articles in magazines such as *The Cycle* and *The Lady Cyclist* in the 1890s. There had been much debate about what women should wear when cycling, an option being referred to as 'rational dress', involving 'divided skirts'. Eleanor had tried this out briefly around 1896 for long-distance riding but later reverted to more feminine attire. She featured in *News of the Wheel* in February 1898 when she was praised for '*encourager les autres*'. In the early 20th century she went on to promote motoring by women, owning her own Gladiator and again receiving her own press coverage, such as when she won the Battle of the Flowers in her Gladiator at Earls Court in 1902. An article in *The Car Illustrated* in July 1902, accompanied by a photograph of Eleanor in her 12hp Gladiator, stated: 'Though driving herself nearly every day in her Gladiator, she normally joins her husband on a bigger vehicle for week-end excursions.'[301]

Mention of Eleanor was made in *The Times* when she drove a 12hp Napier at The Meet of

➢ Eleanor Edge, SF's wife, helped to promote motoring for women and is pictured in June 1902 when she won the 'Battle of Flowers' at Earls Court, London. The flowers on her 12hp Gladiator were, stated *The Car Illustrated*, 'marguerites, yellow iris, Lenten lilies, daffodils, forget-me-nots and lilies of the valley'. *The Car Illustrated (25 June 1902)*

➢ Without the flowers, the neat appearance of Mrs Edge's Gladiator is more readily appreciated. *The Car Illustrated (9 July 1902)*

When this photograph was published in *The Automotor Journal* in 1908, Dorothy Levitt had just taken part in the Prince Henry Cup in Germany with a 45hp Napier. The caption stated: 'With the assistance of her mechanic, Miss Levitt looks after all details of the car herself.' She was SF's personal secretary and they may have had an affair. *The Automotor Journal (1 August 1908)*

the Automobile Ladies Club in 1904, and she was also said to have been present during SF's 24-hour drive at Brooklands in 1907. *The Motor* ran a photograph taken just before he set off on his 24-hour record captioned 'Mrs Edge says good-bye to her husband', which makes one wonder whether one was meant to read more into it than might at first appear.[302]

'Cives', writing in the *Daily Report* in November 1907, described Eleanor as 'the charming lady who was the first of her sex to drive a car in this country'. But in the same article, probably referring to Dorothy Levitt rather than Eleanor, he mentioned 'the charming and beautiful lady who was always sitting at the Napier's steering gear in the many photographs that flooded the papers, and nearly induced us to become a purchaser, under the misapprehension that she was included in the bargain'.

It is known that Eleanor ended up migrating to New South Wales after the separation, although it is not clear why she should choose the country of birth of her husband. It is possible she had relatives of her own there. A shipping manifest records the departure of a 'Mrs S.F. Edge' for Australia on board the *Wakool* on 4 March 1908, but her age was given as 29, whereas Eleanor would have been 35. However, it seems unlikely that there was a different Mrs S.F. Edge travelling alone to Australia at this time, and perhaps Eleanor had lied about her age or there was a simple clerical error.

The 1911 Census of England and Wales shows SF living at Gallops Homestead, described as 'married' but not accompanied by Eleanor, with a cook, his driver, Joseph Blackburn, a 14-year-old girl described, intriguingly, as a 'nursemaid', a 14-year-old stable boy, three female 'visitors' and a 47-year-old servant who was also a dressmaker'!

SF had likely been unfaithful to Eleanor, and it is quite possible that he had had an affair with Dorothy Levitt. She was very attractive, some 14 years younger than SF, and was for a while his personal secretary. She actively raced Gladiator and Napier cars and Napier-powered boats between 1903 and 1908 (see Chapter 7), when she would have spent quite a lot of time 'on the road' with SF. If they were in a relationship, it seems to have ended by the time SF disbanded his racing team late in 1908. There is nothing to suggest they met after that point. In 1909 she published a book *The Woman and the Car*, in which she commends Eleanor as one of the first lady motorists but does not mention SF, to whom she owed her success as a racing driver. After that she largely disappeared from public life, possibly because of illness. She never married and died in her bed from morphine poisoning in 1922 at the young age of 40.

Another indication of possible misbehaviour on SF's part was that, back in 1907, SF had been the plaintiff in a mysterious case against Charles Sultzberger, an employee of D. Napier & Son between 1899 and 1905, who had allegedly called SF 'that white-faced, adulterous cad' and threatened to kill him. Montague Napier had to give evidence under cross-examination that he 'had never heard anyone apply the term 'adulterous' to Mr Edge; it has no application to him'. Sultzberger had also used the terms 'mongrel-waster' and 'dishonourable cheat'. In his evidence, it was clear that Sultzberger felt he had been unfairly treated by the Napier company, but it is not clear why he had a grudge against SF. Sultzberger denied calling SF an 'adulterous cad', and claimed that 'mongrel-waster' was meant to refer to an employee of Napier, but confirmed that 'dishonourable cheat' referred to SF. Sultzberger was found guilty but was released on a bond of £500 and one surety of £200, 'to be of good behaviour'.

In a court case in 1907, the charges against Charles Sultzberger, a disaffected former Napier employee, included libelling and threatening to kill SF. *The Daily Graphic (26 October 1907)*

PARTING WITH NAPIER

It is clear that SF's parting with Napier was not solely of his making. Relations between Montague Napier and SF had been deteriorating for some time. Sales were declining, partly due to competition from Rolls-Royce,[xv] and Montague Napier was incensed by the fact that S.F. Edge, Limited was making more profit per car than D. Napier & Son, Limited. Sales had declined from 801 pleasure cars and 235 taxis in 1911 to 653 pleasure cars, 129 taxis, and 91 business vehicles in 1912 and Napier's profit fell from £57,407 in 1911 to £25,094 in 1912.[303] SF, on the other hand, felt that the quality of Napier's cars was declining and that they were not up-to-date. He even issued a writ against the Napier company in June 1912 claiming 'damages for the sale of bad cars'.[304] Napier's response was that S.F. Edge, Limited was not taking the agreed number of cars. There was also a dispute as to whether the agreement between the two companies was in respect of all vehicles, or just cars. Napier was now producing 'business' vehicles, as it called them, and Montague Napier did not feel these should be sold by SF.

As we have seen, D. Napier & Son, having gained control of S.F. Edge (1907), Limited by November 1909, then sold all 109,000 of its shares back to SF in February 1910. By June 1912, however, the relationship had soured to the point where SF had initiated litigation against D. Napier & Son. It was obvious that neither party would benefit from a public argument over the quality of the cars, so on 17 October, in an attempt to settle out of court, Napier called SF and offered to buy all his shares. A 'long and critical interview took place with Mr Vane[xvi] and Mr Napier. The meeting lasted from 5pm to 10pm.'[305] SF accepted Napier's offer, and on 23 October 1912 an agreement was reached whereby D. Napier & Son would purchase all 152,951 shares in S.F. Edge, Limited owned by SF (which included the 109,000 shares sold to him in 1910) for £160,598 (one guinea per share).[306] The transaction included SF's interest in the Cunard Carriage Co. An important part of the agreement was that SF bound himself over for seven years not to go back into the business of making or selling motor vehicles or engines.[307]

In November 1912, *The Automotor Journal* gave the following tribute to SF: 'Among the pioneers, no man has done more for the industry than S.F. Edge, nor has anyone been a more strenuous advocate of the English car for the English people. True, he has had his axe to grind, but who in business has not?'

---

xv It is of interest to compare the businesses of Napier and Rolls-Royce at this point. Charles Rolls had originally modelled his business on SF's, becoming the sole sales agent for the cars produced by Henry Royce. However, by 1906 Rolls-Royce had acquired the business of C.S. Rolls & Co, and Rolls resigned in 1910 in order to focus on aviation (which led to his early death). From 1907 Rolls-Royce had adopted its one-model policy, focusing all attention on the development and sale of the 40/50 model, christened the Silver Ghost, and soon regarded as the 'best car in the world'. On the other hand, the Napier catalogue for 1911 listed cars ranging from 15hp to 65hp, delivery vans, cabs and marine motors.

xvi Harry Tempest Vane, who was by then the General Manager of S.F. Edge, Limited, and was to become Managing Director and eventually, on the death of Montague Napier, Chairman, of D. Napier & Son.

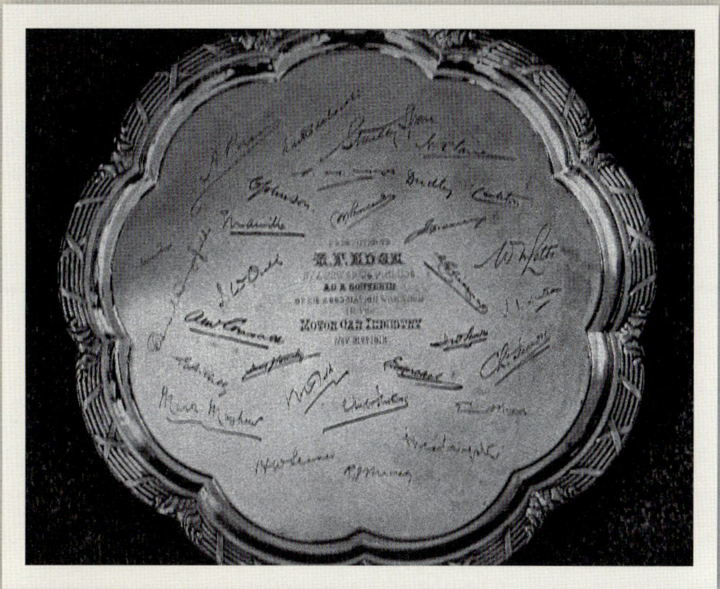

The silver salver presented to SF on his 'retirement' from S.F. Edge, Limited in 1912. Signatories include Harry Vane, Jack Stocks, Ernst de Rodakowski, Charles Jarrott, Claude Johnson, Mark Mayhew, William Letts and Lord Montagu. *Author's collection*

This circular letter sent by SF from 14 New Burlington Street announced his parting from Napier. *The Veteran Car Club of Great Britain*

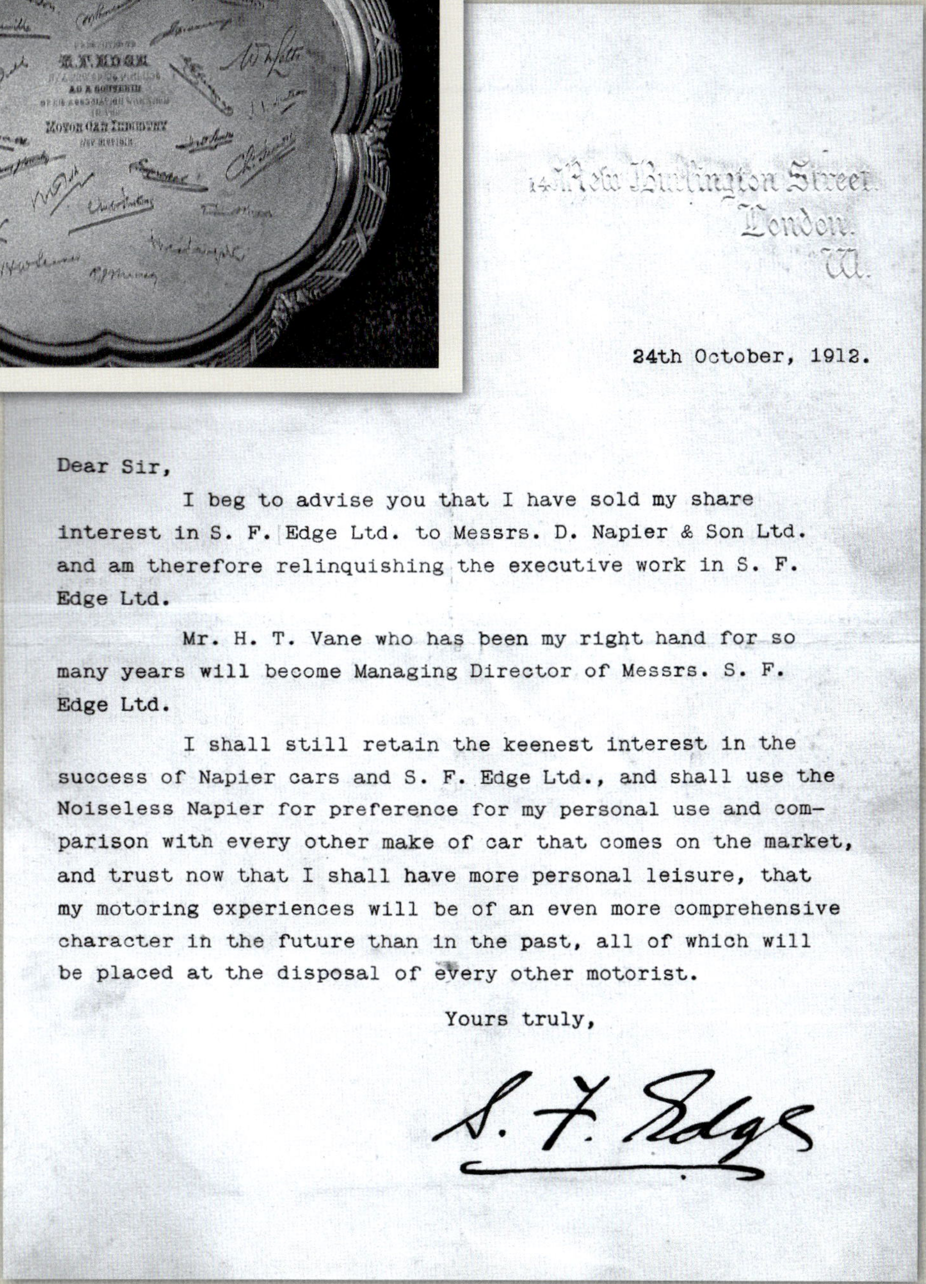

14, New Burlington Street.
London.
W.

24th October, 1912.

Dear Sir,

I beg to advise you that I have sold my share interest in S. F. Edge Ltd. to Messrs. D. Napier & Son Ltd. and am therefore relinquishing the executive work in S. F. Edge Ltd.

Mr. H. T. Vane who has been my right hand for so many years will become Managing Director of Messrs. S. F. Edge Ltd.

I shall still retain the keenest interest in the success of Napier cars and S. F. Edge Ltd., and shall use the Noiseless Napier for preference for my personal use and comparison with every other make of car that comes on the market, and trust now that I shall have more personal leisure, that my motoring experiences will be of an even more comprehensive character in the future than in the past, all of which will be placed at the disposal of every other motorist.

Yours truly,

S. F. Edge

CHAPTER 11
INTERLUDE

Now is an appropriate point at which to pause and reflect on the appearance, character and working habits of SF. In photographs, he was generally formally dressed, wearing a conspicuously high, starched collar with a narrow, plain tie and a three-piece suit. His hair was always neatly trimmed and his dimpled chin clean-shaven, but with bushy eyebrows above penetrating eyes, and a thick moustache. In his cycling days, his moustache was waxed, with prominent points extending on either side, which seemed to be in fashion amongst the cycling fraternity, but once in business the 'points' mutated into 'handlebars' and eventually disappeared.

He was a natural sportsman and a keen cyclist, even in his later years, and his favourite past-time was fishing. He was nearly always accompanied by a dog, even in his office. We have already heard how *Bully* would accompany him to the Anerley Bicycle Club, but he had a succession of dogs over the years. They would travel everywhere with him, and SF was devastated when one, a beautiful Airedale, was killed when it became entangled in an exposed chain on an early car.[308]

He was a prolific letter writer, both to the press and within his office. H.O. Duncan describes how SF would write letters even to his clerk in the next office, and when asked why he did this, his response was, 'Because I might forget what I said, whereas on reference to what was written, no-one can misconstrue my meaning.'

Over many years he would write several letters every week to the press, and he acknowledged that this was a form of self-publicity, the advantage being that it was free. G.H. Smith recounts the story of an editor asking a young sub-editor whether there was much 'overmatter' (material that cannot be used due to lack of space) and being told, 'Yes, forty-seven columns'. When asked what it was about, the sub-editor replied: 'I don't exactly know what it is all about, but it is all signed S.F. Edge.'[309] Appendix 3 has some examples of his correspondence from 1906.

At this point, it is best to hand over to his contemporaries for a first-hand description of his personality and working habits.

Duncan was the most forthcoming, in *The World on Wheels*, when he wrote:

He has sharp, dark, piercing eyes, ever ready to light up into sparkling animation as he talks to visitors or friends upon motor subjects. Few men really understood Edge and he was often considered a 'living enigma'. In other words, one seldom knew if he was angry, joking, or really in earnest. He always had a peculiar manner of being most amiable intermixed with a little sarcasm. It left one wondering whether he had taken the subject under discussion in a really serious manner. He was exacting in his dealings and conducted them with keen swiftness on a fair basis: and he was well-liked by his staff and he knew how to discover merit.

'His hair was always neatly trimmed and his dimpled chin clean-shaven, but with bushy eyebrows above penetrating eyes, and a thick moustache.' *Brooklands Museum Trust*

Everything was confirmed by letter. If it only contained two or three words, it was to the point and there it remained if wanted at any time. Edge is a born letter writer and this may have had a notable influence in his success. A peculiar thing is that all his satellites copied his particular system throughout their advance in life or in their business connections. It was undoubtedly a method that had proved its value.

Edge is a demon for work. He usually started his day by walking to his office, which he reached about nine. Then he began working at high pressure, interviewing a number of callers with wonderful patience, dictating letters and instructing his staff. He handled important deals over the telephone in any odd moments that presented themselves. Too busy to think of lunch, save a sandwich and a bunch of grapes on his paper-strewn table, he worked continuously until 5 pm. Then there were frequently meetings to be attended — Automobile Club Committees or the Society of Motor Manufacturers. If eloquence was not too

> copious at these gatherings, he was free about nine to have dinner and spend the rest of the evening with some business friend making plans for tomorrow or perhaps for many morrows hence.[xvii]
>
> He read all the motor papers carefully from end to end, including the advertisements. This alone took many hours. He was so fully alive to every small detail that he always 'knew that' when friends referred to subjects. Indeed, many were surprised at his intimate knowledge of such variety of topics.[310]

It is noteworthy that this is a description of what might now be known as a workaholic. There is no mention of Eleanor in this, and Duncan was probably describing SF's routine after his separation (although before his parting from Napier), but it might be a further indication of why their marriage ended unhappily.

Duncan also records that SF was a successful amateur boxer, and there are several stories demonstrating that he was quite prepared to defend himself, physically, outside as well as inside the ring.[311]

Smith's description is somewhat briefer:

> Dark-haired, moustached, rather lightly built, but with good shoulders, of good height (5 feet 11½ inches), and with a face that could be terribly earnest and determined if need be, but was more prone to be fully lit up in every feature by animation, almost mischievous humour, or sarcasm so well disguised that the inexperienced victim would often mistake it for approval and support.

For more independent corroboration of this, Murray Graeme wrote in *The Motor World* at the time of SF's parting with Napier:

> Clean cut and limber; head carried stiff as a sergeant-major's at general inspection above the shoulders as square; nose and chin which cry at you truculently; a tight set mouth, which a short aggressive moustache fails to soften; eyes that stab pitilessly from under portcullis brows; closely cropped dark hair — the voice of ages of struggle for self-preservation whispers within you bidding you beware.

Lawrence Stocks, Jack Stocks' son, who was employed by SF in the 1920s, had this to say of SF in an article he wrote for the *Veteran and Vintage Magazine* in 1967:

> S.F.E. was a remarkable personality, as well as being a highly controversial one. In appearance he was tall and slim, yet obviously possessed great physical strength. His principal features were, however, his small, penetrating eyes, black as Indian ink, which peered out from beneath dark and bushy eyebrows, matching his hair and moustache. Yet this formidable-looking man possessed a charming smile, even though I do not recall

---

xvii SF claimed in an article in *The Autocar* of 27 October 1906 that over the seven years [1899 to 1906] he averaged, except when ill and a few days' holiday each year, about 72 hours' work per week.

ever hearing him laugh. A slight dimple in the chin softened the stern aspect which is displayed in most photographs. He was in truth a man who would stand out in any crowd, and a most curious mixture — he could be, and frequently was, a martinet, yet could show an extraordinary consideration for other people. Inflexible on some occasions, he could also be as soft as putty, while he possessed a magnetism which made even his business opponents pleased to see him.'[312]

'He was generally formally dressed, wearing a conspicuously high, starched collar with a narrow, plain tie and a three-piece suit.' *Author's collection*

To end this brief interlude, there is a report by a graphologist, who had been given samples of SF's handwriting to analyse. The report was written by one Lucca Volney in 1911 and read:

> Should be an engineer of some sort and a very masterful, impatient and reckless man. Furious at sloth, or incompetence, never satisfied except with perfection, and ought to love making records of any sort — nerves should be still [*sic*] but he must beware of heart trouble — must be master (or apparently so). A wonderfully magnetic, ambitious and forceful personality, but likely to come to grief, a sort of Icarus, whose ambition may prove his own undoing — but he ought to go very far. Can be absolutely twisted round a woman's finger who is clever enough to study him, as he is developed on one side only. He [is] a kind of modern pirate — it reminds one of *Treasure Island* and that ilk!

As with fortune-tellers, one wonders whether Volney had access to other information in addition to samples of his handwriting. It is not clear whether they met face to face, but Volney almost certainly would have been familiar with SF's exploits, such as the Gordon Bennett race and the 24-hour record. Nevertheless, in the light of the following chapters, it is unnervingly prescient.

CHAPTER 12

GENTLEMAN FARMER

1913 TO 1919

After parting with Napier, SF retreated to his homestead in Sussex and devoted himself to pig farming. One wonders whether the author, Arthur Conan Doyle, was aware of this when writing the short story, *His Last Bow*, published in 1917, in which the famous fictional detective, Sherlock Holmes, followed in SF's footsteps when he retired and took up beekeeping on the South Downs!

Almost immediately a rumour went around that SF intended to enter politics and stand as Unionist candidate for the Hastings parliamentary constituency. Arthur Du Cros, MP, the incumbent, who had succeeded his father, Harvey Du Cros, in the seat in 1908, had announced that he did not intend to stand for re-election.[313] SF quickly scotched this rumour but did not deny that he had parliamentary ambitions and that he would like to champion the cause of Tariff Reform. In the event, Arthur Du Cros decided to stand again and was re-elected as the member for Hastings for a further five years.

Rumours suggested that SF might stand as the Unionist candidate to succeed Sir Arthur Du Cros as MP for Hastings but this did not happen. *Author's collection*

In around June 1913, SF was elected President of the Society of Motor Manufacturers and

▲ SF continued to drive a Napier after he had sold his company to Montague Napier. Here he is seen in a 1913 six-cylinder model, one of the first to be fitted with electric lamps. Note the RAC badge mounted on the radiator and the AA badge fixed to the base of the windscreen. *Clive Boothman collection*

Traders (SMMT), notwithstanding the fact that he was now a farmer, not a motor trader. The Society had been formed soon after the 1902 Gordon Bennett victory. Frederick Simms had organised a luncheon at the Cecil Hotel to honour SF, and it was at an informal meeting immediately after the luncheon that the Society was formed.[314] SF became its Vice President for the first year, followed by two further spells in the post in 1906–07 and from 1908–09 onwards, as well as being Honorary Treasurer in 1905–06. SF's term as President saw the Society's headquarters move to 83 Pall Mall, almost next door to the Royal Automobile Club at 89 Pall Mall.

He also became Chairman of United Motor Industries, Limited. This was a firm formed in 1902 by SF and Montague Napier dealing in motor accessories. G.H. Smith had been the manager of this company in 1900, and in 1913, Ernst de Rodakowski, Manager of Brooklands in 1907, was the Managing Director.

The relationship with Napier must have healed somewhat because, in February 1913, D. Napier & Son, Limited agreed that SF could 'continue acting as adviser on advertising'.[315] But things turned sour again before the year was out and in December SF had gone back to court 'raising a question of construction on a written agreement entered into between the two parties on 23rd October 1912'. The issue was whether SF's involvement in five companies was allowed under the October 1912 agreement, and whether that written agreement was consistent with the verbal agreement that had been reached in the long meeting that took place on 17 October 1912. These companies were United Motor Industries, Limited, the Hertford Street Motor Hiring Company, Ltd (in which SF was said to have 'a considerable interest'), the Electromobile Company, Mercédès, Daimler and Ivel. SF's argument was that none of these companies competed with Napier. However, the case seems to have been dropped before judgement was given.

In March 1914, SF himself was sued for breach of an agreement by one Henry George Burford. Entered into in June 1912, when SF was suing D. Napier & Son, the agreement had been to find capital of £50,000 for a company known as British Business Motors Limited, which somehow was going to be used in the negotiations with D. Napier & Son. SF explained that this was formed 'on a war basis' and he no longer needed it. The jury initially assessed damages in favour of Burford of £3,350, but this was later reduced to £800 with costs.

The court cases did not end there. In December 1914, SF was taken to court by Napier to recover various cups and medals awarded for races won in Napier cars and boats. The case was settled amicably, however, with SF returning most of the cups and medals apart from those that it was agreed he could retain 'on account of a sentimental interest'.

SF stepped down as President of the SMMT on 14 June 1914. Under the constitution he could have continued, but he expressed the view that the tenure of the presidency should be limited to one year.

The First World War

On 4 August 1914, Britain declared war on Germany. With food production now being of great national importance, SF based himself at Gallops Homestead and threw himself into the business of farming, with as much energy as he had applied to selling cars. His main interest was pedigree stock breeding, specialising in large black pigs and middle-weight pigs — but he also bred cattle (Scotch shorthorns), Shire horses, and pure-bred Sussex poultry.[316] G.H. Smith reports that at this time SF had paid as much as 1,250 guineas for a shorthorn bull calf called 'Prince of the Manor'.[317]

SF was said to be the creator of the open-air system of farming. Duncan described this system as follows:

> The whole basis of everything that is bred is to get real health and constitution, combined with good size. The pigs are reared in open woods or pasture, with timber, faggot or corrugated steel huts in which to farrow and sleep during bad weather. Large open and partly covered yards take care of the Shorthorns in winter, and extremely lofty stables, with ample ventilation, are the resting homes of the Shires.[318]

In contrast to his newfound career as a farmer, around this time (late 1914) SF was appointed Chairman of the Cunard Film Co Ltd. This was

Sow and sucklings in their fine-weather paddock at Gallops Farm. *Country Life (13 March 1915)*

apparently a partnership between SF and Ernst de Rodakowski.[319] The company had built a film studio in Wood Street, Walthamstow, in the East End of London. In November 1914, it produced *Danny Donovan, the Gentleman Cracksman*, directed by Wallett Waller (1881–1951) and starring an American actor, Thomas Meighan (1879–1936), with Gladys Cooper (1888–1971) in a supporting role.[320] Other films included *The Smugglers' Cave* and *The Call of the Drum*. At a preview of these three films in November 1914, SF addressed a few remarks to the audience in justification, as he explained, of the company's existence, laying particular stress on the fact that the productions were from start to finish of entirely British manufacture.[321] They produced a few more silent movies but the company was not a financial success and it closed in 1915. SF was also a director of an associated company, Bioschemes, Ltd, which was wound up around the same time.

Not long after the outbreak of war, news must have reached SF that Eleanor, whom he had married in 1892 but been separated from for at least four years (see Chapter 10), had died in Australia on 24 November 1914 from pneumonia, aged 42. Her death certificate states that she had lived for four years in New South Wales. There were no children from the marriage. SF's feelings about her death are not recorded.

Further sad news followed. One of SF's younger brothers, Randolph, died fighting at Gallipoli on 27 August 1915. He was serving as a private in the 18th Australian Infantry Battalion. Another brother, William, also died in 1915, in Australia, but the circumstances of his death are not known.

SF did not sever his connections with the motor trade altogether, and in October 1915 he was elected Vice President of the newly formed Associated British Motor Manufacturers Limited. He continued his usual active correspondence with motoring journals while being equally active corresponding about farming matters. Motoring journals even covered his farming activities, and in November 1915 *Motor News* was promoting his latest catalogue for an auction of pedigree pigs, having 'inspected Mr Edge's farm under his personal conduct'. It even invited 'those of our readers who are interested in farming' to write to SF for advice.[322] He remained a director of the tractor manufacturer, Ivel, tractor production now being a vital industry, with Ivel being one of very few companies supplying tractors.

Whilst there was now no motorsport in Britain, in America it continued unabated. SF must have been disappointed to learn that on 3 June 1916 his 24-hour record set in 1907 was broken by Ralph Munford at Sheepshead Bay near New York. Munford was driving a Hudson Super-Six and covered 1,819 miles in 24 hours, compared to SF's 1,581 miles in the Napier.[323]

In September 1915, SF had become a member of the Metropolitan Munitions Committee,[324] and on 2 January 1917 he was appointed Director of the Agricultural Machinery Branch of the Ministry of Munitions by Dr Christopher Addison, a Liberal MP who had become the Minister of Munitions in 1916. SF's duties were to control both the manufacture and the import of agricultural machinery, a task for which he was clearly well qualified, with his knowledge of commerce and agriculture, although without the right temperament for working in a government department. This was an unpaid position (the press described it as 'lending his services') but would have required SF to spend much time away from his farm.

Changes were also taking place in his personal life around this time. Myra Catherine Martin was born in 1887 in Lewes, Sussex. The 1901 Census shows her, aged 14, living with an uncle and aunt in Tunbridge Wells,[325] her mother, Maria, having died in 1893. By 1911, at the age of 24, she was working as a stenographer (shorthand typist), living as a boarder in St John's Wood, London.[326] At some point she was employed as a secretary by SF. In January 1917, just after SF was appointed as Director of the Agricultural Machinery Branch of the Ministry of Munitions, photographs were published in the press of SF with Myra, who was described as his 'chief assistant', having been his 'secretary in business', and who now, in SF's absence, 'controls the farm and herd of 700 pigs'.[327] One of the photos depicted SF leaning on a farm gate surveying a herd of large black pigs, while another showed Myra Martin feeding some 'young porkers' from a bucket while SF looks on benignly. There was no suggestion of any romantic involvement but the publicity would seem to be an effort by SF to introduce the world to his future wife, for on 17 March 1917 they were married, at Christ Church in Mayfair (just round the corner from SF's office in 7 Hertford Street). Myra also featured in a British Pathé news film about pig-keeping, which can be viewed at www.britishpathe.com under the title 'Hog Farm C 1910s AKA Pig Keeping (1917)'.

➤ Myra Martin at work on the pig farm, circa 1916. She and SF married the following year. *British Pathé*

The Autocar published an interview with SF in February 1917 in which his appointment in the Ministry of Munitions was described as one of 'the most popular made by the present Government'.[328] His duty was described as 'to order and obtain agricultural machinery when instructed by the Board of Agriculture or the Food Controller'. In the interview, SF emphasised the need for food production to be increased through mechanisation in the form of tractors. Tractors were still relatively new and undeveloped, and SF went on to explain the difficulties of increasing the capabilities and supply of them at that time (shortage of materials for local manufacture, and shortage of cargo space in shipping for imports).

Around the same time, *The Motor* had this to say of SF: 'A man whose inflexible will is reflected in his piercing eye, a keen fighter for what he regards as right, and one whose judgement seldom errs, Mr Edge brings to the post to which he has wisely been appointed a new force which should be immensely advantageous to the country.'[329]

Immediately after his appointment at the Ministry of Munitions, the manufacture of agricultural tractors except under special licence was prohibited, it being stated that the agricultural tractor is, in the view of the government, 'as much a munition of war as a gun'.[330] The American car magnate, Henry Ford, was already considering setting up a factory in Cork, Ireland (then still part of the United Kingdom), and the granting of such a special licence was given by Parliament in March 1917, which raised objections from British motor manufacturers. SF, as Director of Agricultural Machinery, was asked to find out if any British manufacturer would organise an enterprise at least commensurate with that of the Ford company.[331] It seems they would not, and construction of Ford's factory went ahead. However, at the last minute the government's priorities changed, with Ford being asked to use the Cork factory for aircraft production, and the tractors were instead produced by Ford in America.

Controversy quickly surrounded SF's appointment at the Ministry of Munitions. It was suggested that he had a conflict of interest due to his connection with the tractor manufacturer Ivel Agricultural Motors Limited, but SF declared in April 1917: 'I am not a director of Ivel Agricultural Motors Limited as on my appointment as Director of the Agricultural Machinery Branch I naturally resigned such an office and also sold the small share interest I had.'[332] Then in August 1917 questions were raised in Parliament over how unofficial tractor trials were held on SF's farm on 28 July. *The Car Illustrated*, however, had this to say: 'The insinuation in the House of Commons that Mr. Edge was acting in his own interests on the occasion of the agrimotor demonstration at Ditchling may be dismissed as the vapourings of a rather foolish, or possibly misinformed, politician of about the average political intelligence.'[333]

In May 1917, the Agricultural Machinery Branch of the Ministry was reconstituted as the Agricultural Machinery Department, and SF was promoted to the rank of Controller. Of more significance, SF's one-time customer, Winston Churchill, was appointed as the Minister of Munitions on 17 July 1917 in place of Dr Christopher Addison. The two strong personalities clashed at an early stage, with diplomacy never being SF's strong suit. He had already fallen out with Sir Arthur Lee, who had been appointed as the head of the Food Production Department of the Board of Agriculture, over matters of policy. A further factor may have been the fact that Churchill, as First Lord of the Admiralty at the time, was held largely responsible for the military disaster of the Gallipoli Campaign in 1915, during which SF's brother Randolph had been killed.

Matters came to a head in October 1917, and the outcome is probably best described, at least from SF's point of view, in a letter SF wrote from 7 Hertford Street, in his usual forthright manner, to Churchill on 18 October 1917, which he copied to the press:

> Dear Mr Churchill,
> You have today appointed a Controller of the Agricultural Machinery Department in my stead, as you have not been able to prevail on me voluntarily to resign my position.
>
> As it is my intention to send this letter to the Press, I wish shortly to recapitulate the history of this change as far as is known to me.
>
> In August of this year, a 'sort of enquiry' was held on your behalf into the activities of my Department. About the end of August, without any charges or complaints having been formulated against me, Sir Arthur Duckham (a member of your Council) sent me two draft letters of resignation for me to sign. This I declined to do, and wrote to you, on September 3rd, giving my reasons for declining to resign, and asking that any charge against me, if one existed, should be stated in writing, and that I should receive a personal hearing from you, which, if you were not satisfied with my explanations, should be followed by a public and exhaustive Enquiry.
>
> As a result, you kindly granted me an interview; you did not formulate any charges whatever, and asked me to 'carry on' until I heard from you again. On October 3rd you wrote asking me to place my resignation in your hands. You were good enough to say, in that letter, that you wished to make it quite clear that my leaving was not due to any cause affecting my probity or capacity, and you even expressed your thanks for the energy and ability with which I had served the Ministry of Munitions in an honorary capacity since my first appointment.
>
> In that letter, you at last indicated (though in the faintest manner) why you are so anxious to dispense with the services of an official to the probity, capacity, energy and ability of whom you testify. I will quote your reason: "The need of making the most convenient and smooth-running arrangement for the discharge of this branch of our work, having regard to the various interests and Government Departments concerned."
>
> As I have worked in the most complete harmony with every Branch and Department of your and other Ministries, from the Heads of which I have received nothing but the most ready and courteous assistance, it is quite evident that the only Government Department you can have in mind is the Food Production Department of the Board of Agriculture.

It perhaps would have been more frank had you stated this fact.

It is a fact that there has been no harmonious working with Colonel Sir Arthur Lee's Food Production Department. I do not wish to burden this letter with the history of such lack of harmony. I merely wish to state that it has nothing whatever to do with personal animosity, as Colonel Sir Arthur Lee and I have only met two or three times in all. The reason of the lack of harmony lies in the fact that, as a business man and a man of engineering and farming experience, I was invited by Dr. Addison, the then Minister of Munitions, to give my assistance to the Ministry, and I therefore considered it my duty to criticise any schemes which I did not think sound, workable and likely to benefit the country. From the very outset of the formation of the Food Production Department of the Board of Agriculture, I saw that Sir Arthur Lee had no coherent or well-thought-out policy, for his various chimerical and window-dressing schemes (as represented by the Tractor-purchase and ploughing-by-night arrangements) could not, in my opinion, however well managed, be of real use.

As, in addition, everything connected with the Food Production Department seemed as ill-managed as it was ill-conceived, I was unable to find it consonant with my duties to your Ministry and to the country to let them develop without sounding the frequent notes of warning which my official correspondence places on record.

I would remind you that it was because of my long business training and experience of practical and motor farming that I was selected for the position of trust which I deemed it my duty to retain until you now compel me to relinquish it.

Sir Arthur Lee's magnificent gift of Chequers Court will doubtless benefit future Prime Ministers, but I fear his activities at the head of the Food Production Department of the Board of Agriculture will prove a very onerous and unremunerative burden to the British taxpayer.

I leave the country to judge whether my opinions are correct. The next twelve months should enable it to do so.

I am, dear Mr. Churchill, yours very faithfully, S.F. Edge[334]

Elsewhere, in the non-motoring press, SF is quoted as saying: 'Soon after I was appointed I found that the bulk of my knowledge was useless, because it would interfere with the political aspirations of the Food Production Department. I gave up my other work, and devoted my whole time to the post without either pay or reward of any kind.' And a journal called, simply, *Food* made the following insightful and supportive comments:

Yet Mr. Edge is no politician. He is anything but talkative, but when he does speak it is to a purpose. No one has ever accused him of suffering from excess of sentiment, and though he would not tolerate favouritism, he bore the reputation for dealing justly with those in his employ. Is it a wonder that Mr. Edge has the confidence of the motor

> industry, and that his criticism of the Food Department is being received very seriously by a great body of people who count very high amongst those who are carrying on the nation's war.

▲ Sir Arthur Lee: SF described him as having no coherent or well-thought-out policy for his various chimerical and window-dressing schemes at the Food Production Department of the Board of Agriculture. *Author's collection*

Sir Arthur Lee, the target of SF's criticism, and just a few months younger than SF, had had a military and diplomatic career before becoming an MP in 1900. He rejoined the army at the start of the First World War, serving in France in 1914 and 1915, and was knighted in 1916. He was appointed Director of Food Production in 1917. Also in 1917, Arthur and Ruth Lee, who had no heirs, bequeathed their home, known as Chequers, to the nation for use as a country retreat for the serving Prime Minister of the day (for which it continues to be used to this day). SF might have felt that this act of philanthropy had influenced senior politicians into giving Sir Arthur an appointment he did not deserve. Lee was made a peer in July 1918, as Baron Lee of Fareham. SF received no honour in recognition of his service.

In writing his letter to Churchill, SF had no expectation of retaining his position so went back to farming with his new wife at Gallops and could start planning what he would do once his seven-year agreement with Napier to stay out of the motor industry expired in October 1919. Before that, in 1918, he bought a further four farms in the area around Ditchling: Glebe Farm and St Helena Farm in Streat, Lambourne Meadow in Plumpton, and Middleton Common Farm in Westmeston.

CHAPTER 13
THE ROARING TWENTIES

The 1920s started on a bright note in SF's personal life, since on 18 June 1920 his first child, a daughter, Jean Myra, was born to his wife, Myra. At this time most of his efforts were devoted to his farming activities from the comfort of Gallops Homestead.

Aged 51 at the end of 1919, SF was a wealthy man but his heart was still in the motor industry. As soon as the non-compete agreement with Napier expired he had started acquiring shares in a company called at that time Auto-Carriers (1911), Ltd, later to become better known simply as AC Cars Limited. Montague Napier, who was by this time a sick man, would not have felt at all threatened by this. He had been living in France since 1917, had sold many of his shares such that he no longer had a controlling interest in D. Napier & Son, Limited, and the company was now being run by SF's former manager, Harry Vane. During the First World War, the company had been asked to build aero engines under contract, mainly the Sunbeam Arab. Believing that Napier engineers could design a better engine, towards the end of the war the company developed a powerful 12-cylinder engine that was named the Lion. By 1920 production of the Lion was its main activity. To hedge its bets, Napier designed and sold a single model of car, with an advanced engine drawing on its aero-engine expertise, but with a pre-war chassis design. The car was known as the T75 or 40-50 and sold at a chassis-only price of £1,750. The company planned to produce an initial batch of 500 cars, but production was plagued by labour disputes, sales were slow, and it ended up making fewer than 200 before abandoning car production for good in 1924.

This did not stop SF from irritating the Napier concern. SF had known Colonel John Stewart Napier OBE (1871–1957) for some time, since the Colonel had been the Chief Engineer of Arrol-Johnston in the early years of the century and had won the 1905 Tourist Trophy in the Isle of Man, driving a car of that make. John Napier was a great-grandson of Robert Napier (1791–1876), a famous shipbuilder on the Clyde, who in turn was a grandson of Robert Napier (1726–1805), Master Blacksmith, from whom Montague

Napier was also descended.[335] Early in 1920 the Colonel and SF formed a company called Edge and Napier, Ltd. They cannot have expected to get away with it, and it appears to have been a frivolous act on their part, confirmed partly by the fact that the paid-up capital was only £100.[336] When interviewed by *The Automotor Journal*, SF was very reticent about what the company's plans were.

Naturally D. Napier & Son, Ltd, which had acquired the company S.F. Edge, Ltd in 1912, was aggrieved by this, and took the new entity to court in April 1920, to 'protect their interests'.[337] The case was settled in November 1920, having

As with Napier before the Great War, advertising by AC Cars under SF's guidance promoted the sporting and endurance achievements of its cars, now with SF's signature prominent. *gracesguide.co.uk*

been won by D. Napier & Son, Ltd. Under the terms of the settlement, Edge and Napier, Ltd was required to change its name immediately to 'some name of which neither the name of Edge nor the name Napier forms part'.[338] This little diversion must have been a waste of time and money for both SF and the Napier company.

Auto-Carriers (1911), Ltd was a very different business from D. Napier & Son, Ltd. It had been founded in 1900 by John Portwine and John Weller, the latter being an engineer, with the former, a butcher by trade, providing the finance. They started by making the Weller car, in South Norwood, near where SF grew up, but this was not a success, and in 1904 they switched to making a commercial vehicle. Called the Autocarrier (hence the name adopted by the company in 1907), it was a tricycle powered by a 5.6hp air-cooled single-cylinder engine, with a large box between the two wheels at the front that could be used for delivering goods. These proved popular, and by 1907 the company had developed a passenger-carrying version, initially with a single seat in front of the driver, but later with two passenger seats (named the AC Tricar, and subsequently the AC Sociable).

In 1911, the factory moved to Thames Ditton, Surrey, to gain additional space, and the company was restructured under the name Auto-Carriers (1911), Ltd. By 1913, Weller had designed a four-wheeled car, fitted with an engine made by Fivet in France, and a few of these were sold before the war dictated that the factory be turned over to the production of shells and fuses. SF had owned one of these early economical AC cars, a 12hp, during the war, and would drive himself to and from Gallops at the weekends when working for the Ministry of Munitions. In 1919 Weller designed what turned out to be a very successful, light, six-cylinder engine of 1,991cc, which would have appealed to SF.

By February 1921, SF had built up his interest in Auto-Carriers (1911), Ltd to the point where he was offered a seat on the Board, with the intention, in his words, of 'going deeply into it'.[339] According to Duncan, after SF joined the company he 'applied himself to cleaning up the commercial side, cutting down unnecessary expenditure and getting twenty shillings' worth of material and labour for every pound spent'.[340] SF also introduced a Mr Thomas G. Gillett, who became the works manager and a director in July 1921.[341] By December of the same year, SF's appointment as Chairman of the Board and Governing Director was confirmed, while Portwine and Weller resigned.[342] This was an executive position, and he would now be spending most of his time back in an office, furiously writing internal memos and letters to the press as in days past.

It was, however, very different from his days in charge of a relatively small team at S.F. Edge, Limited, when all he had to worry about was selling cars. Now he was in charge of manufacturing the cars as well as selling them. The motor industry had also changed beyond recognition from the time he sold out to Montague Napier. In 1911 the total number of motor vehicles of all types produced in the United Kingdom was 19,000, of which almost 1,000 had been made by D. Napier & Son, Limited. In 1922, 73,000 vehicles were produced, and by 1927 production was more than 200,000.[343]

Naturally, SF reverted to publicity-seeking stunts, especially racing successes. The company employed several competition drivers, including S.C.H. (Sammy) Davis, who went on to be a successful driver for Bentley, winning the Le Mans 24 Hours in 1924, while at the same time being employed as a journalist for *The Autocar*. Other drivers included Sydney Westhall, J.A. Joyce, G. Brownsort and A. Noble. Sammy Davis had this to say about two of them:

When S.F. Edge took over, Noble and Brownsort proved more than a match even for this man, who was one of the most experienced in the whole motor industry. An argument between them was pure delight to listen to. Since no one was ever able to argue with Edge — and since he knew this — it was a joy to watch the bewilderment which came over him as most unanswerable logic failed lamentably to even scratch the surface of Noble's and Brownsort's own convictions. Edge undoubtedly considered that these two men were the oddest he had ever met, although I think he looked upon the whole crowd of us as pretty odd.[344]

SF joined the Board of AC Cars in 1921 and became deeply involved in the company's ups and downs throughout the decade. He is pictured that year at the wheel of an AC 1.5-litre open two-seater. *Motoring Picture Library, National Motor Museum*

One other driver was H.G. (Harry) Hawker, who raced as an amateur in his spare time while running the company he owned with Tommy Sopwith that went on to build such icons as the Hawker Hurricane. Sadly, Hawker did not live to see the success of his eponymous company, dying in an air crash on 12 July 1921. Shortly before, in June, Hawker had used a specially developed AC to set a world record for a 1,500cc car of a flying half-mile at 105.14mph.

SF was keen for his own 24-hour record of 1907 to be bettered. The attempt was to be undertaken back at Brooklands but had to be driven in two periods of 12 hours each on successive days (known as the 'Double-Twelve') because night-time driving at Brooklands had been banned after the 24-hour record. Cars had to be locked in a '*parc fermé*' between the two 12-hour runs.

The first attempt was on 27 September 1921, in AC's new six-cylinder 2-litre model, with Brownsort and Noble sharing the driving. This was before SF became Governing Director, otherwise he probably would have insisted on being the sole driver. Several new records were taken on the first day, but at the start of the second day a heavy mist lay on the track. Noble had become unwell and was unable to drive, but Brownsort set off at 7.40am, to be relieved after some time by Sammy Davis. Then there was a delay while the petrol tank was replaced due to a leak. As a result of the delay, it would have been necessary to drive at 85mph to beat the record. This was too much for the little car and the engine overheated, leading to a seized piston and a broken con-rod after 1,192 miles. A short film clip of this attempt can be viewed at www.britishpathe.com under the title 'Small Car Test 1921'.

Another attempt was made on 24 and 25 May 1922. An AC with an Anzani engine driven by Joyce and Day, the latter probably also an employee of AC, would have to share the track with an Aston Martin driven by Lionel Martin on the first day. On the second day the AC set off on its own at 7am and lapped faultlessly for 11 hours and 20 minutes until it, too, 'blew up'. But that was good enough to set a new 'Double-Twelve' record as 1,709 miles, 1,234 yards had already been covered, 128 miles more than SF had achieved in 24 hours in 1907.[345]

SF was determined to win back the record himself, and another attempt was made on 19 and 20 July 1922. This time SF would be the sole driver. He acknowledged that as he was now 54, a solo 24-hour continuous drive would have been tougher than it was for him in 1907, but was confident he could manage the two 12-hour stretches. *The Motor* agreed to SF's suggestion that they give him a 'little copper medal' if he succeeded and that he would give the Motor Trade Benevolent Fund £100 if he failed.[346] Surprisingly, he chose to drive a car other than an AC, and one that was not British: a Dutch Spyker fitted with a six-cylinder Maybach engine of 33.5hp. It was built, on a standard chassis, as a racer, with a streamlined body with two bucket seats. SF explained that he wanted to drive a six-cylinder car of smaller engine capacity than the Napier, but he must also have been influenced by the recent failures of ACs to complete the distance. *The Motor* cheekily offered him a second medal if he could beat his record on a car of British manufacture.[347]

SF may have had a financial interest in the British agency for Spyker[xviii] but he definitely knew the manager of it, Colonel Sam Janson, who had been the Managing Director of Hertford Street Motor Hiring Co, Ltd in 1914.[348] At the

---

xviii Grace's Guide records that in 1921 the old-established firm of Angus-Sanderson was reorganised 'with backing from British Spyker Co and Tylors under the control of S. F. Edge becoming Angus-Sanderson (1921) Ltd'.

start of the war, Janson enlisted with the Army Service Corps before transferring in 1917 to the Royal Flying Corps, where he served as Deputy Director of Transport at the same time as Lt Col Charles Jarrott served as Inspector of Transport.

SF agreed that, at the same time as he was making his attempt, Gwenda Janson, Sam's wife, would attempt to set a 'Double-Twelve' record of her own riding a 2¼hp Trump-JAP motorcycle, which she did successfully, covering 1,071 miles in the 24 hours at an average speed of 44.65mph.

Gwenda Mary Janson, *née* Glubb, was an interesting lady. Born in Preston in April 1894, she was the daughter of Major-General Sir Frederic Glubb and elder sister of John Bagot Glubb, who went on to become Lt-General Sir John Bagot Glubb, known as Glubb Pasha, Commander of the Arab Legion, from 1939 to 1956. During the First World War, Gwenda served with distinction with the Scottish Women's Hospitals as an ambulance driver. In 1915, she was present during the Great Russian Retreat and the Serbian Retreat to Albania, being awarded both the Cross of St George and the Cross of St Stanislaus. By 1918 she was stationed at RAF Hurst Park as a driving instructor where she caught Lt-Colonel Janson's eye. They married in 1920 but were divorced by 1923.

SF's run in the Spyker went without incident, and with only two tyres being changed (both having been punctured by metal objects), unlike the 1907 attempt in the Napier when 24 tyres were changed. For the first 12 hours he was accompanied by Thomas Gillett, the works

DOUBLE 'DOUBLE 12'

When a 250cc motorcycle and a 5.7 litre car shared Brooklands for a unique record

Left: Mrs Gwenda Janson (later Mrs Stewart, then Mrs Hawkes) with her 250cc Trump-JAP motorcycle and S.F. Edge with his 5.7 litre Spyker, seen on the occasion of their simultaneous Double 12 hour record attempts at Brooklands in 1922. *(Photo, courtesy of Frank H. Frisbee)*

22

In 1922, SF made a 'Double-Twelve' record attempt at Brooklands with a 5.7-litre Spyker at the same time as Gwenda Janson, wife of Colonel Sam Janson, manager of Spyker's British agency, went about the same feat on a 250cc Trump-JAP motorcycle. *Brooklands Museum Trust*

manager of AC. For the second stint he was accompanied part of the time by a mechanic from Spyker and part of the time by a wireless operator, who experimented by sending wireless messages to the 'depot' (pits) while the car was circulating at 80mph. The wireless aerial was allowed to trail behind the car, with the result that it wore away during the run and the experiment had to be abandoned. The rest of the time, messages were passed by the mechanic writing notes on paper that he screwed up in a ball and dropped on the track as the car sped past the depot.

Almost the entire workforce of AC turned up in a fleet of char-à-bancs to cheer their chief. During the 24 hours' running time he covered 1,782 miles 1,006 yards at an average speed of 74.27mph, compared to his 1907 record of 1,582 miles at 65.91mph.[349] *The Motor* described it as a 'most remarkable feat' and a 'fine physical effort'.

Not satisfied with that, and maybe in response to *The Motor's* taunt about using a British car, SF was back at Brooklands on 31 August 1922 in a 40hp Lanchester. He set new records in the first five hours, but soon after that the steering failed. The car swerved dramatically, but SF managed to keep it under control, having a lucky escape from what could have been a fatal accident. Maybe this, and the fact that he was now a father, was what persuaded him to give up racing and record-breaking once again. The AC drivers continued to compete, however, with many successes over the next five years.

On 6 October 1922, Myra gave birth to their second daughter, Sonia Frances Edge.

Throughout this period, SF was still very much involved in pig farming, although he was finding it more difficult to make a profit. In articles published in 1921, he offered to hand over £20,000 to a committee of his workpeople and leave the management in their hands: 'Let them see if they can pay wages out of profits in the face of falling markets. Some of my own people think I am living on them. The bald truth is they are living on me.'

It seems his workpeople did not take up the offer and in 1922 he formed a company, S.F. Edge's Pig Farm Limited, which he floated on the London Stock Exchange in December of that year. The capital of the new company was made up of 60,000 8% preference shares of £1 each and 100,000 ordinary shares of one shilling each (£65,000 in total). The prospectus was offering £60,000 of 7% First Mortgage Debenture Stock and 20,000 of the preference shares. The new company was to buy the pig-rearing business of SF, the livestock farms of Ifold Herds, Ltd, and the pig business of Brigadier-General A. Symons. It would take over several farms, including Gallops, with over 2,000 pedigree pigs and a total acreage of 1,012, making it the largest pig farm in the United Kingdom. The land and buildings were valued at £35,502 and the livestock at £39,762, with SF receiving £24,762 and Symons receiving £50,502, part of which would be paid in the form of shares, SF receiving 9,880 ordinary shares, and Symons receiving 20,120 ordinary shares.

It was made clear that SF would still take a practical interest as a large shareholder, and chairman. The other directors were Brigadier-General Symons and the Rt Hon The Earl of Clanwilliam. The financial press was generally not very enthusiastic about the investment opportunity, deeming it to be 'highly speculative', and it is not known to what extent the shares and debentures were taken up.

Around this time a 'disastrous fire' broke out at Gallops Farm (this was a separate building from the Homestead). The main building was saved, but the loss was estimated at £2,000.

SF retained Gallops Homestead as a weekend retreat, but from 1923 he and Myra lived during the week at The High House, Thames Ditton, within walking distance of the AC factory.

Accompanied in the Spyker by Thomas Gillett, SF's two 12-hour runs at Brooklands saw him cover 1,782 miles at an average speed of 74.27mph. *Motoring Picture Library, National Motor Museum*

As if running a large farm in Sussex and a car factory in London was not enough, SF went on to buy another car maker in 1923. Cubitt's Engineering Company Limited was founded in 1920 with the intention of mass-producing a simple, rugged, car along American lines, which it did in its factory in Aylesbury. However, it failed to achieve the volume of sales required. SF acquired an interest in 1922 and at a meeting of creditors in May 1923, Sir Arthur Whinney, a prominent Chartered Accountant, told them that 'if the company got upon its legs', SF was prepared to take charge. SF was soon after appointed Managing Director, bringing in the aforementioned Col John S. Napier as a director and designer, and by August it was reported that 'under the direction of SF the original programme of the company has been considerably reshaped'.

Unrelated to this, in June 1923 The Rapson Tyre Company announced in its prospectus that 'Mr S.F. Edge is to be Commercial Consultant for £500 per annum and 1% of gross trading profits'. This company went on to build a tyre factory in Launceston, Tasmania, by 1928, but it was not a commercial success and was eventually sold to Dunlop in 1932.

SF's plan was ultimately to merge AC and Cubitt's, and he got as far as arranging for the Anzani engines fitted in ACs to be produced by Cubitt's under licence. In January 1924 he told the press 'I hope by the end of 1924 to have the two companies ready for coalition', but that 'we must have £100,000 to £150,000 to carry out the plans we have for expansion. The general body of shareholders has given no assistance, and if it still neglects to do so we must look elsewhere'.

Not long after this, SF was hospitalised at what must have been a stressful time for him. Duncan reckoned that in his early years at AC, SF had been working 16 to 18 hours a day, five days a week. Details of his ailment are not known, but in May 1924 he wrote to *The Motor*: 'It is very nice to be away from surgeons and doctors and amongst motor matters again'.[350] He later revealed that he was told by his doctor that he must not work at weekends as well as during the week.

Then, still in May 1924, Philip Snowden, Chancellor of the Exchequer, removed the 'McKenna Duties' on imports of motor vehicles and other goods that had been introduced in 1915 as a war-time protective measure by Reginald McKenna, Chancellor at that time. As a result of the removal, imports of vehicles surged and the British manufacturers suffered. Some manufacturers, such as Morris, had to reduce their prices to compete, while Austin was saved by the recent introduction of the popular Austin Seven.

Cubitt's Engineering was particularly vocal in its opposition to removal of the duties, no doubt led by SF, and wrote to the Prime Minister and Chancellor of the Exchequer in May 1924:

> The staff and employees of this company held a meeting at Southern Works, Aylesbury, on Thursday, May 1, for the purpose of considering the proposed abolition of the McKenna duties on motor-cars. The shop stewards themselves, in conference, drafted the following resolution, which was placed before the above meeting and carried enthusiastically:- 'That we, the workers of Cubitt's Engineering Company, Aylesbury, are of the opinion that the time has not arrived for the abolition of the McKenna duties, and we strongly urge the Government, if they have no wish to cause distress amongst the workers of the motor-car industry, to retain the McKenna duties for an indefinite period.'
>
> We earnestly hope that you will most seriously consider the above appeal from our workers. We view the future with the most serious anxiety, unless your further deliberations result in distributing the abolition of this import duty over a considerable number of years.
>
> Before the introduction of the Budget a decision had been taken to reduce the prices of Cubitt British cars with the object of further increasing production and thus reducing overhead charges per car. The new rates, which range from £310 for the 16 h.p. two-seater touring car to £515 for the 16 h.p. landaulette, came into operation on May 1, but the manufacturers now announce that if the McKenna duties are removed in August as threatened it may defeat their object of increased sales, in which event they reserve to themselves the right to rearrange their prices accordingly.[351]

The removal of the tariffs went ahead nevertheless. Following a General Election held on 29 October 1924, Ramsay MacDonald's government was replaced by one led by Stanley Baldwin, and SF's nemesis in the Ministry of Munitions, Winston Churchill, was appointed Chancellor.[xix] The

xix In November 1923, SF had been a guest at a Ministry of Munitions Reunion dinner at the Trocadero Restaurant — scene of the announcement of the six-cylinder Napier by SF in 1903 — which Winston Churchill also attended. It would be interesting to know if they were on speaking terms at the dinner.

➢ SF relaxes at Gallops Homestead during the summer of 1925. *Michael Cooke collection*

motor industry had started to recover towards the end of 1924 when Churchill announced that he would be putting the duties back on again. While this would have been helpful in the medium term, in the short term it produced another flood of imports in anticipation of the reimposition of the duties.

By June 1925, a winding-up petition against Cubitt's was presented by the Earl of Dudley's Round Oak Works Limited (suppliers of steel) and the company was declared bankrupt. SF and the other investors were thought to have lost a lot of money. The only memorial to this venture is a road named Edge Street next to Cubitt Street, running through the site of the old factory in Aylesbury.

To add to his woes, SF's father had died in Australia on 19 June 1924.[352] Little is known about Alexander Edge or why, at the age of 28, having been born in New South Wales, he decided to move his family to England. The 1891 Census describes his occupation, unhelpfully, as 'living on own means', although SF described him as being a merchant. In October 1892, he had moved back to New South Wales with most of his children, leaving just SF in England. Seaton had returned to England at some point and in 1907 was living in a flat in Whitehall Court owned by SF, but he died in 1910 in Devon. Alexander's other sons, Kelburne, William and Randolph, had also predeceased him.

Alexander had been a keen cyclist, however, and the Anerley Bicycle Club *Gazette* had this to say:

> Pa Edge passed away at Sydney, end of June, at the ripe age of 81. For many seasons he was a constant supporter of our Club Runs and in spite of his years, even ran in some of the races. He was a wonderful sticker on his tricycle, a keen sport and a worthy father of a whole string of speedy Anerley men, SF Edge, KE Edge [Kelburne], ST Edge [Seaton], etc.

In the summer of 1925, SF and Myra hosted 38 members of the of the Anerley Bicycle 'Old Boys' Club (including G.H. Smith) to a reunion at Gallops Homestead. They took tea under a marquee on the lawn, after which they admired the replica of the Gordon Bennett Trophy won in 1902, together with another trophy for the Champion Sow of Sussex.[353]

Towards the end of 1925, the AC company was also in financial difficulties, and SF called a meeting of creditors on 4 December. At this point SF had put £106,869 cash into the business, and taken over a liability to the bank of £60,000. For some time, 80,000 of the 180,000 shares in the company had been owned by Vauxhall Motors, which had recently come under the control of General Motors Ltd. SF revealed that he had met with the solicitors representing Vauxhall early that morning and agreed to purchase their shares (for £4,000). However, he would only do this if the creditors were willing to support him. The outcome was that a moratorium of four months for paying the creditors was agreed upon, and SF acquired the shares from Vauxhall.[354] It is not known how many shares he already owned, but the purchase of that block must have put him fully in control.

Just 12 months later, on 7 December 1926, SF, as a debenture holder, had a receiver appointed, as

An AC model introduced in 1927 was this special drop-head coupé named the 'S.F. Edge Special'. *Author's collection*

the company was unable to pay the weekly wages of £3,800. The *Financial Times* reported that the company had a total deficiency of £362,795, and voluntary liquidation was confirmed.[355] The business continued to trade under the receivership of H.W. McLaren until February 1927, when SF formed a new company, A.C. (Acedes) Cars, Ltd with a capital of £140,000 which bought, at auction, the whole of the business of A.C. Cars, Limited, including goodwill, for £135,000 on 16 March 1927.[356]

The company thrived for a while, producing a range of four-cylinder and six-cylinder models ranging in price from £350 for the Royal Open two/three-seater to £585 for a long-chassis coach-built saloon. Another popular model was the 'S.F. Edge Special', a drop-head coupé introduced in 1927. The company was a major carmaker at this time, although not in the league of the mass producers such as Morris and Austin.

An AC was the first British car to compete in the Monte Carlo Rally, in 1925, driven by the Hon. Victor Bruce. He was placed 12th that year but won in a six-cylinder AC in 1926, going on to win the Monte des Mules hill climb.[357] Shortly after that rally, he married Mildred Petre, a very adventurous lady who entered the 1927 Monte Carlo Rally in an AC Saloon, starting from John O'Groats. Driving for 72 hours virtually non-stop, she came sixth overall and won the Coupe des Dames. From Monte Carlo she continued with her husband on an endurance trial, which took her through Italy, Sicily, North Africa, Spain and back to France.

On 9 July 1927 she and her husband were off

A superb competition success for AC came in 1926 when the Hon. Victor Bruce (seated) and co-driver Bill Brunell (behind) won the Monte Carlo Rally in a six-cylinder 2-litre model. *Motoring Picture Library, National Motor Museum*

SF bids farewell to Mildred Bruce on 7 July 1927 as she embarks on her journey with her husband, the Hon. Victor Bruce, to the Arctic Circle in an AC saloon. *Courtesy of Rinsey Mills*

➢ Lord Montagu prepares to take SF for a spin in his AC before driving it to the South of France. *The Auto (16 February 1928)*

again in the same car, this time with a mechanic, departing from London and driving through France, the Netherlands and Scandinavia to get to the Arctic Circle, where she planted a flag.

In December 1927, Mr and Mrs Bruce took a six-cylinder AC to the Montlhéry track in an attempt to cover 15,000 miles. The first day was completed at a promising average of 78mph, but then bad weather set in, rain being followed by fog, sleet and snow in succession. On the fifth day, J.A. Joyce had to step in as a third driver as the two Bruces were exhausted. However, the attempt was successful, with the previous record for 15,000 miles being beaten by 48 hours 28 minutes.[358]

Early in 1928, SF's close friend, G.H. Smith, published a short biography of SF, titled *Selwyn Francis Edge, The Man and Some of the Things He Has Done*. It was a small booklet of some 50 pages and dealt mainly with SF's cycling, motoring and business achievements. It was printed by H.R. Grubb, Ltd of Croydon, for 'private circulation', and distributed free of charge. It is quite likely that SF met the printing costs. The last paragraph read: 'We will not write "Finis" for we have a strong feeling that the last word and the last exploit of S.F. Edge is not yet.'[359] Sadly, SF's last exploits were close at hand.

Charles Jarrott was appointed as a director of A.C. Cars Limited in October 1928. The company had made a small profit (£2,264) in the year to September 1927, but a loss of £24,190 in the following year, and a further loss of £38,874 in the year to September 1929.[360] The Wall Street crash in October 1929 was the final straw for the business, and it went into voluntary liquidation for the second time before the end of 1929. Although the assets were later purchased by

SF with one of his succession of Bull Terriers — this is *Bonzo* — outside AC's premises in Thames Ditton. *Michael Cooke collection*

the Hurlock brothers in 1930 and the company continued to produce fine cars, SF lost most if not all of his investment in AC. He wrote to his employee, Lawrence Stocks, at the time:

> I am sorry to say that the bank has put in a Receiver to this company and the whole business will be sold up. It may be fresh money will be found to carry on but at present I cannot say. It has been a very bad job for me as I have lost about £200,000 in it — the whole of my fortune.[361]

His total losses were probably a lot more than £200,000, as he had previously invested, and lost, money in Cubitt's. St John Nixon was later to describe SF's investment in AC as his biggest mistake: 'The business thrived for a time and Edge poured a large part of his fortune into it, and he died a comparatively poor man.' His health had not been strong since his surgery in 1924, and after relinquishing his interest in AC, he had no further involvement in the motor industry, nor in public life generally.

Between 1923 and 1928, SF had been residing at The High House, Thames Ditton, very close to the AC factory, and he likely sold Gallops Homestead around the end of this period. By 1930, he and his young family had moved back to the Farnham area, living at Dentdale, Corry Road, Beacon Hill, Hindhead.

In 1929, SF had the strange experience, for the second time in his life, of reading of his own death in the press. On 27 February, a French motoring magazine, *L'Auto*, published in Paris, reported SF's death. It turned out that it was T.A. Edge, a fellow cyclist but not related, who had died.

Later that year SF hosted a reunion of the Anerley Bicycle Club on a steamer between Weybridge and Kingston.

➢ This studio photograph, taken in 1928, first appeared as the frontispiece of G.H. Smith's biography of that year and again in 1934 as the frontispiece in SF's own book *My Motoring Reminiscences*, with the simple caption 'Myself'. *Motoring Picture Library, National Motor Museum*

CHAPTER 14

SUNSET

By the start of the 1930s, when SF was 61 and Myra was 42, he had sold most of his business and farming interests and settled into retirement looking after his two daughters, Jean, 9, and Sonia, 7. This did not stop him corresponding in the press, though, particularly the motoring press. In February 1931 he wrote a long article in *The Daily Telegraph* in which he suggested that 'our railways should be turned into motor-ways'. He was showing his usual foresight in predicting both the decline of the railway system and the coming of motorways; Britain's first motorway was not opened until 1956, albeit not on the track of a railway. The article created considerable discussion and correspondence. Around the same time, a second edition of G.H. Smith's little book was published, still for distribution free of charge.

On 22 January 1931, Montague Napier, with whom SF had been so closely associated in business for some 13 years, died at his villa in Cannes, France, at the age of 60. Although they fell out in 1912, in 1904 Montague had named his first-born son Selwyn Montague Napier, showing

SF's two sisters, Marguerite ('Daisie') and Mary, spent their adult lives in Australia, where they are pictured, in Sydney, probably in 1933. *Michael Cooke collection*

how close they must have been at that time.

In 1932, SF decided to visit his two sisters, Mary, 58, and Marguerite (also known as 'Daisie'), 48, who had been living in Australia since moving there in 1892. His four brothers had also migrated back to Australia (Kelburne and Seaton are recorded as being in partnership as 'Edge and Edge' in Sydney in 1903),[362] but at this point all four had passed away and his two unmarried sisters were his only surviving siblings. His aunt, Catherine, now aged 89, was living with his two sisters. He travelled with Myra and they reached Australia in November 1932, arriving back in England, from Brisbane, on the SS *Cathay* on 23 March 1933.

This was one of two visits to Australia in his retirement, but in between the two, in 1934, *My Motoring Reminiscences* was published by G.T. Foulis & Co., Ltd. SF is given as the author and must have devoted much time to providing the material for the book, mainly from memory, but it is generally believed that the book was ghost-written by St John Nixon. This is more or less confirmed by the acknowledgement at the beginning, which reads: 'I wish to express my sincere thanks to my old associate of the Thousand Miles Trial, St. John Nixon, for all the help he has given me in the writing of this book.'[xx] The Foreword was written by Earl Howe, a politician and motor racer who had recently won the 1931 Le Mans 24 Hours in an Alfa Romeo, and includes mention of SF as 'an absolute hero'. The book was dedicated to the memory of Earl Balfour,[xxi] 'whose advice, assistance, and encouragement in the early days of motoring was of inestimable value to me'. This is somewhat enigmatic, since there is no mention of Earl Balfour within *My Motoring Reminiscences*,

An advertising poster for SF's book *My Motoring Reminiscences* featured an illustration of the Napier in which he set his 24-hour record of 1907. *National Motor Museum Trust Library*

xx The National Motor Museum at Beaulieu also has a file of correspondence between SF and Nixon, in which Nixon is checking various facts mentioned in the draft. Nixon has typed out his questions and SF has responded in his notoriously illegible handwriting.

xxi This would be Arthur James Balfour (1848–1930) who had been Prime Minister from 1902 to 1905, and Foreign Secretary from 1916 to 1919.

SF with his friend E.M. Mayes (right), with whom he visited Tasmania in early 1935. They are pictured at a garden party at Government House in Hobart, with an unknown guest between them.

and no indication of him having an interest or involvement in the early days of motoring. It is a mystery as to what advice he might have given to SF, although Balfour had bought a 9hp Napier car in 1902, just after he became Prime Minister, and went on to buy several more, which would have provided good publicity.

SF remained a very private individual, and the book stuck closely to 'motoring reminiscences'. These cover the period from 1895 to 1913, so make no reference to his time running AC Cars, although he did briefly mention his Double-Twelve record in the Spyker in 1922. The only mention of his family is the photograph of Eleanor as a passenger in his Coventry Motette, captioned 'my first wife (deceased)', leaving the reader to infer that there was a second wife.

Having got his book into the bookshops, SF left, on 28 December 1934, on a second overseas trip. He described it as a visit to Tasmania 'with my friend, E.M. Mayes to sample the fishing'. The fishing must have been successful because Mayes subsequently published a small booklet of 23 pages titled *About Giant Trout in Tasmania*, and described as 'Extracts from the diary of the author whilst on a fishing holiday to the Great Lakes, Miena, Tasmania February, 1935.' They travelled back through Bombay, leaving there in March 1935, but not reaching home until May 1935.

The Veteran Car Club of Great Britain had been founded in 1930 following the London-to-Brighton run of that year. Although SF was not involved in its formation (but the former driver of AC Cars, Sammy Davis, was one of the founders), he actively supported it, and in 1938 recorded that he usually attended 'the various rallies organised by this excellent club in the position of judge'.[363] SF, Charles Jarrott and J.W. Stocks (the 1903 Gordon Bennett team) were Guests of Honour at a dinner held by the Club in November 1936 to mark the 40th Anniversary of the original Emancipation Run, held on 15 November 1896. St John Nixon was to become, first, Editor of the Club's *Gazette* and then Secretary of the Club in the late 1940s. Nixon owned an 1898 De Dion Tricycle that he campaigned enthusiastically in many of the Club's events, while Sammy Davis owned a Bollée, similar to one of SF's early cars.

Brooklands was becoming a bit dated by 1936. The Donington Park circuit had been built in 1931 and was becoming the premier race circuit in Britain, with a Grand Prix first held there in 1935. To make Brooklands more modern, it was felt that the venue needed something more akin to road racing along with the banked track. Sir Malcolm Campbell designed a route with plenty of sharp bends that used the Members' Banking but cut across from the Railway Straight, skirting round the aerodrome and crossing the Finishing Straight before getting back to the Members' Banking. The work was carried out during the winter of 1936/37 and the official opening of what was now called the Campbell circuit took place on 20 April 1937. The tape was cut by Dame Ethel Locke King, DBE, and then SF, with one of his daughters, drove on the new road in a 1903 Gordon Bennett Napier, loaned for the occasion by the Blake brothers.[364]

This was probably the last public event SF attended. In June 1938 he wrote a sad letter, published by *The Motor*, which read: 'I am sorry to tell you that I may not drive a car again, and this after driving for 42 years, from 1896, without an endorsement. My heart has given out and I am liable to faint, so it is not safe to drive. Hence, I stop, I much regret to say.'[365] The editor added a note explaining (as though worried that his readers may already have forgotten him) that SF 'was a maker of motoring history, a pioneer. Won the Gordon Bennett race in 1902'. And in the *Daily Sketch* of 16 June 1938, SF is quoted as saying 'the old heart, she's missing a bit. I get fainting fits, and there's no room for fainting drivers on the roads today. I shall miss driving. I love it — always have. But the missus will have to take the wheel now.'

After the outbreak of the Second World War but before the fall of France, SF and his family chose to stay in a hotel in Eastbourne on the Sussex coast from October 1939.[366] The reasons are unclear, but maybe it was thought to benefit his health. On the evening of Sunday, 11 February 1940, SF and Myra attended a concert at the Winter Garden. His heart was troubling him, so when they returned to the hotel he went straight to bed. At 12.30am a porter heard a crash of glass, and it was found that SF had fallen from the wide-open window of his bedroom through a glass canopy onto steps 37 feet below.[367] He died shortly afterwards in the Princess Alice Hospital, Eastbourne, on 12 February 1940, aged 71. The house surgeon at the hospital, Dr G.R. Staley, gave evidence at the inquest stating 'Mr Edge was admitted to the hospital in the early hours of Monday morning with multiple injuries, due to the fall. He died without regaining

SF with his daughters, Sonia (left) and Jean, in April 1936 at Dentdale, which had been their home in Hindhead, Surrey since 1930. *Michael Cooke collection*

⮜ Dame Ethel Locke King cuts the tape at Brooklands for the opening of the Campbell Circuit in 1937. The car is one of the 1903 Gordon Bennett Napiers with SF at the wheel and St John Nixon standing beside it. *Brooklands Museum Trust*

➤ The opening of the Campbell Circuit at Brooklands in 1937 was probably the last public event SF attended. Here he is in the 1903 Napier, with St John Nixon back on the floorboards. *Michael Cooke collection*

consciousness. The cause of death was a fracture of the skull.' The possibility that this was suicide was considered, as he might well have been suffering from depression caused by ill health, having been such an active man in his prime. The coroner, Dr E.F. Hoare, however, returned a verdict of death by misadventure, saying he 'did not find the slightest suspicion of suicide' and noting that if SF had jumped from the window, he would have missed the canopy, so it was clear that he had fallen, as a result of a heart attack.

His body was cremated at the Brighton Crematorium on 16 February. Those attending the funeral were few in number, attributable in part to the bad weather, the distance from London, and the fact that the country was at war.

Other than Myra, her two daughters (aged 19 and 17) and some other relatives, those of his contemporaries present were Mr A.G. McKechnie, Mr R. Moffat Ford, Captain Hubert Egerton, Mr Charles Gazzard (of the Circle of Nineteenth Century Motorists) and Mr St John Nixon. The Automobile Association was represented by Mr C.D. MacWilliams, the Royal Automobile Club and Society of Motor Manufacturers and Traders by Mr E.J. Appleby, *The Motor* by Mr Selwyn Sharp, and the Anerley Bicycle Club by Mr W.P. Harmsworth.

Charles Jarrott, G.H. Smith, Harry Vane and H.O. Duncan were notable absentees, perhaps due to ill health or other commitments. St John Nixon was disappointed by the low turn-out for his friend and mentor, and in a letter to *The Motor* wrote.[368]

> I was somewhat shocked to find the extremely small gathering at his funeral of those of his old associates who knew him when he was at his zenith. The charitable-minded may explain this apathy towards the passing of one of the fathers of the British motor industry by pointing to the prevailing war conditions, and to the fact that many of his old colleagues have themselves solved the great problem, but in glancing round the motor industry today I can find more than one whose first step to fame and fortune was solely due to Edge.
>
> Surely it is rather deplorable that British motor racing and more particularly Brooklands was unmoved by the passing of one who saved the situation in 1907; had it not been for Edge, Brooklands would today be but a memory of a bungled attempt to introduce motor racing into this country, yet so far as I am aware, not an official nor a solitary member of the modern racing school was present to pay homage to a great man.

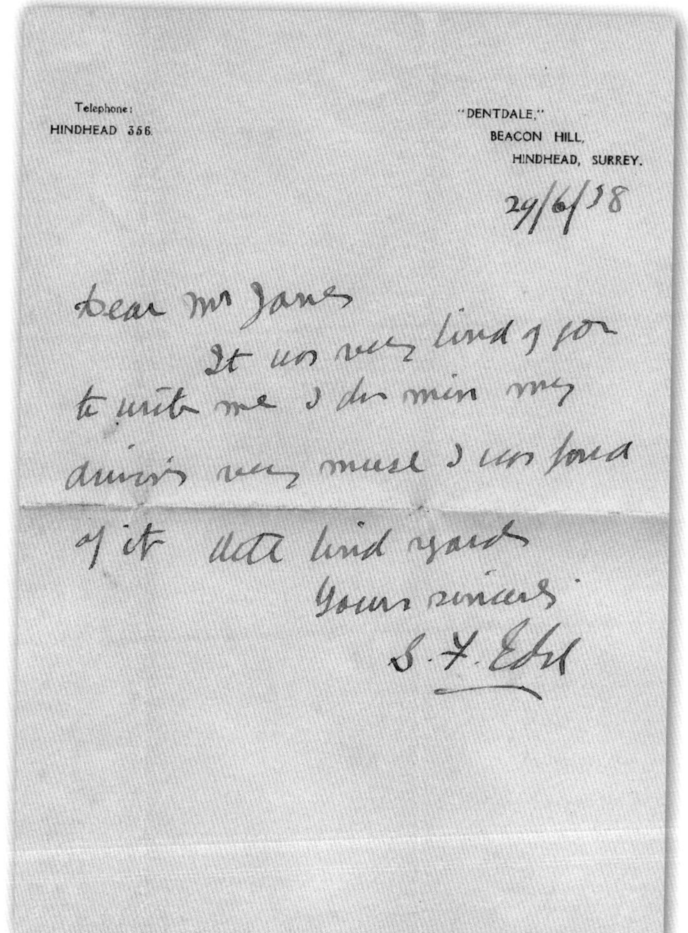
Telephone:
HINDHEAD 356.

"DENTDALE,"
BEACON HILL,
HINDHEAD, SURREY.

24/6/38

Dear Mr Jones
It was very kind of you to write me I do miss my driving very much I was fond of it All kind regards
Yours sincerely
S.F. Edge

⮝ In SF's barely legible writing, with no punctuation, this letter — sent to a Mr Jones in 1938 — reads: 'It was very kind of you to write to me I do miss my driving very much I was fond of it.' *Clive Boothman collection*

Sic transit gloria.

POSTSCRIPT

Myra continued to live in Hindhead with her two daughters until after the war but later moved to Bexhill-on-Sea. She played an active role in the Veteran Car Club of Great Britain, and was appointed as one of its Vice Presidents in 1947, jointly, and most appositely, with Sammy Davis. She donated some of SF's cups and awards to the club, including a replica he had had made of the Gordon Bennett Trophy. She also donated several large volumes of press cuttings that SF had collected over the years.

In a letter to the President of the club at that time, G.J. Allday, St John Nixon wrote:

> My wife and I have known Mrs Edge for a great many years. She is a very kind-hearted, nice woman, but she is highly imaginative and she has the unhappy habit of exaggerating fearfully, so what she tells you must be taken 'cum grano salis'... She was extremely kind to my mother during her life time [Blanche Nixon had died in 1939, shortly before SF's death]. She used to send the car into Brighton for her two or three times a week and my mother used to go and stop with them when they were in Ditchling.

Being resident in Bexhill-on-Sea, Myra suggested to the Veteran Car Club that they hold an event there in 1954 to commemorate the 50th anniversary of the 1904 Speed Trial. She played an active role in organising the event and donated to the club the trophy that SF had won in 1904 as a 'Perpetual Challenge Trophy'.

Myra Edge in 1938: she was 19 years younger than her husband and outlived him by 29 years. *Michael Cooke collection*

In the 1960s, Myra was struck down by an illness that eventually immobilised her completely and she passed away in March 1969, aged 82, in a nursing home in St Leonards-on-Sea. Her ashes are buried at All Saints Church, Tilford, near Frensham, Surrey, along with those of SF and his cousin Cecil.

SCORECARD

Looking back on SF's life, how should he be judged? Like everyone he had his strengths and weaknesses, his friends and his enemies, and his share of successes and failures.

His weaknesses might be considered to include his personality, often described as 'bombastic', which is probably unfair. Certainly he held strong opinions and was not afraid to voice them, often in the cause of publicity for his own personal brand as much as the product he was selling. Coupled with this he could demonstrate a lack of tact and diplomacy, as evidenced by his unhappy parting from the Ministry of Munitions. There is also evidence that he grew increasingly stubborn and inflexible. However, he made several life-long friendships, friends who were intensely loyal to him, and to whom he returned the loyalty. As St John Nixon pointed out, there were many 'whose first step to fame and fortune was solely due to Edge'. Among these would be included Nixon himself, G.H. Smith, Harry Vane, Cecil Edge and Jack Stocks. He was also, on the whole, popular with his employees. Against this was his propensity to take his friends and colleagues to court, the prime example being when he sued Harvey Du Cros, his mentor and financial sponsor in the early years, for half the profits of the Panhard agency.

There is the likelihood that he treated his first wife, Eleanor, poorly, but his second marriage seemed to be a happy one, and Myra Edge remained loyal to his memory long after his death, making sure he was remembered at least by the Veteran Car Club of Great Britain.

SF in later life. *Michael Cooke collection*

His strengths were first and foremost as a successful salesman. He had tremendous energy, drive and commitment, to the extent that it affected his health as early as in his 20s. He also showed great foresight, first in seeing that success as a racing cyclist would promote his own brand and make him a more successful salesman, then in foreseeing the potential of the pneumatic tyre, first for cycles and then for motor vehicles, followed by his recognition, in the 19th century, that the future of personal mobility lay with the internal combustion engine. Perhaps most significant of all was his recognition of the skills of Montague Napier and the potential of his company as a car manufacturer.

His failures were as a civil servant, to which he clearly was not suited, but nevertheless he volunteered for his wartime role in the hope that his skills and experience could help the war effort in addition to his work as a pig farmer. His much more costly failure was his inability to make a success of the AC and Cubitt car businesses, but they were not the only car companies to fail during the 1920s, which were difficult times for the motor industry. Changes in tariff laws clearly had a damaging effect, exacerbated by the Wall Street Crash of 1929.

His successes started with his very fruitful career as a racing cyclist, his winning of the Gordon Bennett race in 1902 followed by his solo 24-hour record at Brooklands, repeated as the 'double-twelve' in 1922. His motoring successes were not due to any great skill as a racing driver but were more a matter of determination and endurance. Indeed, he gave up motor racing at quite an early stage and chose to focus more on trials and, for a short spell, managing a successful motor racing team. Financially, the most successful years, during which he made his fortune, were the first decade of the 20th century, when he simultaneously ran several businesses and agencies.

◄ The gravestone of SF, his cousin Cecil and second wife Myra at All Saints, Tilford, near Frensham, Surrey. *June Cooke*

Born into a relatively humble middle-class family, albeit with a commercial background, and with limited formal education, he found himself, as an early automobilist and car salesman, mixing with the wealthy upper class of British society. His weekends in the 1890s spent at Harvey Du Cros's country house, shooting and fishing, clearly gave him a taste for that style of living, and as soon as he could afford it he bought his own country estate, first at Tilford, then at Gallops Homestead, where he could hold his own weekend house parties for his friends. But he probably found that he was never accepted as an equal by his customers.

He must have been disappointed and perhaps bitter at the fact that he never received public recognition. His 'right-hand man' at S.F. Edge, Limited, Harry Vane, ended up with a CBE, and his former lodger, Charles Jarrott, was made an OBE, but SF (and Montague Napier) got nothing — not even a blue plaque on the house in which he grew up. The last ten years of his life, in reduced circumstances, although not poor, and in failing health, must have been a sad and frustrating time for him, alleviated only by the joys of fatherhood and the support of his second wife. But all said and done, he clearly made a huge contribution to the development of the motor industry in Britain and to motor sport in its early years and deserves to be remembered.

APPENDIX 1
FAMILY TREE

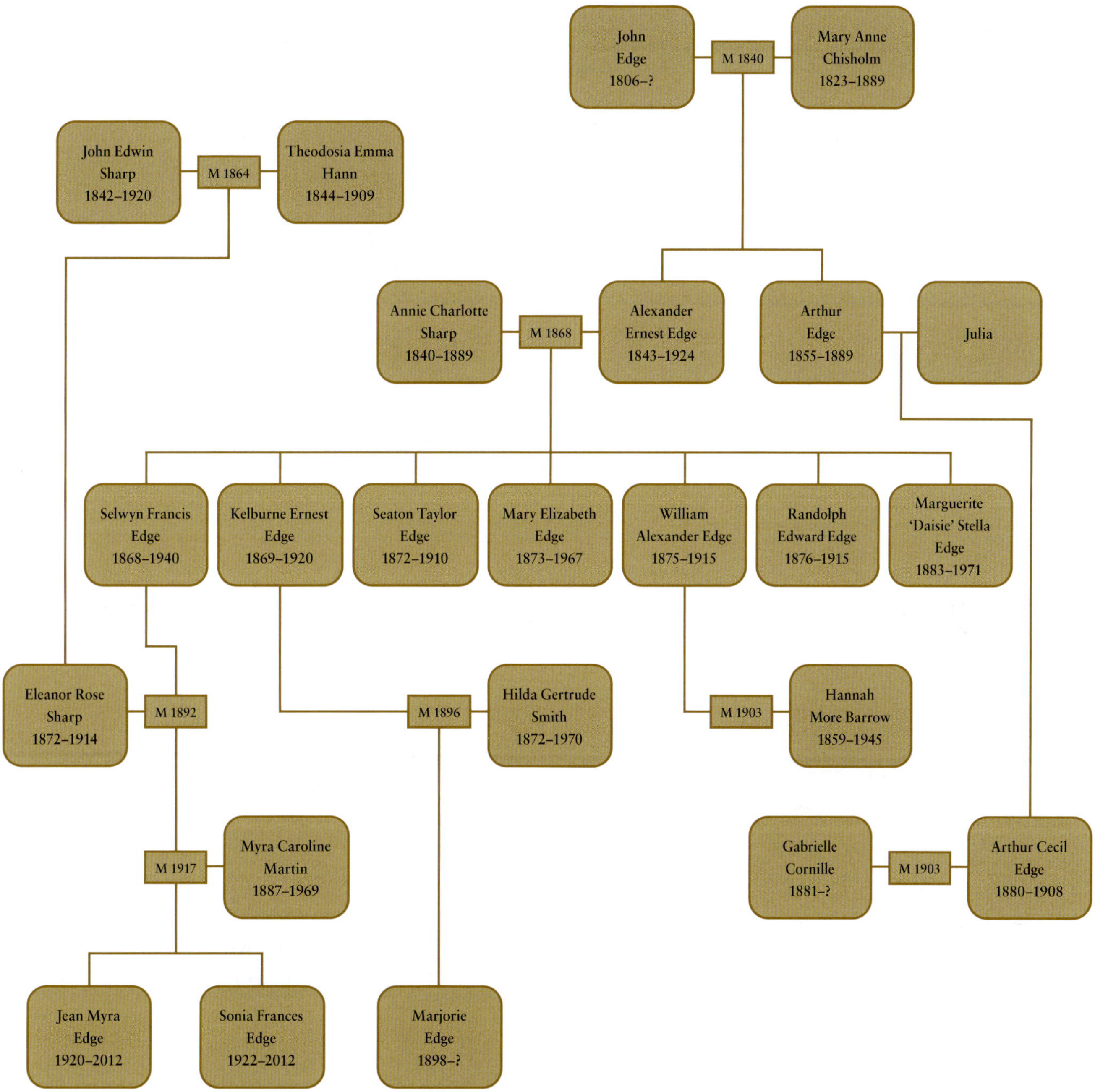

APPENDIX 2
PERSONALITIES

Dr Joah Edward Lionel Bates (1867–1930) was born in Croydon but seems to have spent almost the whole of his life residing at 113 Central Hill, Upper Norwood, less than a mile from SF's childhood home. He was an early and active member of the Anerley Bicycle Club, where he was known as 'Jelly' Bates. He regularly raced against SF, and sometimes with him on a tandem. He trained as a medical student at Guy's Hospital, becoming an MRCS in 1904.

J.E.L. Bates — racing at Paddington in 1889 with SF acting as 'starter'. *The Veteran Car Club of Great Britain*

William Harvey Du Cros (1846–1918), known as Harvey Du Cros (pronounced 'Do Crow'), was born in Dublin. Although of small stature, Du Cros was a boxing and fencing champion. He also became President of the Irish Cyclists Association.

He had six sons. The first two, Alfred and Frederick, were twins, born in 1868. They were followed by Arthur, Harvey (Junior), William and George. The six boys formed a team of racing cyclists known as the Invincibles.[369]

He retired as a partner in a paper-manufacturing business at the age of 40.[370]

In 1889, with John Boyd Dunlop and others, Du Cros established the Pneumatic Tyre and Booth's Cycle Agency as a public company based in Dublin and served as Managing Director. Soon after, the company opened a large factory in Coventry and employed SF from 1893 until 1899. It was succeeded by the Pneumatic Tyre Co in 1894, which was then refloated for £3 million as the Dunlop Pneumatic Tyre Company in 1896, with Du Cros continuing to be closely involved. By this time he had settled in England but had sent five of his sons to different parts of the world to represent the company, with only Arthur remaining in England.

It was SF who convinced Du Cros of the prospects for the motor industry and persuaded him to invest in the Motor Vehicle Company, which eventually

Harvey Du Cros. *The World on Wheels*

became S.F. Edge, Limited.

Du Cros was Member of Parliament for East Sussex from 1906 to 1908, when he was succeeded by his son Arthur. He died in Ireland in 1918.

Herbert Osbaldeston Duncan (1862–1945) was born in London and was a step-grandson of George Osbaldeston (1786–1866), a successful breeder of racehorses and Master of the Quorn Hounds. His maternal grandmother, Elizabeth Cornes (1806-1878) had married Thomas Williams in 1822 and Duncan's mother, Mary Williams, was born in 1823. Elizabeth then married George Osbaldeston in 1851, after the death of Thomas Williams, but before the birth of her grandson, Herbert.[371] Duncan was another successful racing cyclist, having been given a bicycle by his grandmother for his 15th birthday. He started racing in England in 1879, but from 1882 he raced extensively in France, and later in Germany and Austria. A Francophile by this time, he must have been fluent in French because in 1885 he founded a French cycling journal, *Veloceman*, and contributed as a journalist to other publications.

In 1887 he took up a job as 'Continental Representative' for Rudge & Co. in Paris. He also held a similar position for Humber & Co. (then making bicycles) for a while. He was then appointed Commercial Manager of Lawson's British Motor Syndicate and helped Lawson organise the International Motor Exhibition at the Imperial Institute in 1896. When things were not going so well for Lawson, Duncan left and became the Managing Director in France for the British company, De Dion-Bouton Limited, remaining in that position until 1916.

In 1926 he published his idiosyncratic 1,200-page *The World on Wheels*. Liberally illustrated, it comprises a collection of essays, memoirs and anecdotes, with biographical information on many individuals, living and dead, including SF, whom he knew well. Not one to hide his light under a bushel, the book even includes a section on 'One of the best known Cycle and Motor Pioneers, Herbert Osbaldeston Duncan'.

The tome starts with 'the origin of the wheel', takes the reader through the ages of steam, cycling and internal combustion, ending up with an essay on 'Modern Roads and their Development'. In the flowery language of the Preface: 'This unique work enters into the spirit of the past and penetrates the personal motives and innermost aspirations of those who have helped to make the present what it is.'

Arthur Cecil Edge (1880–1908) was known as Cecil to distinguish him from his father, also Arthur, who was the brother of SF's father. Like SF, Cecil was born in New South Wales. By 1900 he was living in England

◀ H.O. Duncan. *The World on Wheels*

➤ Cecil Edge — driving the Napier known as *Samson. Courtesy of Graeme Cocks*

and rode as Jack Stocks' passenger in the Thousand Mile Trial that year. He was employed by SF, and he rode as SF's mechanic in the Gordon Bennett races of 1902 and 1903, thereafter regularly competing in Napiers. He married in 1903 but died from consumption in 1908, aged 28. He died at Uplands, Tilford, near Farnham, which was owned by SF at that time.

Charles Jarrott OBE (1877–1944) was born in Pimlico, London, and initially trained to be a solicitor. He was introduced to SF by Harry Lawson, whose secretary he had become, in 1896, and for a while he lodged with SF and Eleanor at 7 Tavistock Chambers. He organised the second London run of the Motor Car Club to the Sheen House Club that took place on 29 November 1897 to mark the first anniversary of the Emancipation Run.[372] He organised some of the earliest motor races in Britain and went on to be a successful motor racing driver. In 1902 he won the first international motor race to be held on a closed circuit, the Circuit des Ardennes, driving a 70hp Panhard. He married Violet Vyner, Countess of Rosslyn, in 1903.

Charles Jarrott — with Montague Napier on a 12hp Napier circa 1902. *Author's collection (photo by Argent Archer)*

With William Letts he founded, in 1904, Charles Jarrott and Letts, Limited, a company that held the agency for De Dietrich cars, but he was also a director of most of SF's companies. Before that, he traded in his own name from 45 Marlborough Street, London, holding a 'Special Agency' for Napier Cars as well as being sole English Concessionaire for De Dietrich Carriages. He drove a Napier in the 1903 Gordon Bennett race in Ireland but was seriously injured in an accident. In 1906 he wrote *Ten Years of Motors and Motor Racing*. In a later edition he explained that he gave up motor racing since 'it was only after racing at Brooklands that I realised that it was not so much motor racing which appealed to me — it was the road'.

Jarrott was a founder, in 1905, of the Automobile Association, and Chairman from 1922. He resigned from Charles Jarrott and Letts, Ltd in 1909, but later became a Director of Crossley Motors Limited, with which William Letts was closely involved. He accompanied SF on his motor tour in South Africa in 1912. During the First World War he was Inspector of Transport in the Royal Flying Corps, attaining the rank of Lieutenant-Colonel. He was invested as an Officer of the British Empire in March 1918, presumably in recognition of his war service.

He was a good friend of SF, who described him as a brilliant racing car driver, and they worked closely together for many years. But in *My Motoring Reminiscences* SF was critical of Jarrott for 'being content to drive foreign cars'.[373] They had also 'agreed to disagree' over the merits of six cylinders, although SF was in no doubt that he had been proved right (see Appendix 3).

Harry John Lawson (1852–1925) was the son of a preacher, and only five feet tall, with a boyish face (Duncan says he was known as 'the little man').[374]

Harry Lawson. *The World on Wheels*

He was another who came to the motor business via cycling, and he was president of the Watford Cycle Club in 1893. He also took a major part, with Harvey Du Cros, in the reconstruction of the Dunlop Pneumatic Tyre Company, Ltd, which made him a wealthy man. His goal was then to monopolise the motor industry in Britain, which he thought he could do by buying up every patent he could get hold of. SF said of him that 'he paid away ten thousand pounds as the ordinary man would a five-pound note'.[375] He founded the British Motor Syndicate, Ltd in 1895, the same year as the first car was imported into Britain. He then floated the Great Horseless Carriage Company in the spring of 1896 and organised the International Motor Exhibition at the Imperial Institute, South Kensington, later in the year. He also bought the Daimler Motor Syndicate from Frederick Simms (qv) and founded the (British) Daimler Motor Company.

Perhaps his greatest claim to fame is as the organiser of the first 'London-to-Brighton run' in November 1896. None of his businesses, except Daimler, was successful, and he came to be regarded as a fraudster in financial circles, serving time in prison in 1905 and again in 1918. His master patents were challenged in court, and he ended up selling them to SF for a modest amount (which SF borrowed from Montague Napier) in 1907, after which he faded from the business scene.

SF said of him: 'Lawson was undoubtedly a clever man: his weakness was in his failure to foresee the type of motor vehicle which would eventually become popular.'[376] An example of this was Lawson paying £20,000 in 1896 for the rights to manufacture the Bollée motor tandems in Britain. The original drawings were lost in a fire at the Coventry works, and there was some delay before Bollée sent over replacements and production of the Coventry Motette could start, but the designs became outdated within a couple of years.

Dorothy Elizabeth Levitt (1882–1922), believed to be the daughter of a tea dealer, Jacob Levi,[377] was employed initially in the typing pool at 14 New Burlington Street. There she was spotted by SF, who made her his secretary. He arranged for her to learn to drive and she took part in a Glasgow-to-London Non-Stop Trial in May 1903. Later she won her class in SF's 12hp Gladiator at the Southport Speed Trials held in October 1903. She was fined £5 in November 1903 for driving at a 'terrific pace' in Hyde Park.

Dorothy Levitt. *The Woman and the Car*

She piloted the speedboat *Napier* in the first International Harmsworth Trophy. She competed in motor races in Blackpool and Speed Trials at Brighton in 1904 and took the Women's World Speed Record in Blackpool in 1905 driving a 100hp Napier at 90.88mph. In March 1905 she drove a De Dion-Bouton from London to Liverpool and back accompanied only by an official observer and her Pomeranian dog, *Dodo*.

Levitt was elected as a founder member of the Brooklands Automobile Racing Club in 1907 but as a woman was barred from racing there. Her last year of motor racing was 1908, during which she drove a 45hp Napier at the Herkomer Trophy Trial in Germany, after which SF withdrew his team from racing. After writing her book *The Woman and the Car* in 1909, she went on to take flying lessons in France but was not able to obtain a pilot's licence. She died in London in 1922 at the age of only 40.

◄ John Scott-Montagu. *Vanity Fair (8 October 1896)*

John Walter Edward Douglas Scott-Montagu (1866–1929) succeeded to the barony as the 2nd Lord Montagu of Beaulieu on the death of his father in 1905. Educated at Eton and Oxford, he then spent a year working for the London and South Western Railway to learn practical engineering and engine driving (during the General Strike of 1926 he volunteered as an engine driver on the railways). He was a Member of Parliament for New Forest from 1892 to 1905 and campaigned for the rights of motorists. In July 1899 he was the first person to drive a motor car into the yard of the House of Commons. Two months later he took the Prince of Wales, soon to become King Edward VII, for a drive in his new Daimler, and later in the same year he competed in the Paris–Ostend road race. He also took part in the Thousand Mile Trial in 1900. Montagu was interested in all forms of transport, and in 1902 he launched a high-quality weekly journal titled *The Car Illustrated, a Journal of Travel by Land, Sea and Air.*

Montague Stanley Napier (1870–1931) was the grandson of David Napier, founder of D. Napier & Son. A keen cyclist in his youth, he was particularly fond of the 'penny-farthing' machine and continued to ride one for pleasure long after they had become unfashionable. When his father, James, died in 1895, Montague, being the youngest son, did not inherit the business, but was able to buy it from the estate with financial assistance from his mother. Its precision engineering work had mainly involved making weighing machines and printing presses but the firm was almost moribund when Montague took it over.

It was SF who encouraged him to go into car manufacturing, and D. Napier & Son was one of the early British manufacturers in an industry that at the time was dominated by French companies such as Panhard et Levassor. An introvert who, in SF's words,

⋖ Montague Napier. *The World on Wheels*

'never sought the limelight',[378] he was happy for SF to handle the marketing and sales side of the business, which was always done through SF's own company until bought out by D. Napier & Son, Limited in 1912. Again, with SF's encouragement, D. Napier & Son was the first company to successfully produce a six-cylinder car and made 'the best car in the world' until Rolls-Royce claimed the epithet for the Silver Ghost.

SF described him as 'a man of striking appearance; standing nearly six feet in height with a face not unlike an apostle', but with a keen sense of humour and a dry wit.[379] SF said of Napier that he was a keen lover of workshop discipline: his one thought in life was to have a perfect workshop where he could carry on his experiments. He was clearly camera-shy, and remarkably few photos of him survive.

Lawrence Stocks also comments on Montague's 'almost messianic appearance', and that he was 'addicted to eccentricities of dress, his normal attire including a Norfolk jacket, knickerbockers, and a white tie of immense width'.[380]

Montague married Alice Paterson, a school governess, in 1903 and they had two sons (the first of whom was named Selwyn Montague Napier) and two daughters, but separated in 1922. Mrs Napier was pictured in *The Autocar* at the helm of *Napier Minor* in 1904, with her husband tending the engines. They lived at that time in a large house on Wimbledon Common.

During the First World War, Napier's health began to decline, probably from overwork (but he might also have had cancer), and he moved to Cannes, France, where he lived until his death in 1931 at the age of 60. His estate was worth more than £1 million, the income from which was left to his nurse, Norah Fryer. Sir Harry Brittain, one of the directors of D. Napier and Son, contributed to Montague's obituary in *The Times*, stating:

> Montague Napier was an illuminating instance of mental brilliancy surmounting bodily pain. For years past, under doctor's orders, he had been forbidden the climate of his native land, and as an invalid passed his days on the shores of France; but never for a moment did his active mind relax, and his keen, inventive brain was concentrated upon the development of engineering problems, the subject of all others to which he devoted his life. As one of his old colleagues I lament the passing of an outstanding engineer, of a thoughtful, competent genius of his class. I still more lament the passing of the man. This handsome, great-hearted Briton possessed also a genius for friendship. It was a joy and an education to be with him. A great lover of books, he was a deep thinker, sure of himself and his conclusions, and so obviously a master of the subjects which interested him. As long as health was granted to Napier he revelled in all physical exercise and was the keenest of yachtsmen. He had the mind of a philosopher, enjoying most the simple things of life. When illness struck him down he accepted it, with fortitude — and worked quietly on.[381]

At the turn of the century, Montague Napier and Henry Royce (1863–1933), soon to enter partnership with Charles Rolls, probably did not know each other, but their careers were to follow very similar paths. Although Royce was from a very humble background and was largely self-educated, while Napier was from a wealthy middle-class family and had learnt his skills from his father, both had become perfectionist engineers. Neither was much interested in the commercial and marketing side of the business, believing that if theirs was the best product, customers should come to them. Both later moved into aero-engine design as a result of the First World War, both fell into ill health, probably because of over-work, and both of them set up drawing offices, separately, in the south of France, where they would each spend most of the year from the 1920s until their deaths in the early 1930s.

◄ St John Nixon — on his De Dion-Bouton in 1933. *From My Motoring Reminiscences*

St John Cousins Nixon (1885–1970) was the son of Alfred and Blanche Nixon, who married in 1869. They were residing in Belvedere Road when the Edges arrived from New South Wales,[382] and the two families became close friends. One of St John's early memories was of 'Uncle Selwyn' bringing his fiancée to their house shortly before his marriage in 1892 (by which time the Nixons had moved out of Belvedere Road). Alfred Nixon was a fellow member of the Anerley Bicycle Club and was a long-distance tricycle rider.

St John, who was born on 17 August 1885, had been racing tricycles from an early age and was racing motor tricycles in 1900, particularly a De Dion-Bouton. He went to work for SF in 1900 at the age of 14 and was his riding mechanic for the Thousand Mile Trial that year. Later he worked in the motor insurance business and from 1912 until his retirement in 1946 he was in charge of the motor department of Law Union Rock Insurance (his father also worked in insurance). During the First World War he was the officer in charge of petrol tractors on light railways, spending some time in France. He married Nellie Thomson in 1922, and SF was their son's godfather.

He was the youngest member of the Circle of Nineteenth Century Motorists, founded in 1927, and went on to become a prolific author on motoring history. His publications include *The Invention of the Automobile* (1936), *Romance Amongst Cars* (1937), marque histories of Daimler (1946) (helped by his fluency in German) and Wolseley (1949), *The Story of the SMMT* (1952), *The Simms Story* (1955) and *The Antique Automobile* (1956), as well as being the ghost writer of *My Motoring Reminiscences*. When the Veteran Car Club of Great Britain was founded in 1930, he became its Librarian, first Editor of the *Gazette* and then Secretary. He was a regular entrant in the London-to-Brighton Run on his 1898 De Dion-Bouton tricycle. He also re-enacted the Thousand Mile Trial, driving an 1899 Wolseley that had been owned by Herbert Austin, in 1950, 1960 and 1970, the last being just a few months before his death at the age of 85.

Charles Rolls — on a 1902 Mors. *Author's collection (photo by Argent Archer)*

Charles Stewart Rolls (1877–1910) was the youngest son of Lord and Lady Llangattock. After Eton he studied Mechanical and Applied Science at Trinity College, Cambridge. He was a keen cyclist and was Captain of the Cambridge University Bicycle Club in 1897. He bought his first car, a Peugeot, in 1896, while still an undergraduate. He entered a Panhard in the Thousand Mile Trial in 1900 and rode as SF's mechanic in the Paris–Toulouse race in July of that year.

For a while his career seemed to mimic SF's. He set up his own sales company, C.S. Rolls & Co, agents for Peugeot and Minerva. Looking around for a British manufacturer to represent, he was famously introduced to Henry Royce in 1904 and soon entered into an agreement to take all the cars Royce could produce. However, unlike SF with Napier, Rolls was able to persuade Royce to incorporate his name so that the cars were sold as Rolls-Royces. By 1907 Rolls-Royce Limited had bought out C.S. Rolls & Co., five years before Napier bought out S.F. Edge, Limited.

Not long after this, Rolls' attention turned first to ballooning and then to powered flight, making his first flight, with Wilbur Wright as the pilot, in 1908. Soon after that, he bought his own Wright Flyer. He was the first pilot to make a non-stop double crossing of the English Channel in June 1910. Just a month later he was displaying his Wright Flyer at Bournemouth when the tail broke off, and he fell to his death.

SF described Rolls as 'an exceedingly nice fellow and a great sportsman, with absolutely no sense of fear or danger'.[383]

Frederick Richard Simms (1863–1944) was born in Germany and worked there as a young man. He became friends with Gottlieb Daimler and was a director of Daimler's company until 1892. When he left, he acquired the rights to make Daimler cars in Britain and formed the Daimler Motor Syndicate. However, that company never made any cars before the rights were sold to Harry Lawson's British Motor Syndicate, Ltd, at a significant profit for the investors in the original syndicate. He was a consulting engineer, enthusiastically promoting the motor industry in Britain, and it is said that he invented the words 'motorcar' (as opposed to 'autocar') and 'petrol' (as an alternative to motor spirit or gasolene).

Regarding the Motor Car Club, of which Lawson was President, as little more than a commercial enterprise for Lawson's benefit, Simms was the driving force behind

Frederick Simms. *From Romance Amongst Cars*

the formation of the Automobile Club, paying many of the initial expenses from his own pocket. Eventually, after much lobbying by him, a meeting was held on 10 August 1897 at which the Automobile Club of Great Britain was formed, and by 1907 it became the Royal Automobile Club. Simms went on to found the Society of Motor Manufacturers and Traders in 1902 and was its President for the first two years of its existence.

With the German, Robert Bosch, he developed the low-tension magneto and set up manufacturing facilities for magnetos in Britain and the United States of America. In 1913 he also established Simms Motor Units, which produced motor accessories as well as magnetos. SF described him as 'a well-read and cultured man who threw his whole life into the cause of automobilism'.[384]

George Herbert Smith (1862–1946), like SF generally known by his initials 'GH', was a great-grandson of King George III. After school in Hammersmith, he entered the wine trade and later worked for a bank. SF met him when out cycling in Kent in the summer of 1886 and invited him to join the Anerley Bicycle Club, of which GH became the President in 1914. GH was a very active cyclist in the 1890s and kept a detailed diary throughout this period, recording the mileage cycled each day. He was Best Man at SF's wedding to Eleanor Sharp in 1892 and often cycled long distances with them. He wrote a short poem at the time, the last lines of which read: If true what folk allege, We always knew that Edge was sharp, Now Sharp will soon be Edge.

When SF was appointed London Manager for Dunlop tyres, Smith agreed to become an international sales representative for the company and travelled around the world (with his bicycle). In 1900 he was the Hon Secretary of the Motor Trades' Association, with offices in Holborn Viaduct. Later, he was appointed manager of United Motor Industries, Ltd, a company

◄ G.H. Smith on his wedding day. *Courtesy of Penny Morris*

started by Montague Napier and SF, where he remained for several years, developing it into one of the largest motor-accessory businesses in Britain.

His first-born son, born in 1902, was named George Selwyn Smith.

In 1928 he printed a small booklet titled *Selwyn Francis Edge, the Man and Some of the Things He Has Done*, for private circulation, free of charge. A second edition was printed in 1931. He also wrote an informal history of the Anerley Bicycle Club in 1929. In an obituary published in *The Motor Trader* in 1946, St John Nixon wrote: 'Never was there a man with higher principles or a more sincere nature than 'G.H.' Even a modest exaggeration would have been foreign to his nature.'

John (Jack) William Stocks (1871–1933) was born in Hull, where he took up cycling in 1888, joining the Hull Bicycle Club in 1889. After a spell working in Hull Post Office, he joined the John Griffiths Cycle Corporation in 1893, first in Newcastle, then moving to London under SF.[385] During this time he became a member of the Catford Cycling Club, and was a successful racing cyclist, holding several records and often racing against SF. In 1897 he raced on a bicycle against a New Beeston

Jack Stocks. *The Automotor Journal (21 May 1904)*

motorcycle on a track in Coventry. Stocks covered 27 miles 300 yards in one hour, beating the motorcycle by a small margin. Later in that year he retired from cycle racing and wrote a book *Stocks on Training.*

He worked for a while for the Ariel Cycle company in Birmingham, but with a stint in Ireland. In 1902 he was appointed Manager of De Dion-Bouton Limited and later became a Director. In April 1902 he drove a 9hp De Dion-Bouton, accompanied by Roger Fuller, from Land's End to John O'Groats in a total time of 2 days, 14 hours 25 minutes.[386] He also raced Napiers, taking part, unsuccessfully, in the 1903 Gordon Bennett race in Ireland. His wife and son were living in Hull at the time and while out shopping saw a newspaper placard with the headline 'Stocks killed', but when they reached home they found a telegram reading 'Car smashed, all gay, no more racing for me today, Jack'.[387]

When war broke out in 1914, he obtained a commission in the Royal Naval Volunteer Reserve and saw service in France. He resigned his commission in 1916 and took up the position of General Manager of Ariel Works, Ltd, later setting up his own car agency and garage in Birmingham.[388] He remained an active motorist to the end of his days, driving 2,010 miles in six days in 1932 in a Model B Ford. His son, Lawrence, was employed by SF at AC in the 1920s.

Harry Tempest Vane CBE (1875–1943) was born in Kennington, London, the son of a tailor, and worked under SF at the Dunlop Pneumatic Tyre Company in the last years of the 19th century. In 1904 he was appointed as Secretary of the Dion Dunlop Motor Company and went on to become the General Manager of S.F. Edge, Limited. When D. Napier & Son, Limited acquired S.F. Edge, Limited in 1912, he was appointed as General Manager of the parent company and soon became joint Managing Director, with Montague Napier. He was made a CBE in 1917 for services to the Ministry of Munitions, at about the same time as SF was being relieved of his duties by Winston Churchill.

Vane became Managing Director of D. Napier & Son, Limited after Montague Napier's death, but resigned in 1932 when he disagreed with other Directors' proposals to get back to producing cars by acquiring the services of W.O. Bentley. Vane's resignation proved to be needless: Rolls-Royce out-manoeuvred Napier, so Bentley, against his wishes, had to work for Rolls-Royce instead, and the Napier company stuck to making aero engines.

Harry Vane. *The Automotor Journal (2 November 1912)*

APPENDIX 3
THE SIX-CYLINDER DEBATE

The first six-cylinder Napier had been produced in 1903, but as late as 1906 there was a vigorous, and somewhat acrimonious, debate between SF and his 'old friend' (and co-owner of the De Dion-Bouton British agency), Charles Jarrott, conducted through the pages of *The Autocar*. The correspondence is reproduced verbatim below as it is a good example of SF's style of correspondence (to some extent imitated by Jarrott), which at times could be patronising and include more than a hint of sarcasm.

The Autocar, 24 November 1906, page 732. Jarrott restarted the debate following a 'Town Carriage Competition' that had recently taken place:

> Some time ago I entered into a very interesting discussion in your columns with Mr. S.F. Edge in regard to the merits and demerits of six-cylinder motors. I pointed out that, in my opinion, the six-cylinder motor possessed no features of advantage which were not possessed by a four-cylinder motor equally well made, while, at the same time, in the six-cylinder, many disadvantages were in evidence. [Jarrott went on to summarise the findings of the recent 'Town Carriage Competition'.]
>
> Capt. Deasy's trial of a four-cylinder car against a six-cylinder proved some time ago the fallacy of the idea that with a four-cylinder car it was necessary to change speed oftener than with a six-cylinder, and now I think Mr. Edge has proved, through entering a six-cylinder car in the first competition in which the various points set out above have been carefully considered, that, so far from a six-cylinder car having advantages over a four-cylinder, it is, on the contrary, not as good — at least as six-cylinder cars are made at the present day.

The Autocar, 1 December 1906, page 814. This was like a red rag to a bull, and SF responded:

> I am surprised to see my old friend, Mr. Charles Jarrott, writing on the respective merits of six *v.* four cylinders, and I do not propose to argue the matter with him. The fact that seventy-eight of the leading manufacturers of the world have copied the six-cylinder principle is quite sufficient for me, and with all due deference to Mr. Jarrott's opinion, I think the six-cylinder principle will become absolutely universal for all powerful cars, and I only wish for Mr. Jarrott's own sake that he had appreciated the six-cylinder principle previously, so that he might not have to bolster up powerful four-cylinder cars, which I could understand if he was interested in a tyre factory and wished to use up as many tyres as possible.
>
> Mr. Jarrott has previously given me advice that good motor cars cannot be manufactured in Great Britain, and on this point I think he is hopelessly wrong. He has also previously written and said that powerful cars cannot be satisfactorily built with a live axle, and on this point I consider he is utterly and hopelessly wrong, as for the last two years nearly every important big road race has been won upon cars fitted with a live axle and direct drive as introduced by Mr. Napier in 1902.

My opinion of Mr. Jarrott as a prophet is not nearly as good as my opinion of him as a sharp businessman who is doing his best to hold up the powerful four-cylinder trade in its declining years.

My best advice to him is to hurry up and change, and not waste time in trying to decry the six-cylinder principle which is now an assured success.

A visit to the Napier works at Acton would, no doubt, somewhat surprise him, where he could see some 1,200 people engaged in the making of six-cylinder motor cars.

The Autocar, 15 December 1906, page 895. Back to Jarrott:

It is seldom that Mr. Edge declines to argue as to the merit of any particular article which he may at the moment be selling, but I do feel that he is in very great difficulty in trying to explain away the success of the four-cylinder cars over the six-cylinder in the recent Town Carriage Competition of the Automobile Club. It must be remembered that that competition was the very first held in which the comparative merits of the two types of vehicle could be carefully judged, and it would have been impossible for a more complete contradiction to have been made of the exaggerated claims made by Mr. Edge during the last two years as to the superiority of the six-cylinder over the four-cylinder system.

I myself thought that perhaps he might have some reasonable explanation for the failure of the six-cylinder car to score over its four-cylinder rivals, but, whilst I sympathise with him, I regret that he should have evaded the whole matter.

Mr. Edge has taken up the point that the four-cylinder car is more destructive on tyres than the six-cylinder, and suggests that my attitude cannot be understood unless I am interested in a tyre factory. During the recent show I was voluntarily informed by two users of six-cylinder cars — the names of which I need not state — that in one case the tyre bill had amounted to over £350 in twelve months, and, in the other, nine months' running had resulted in a total expenditure of over £400 for tyres alone. I am wondering if any four-cylinder car could beat this record.

It is very difficult to argue with an opponent who mis-quotes what has been said before, but I would like to challenge Mr. Edge to produce any letter of mine or statement of mine in which I ever suggested that it was impossible for good motor cars to be manufactured in Great Britain. What I did say was that motor cars in this country two years ago — the time I wrote my letter — were not as good as many of their foreign rivals.

I have never posed as a prophet, as to do this it is necessary to possess an imagination, and in this direction I am always prepared to receive ideas from Mr. Edge.

Six cylinders possess certain advantages over four, but there are certain disadvantages, and these disadvantages were clearly demonstrated in the Town Carriage Competition previously referred to by me.

The Autocar, 22 December 1906, page 923. A.E. Cohen waded into the debate on Jarrott's side:

Mr. Jarrott proved so ably and conclusively by incontrovertible facts, the relative merit of the six, as compared with the four-cylinder car, that I should have imagined it would have been better had Mr. S.F. Edge remained silent for once. But, as usual, instead of adducing anything approaching an argument in his letter he confines himself to crying 'stinking fish', which is rather a favourite proceeding with him when no argument is possible. I venture, therefore, to encroach on your valuable space to submit one or two facts to Mr. Edge's notice. He boasts that seventy-eight of the leading manufacturers of the world (sic) have copied the six-cylinder principle. I would like to point out that probably eighty per cent of these seventy-eight manufacturers are located somewhere in the British Isles, and that over fifty per cent of their productions have never been tried on the road. Of the remainder, produced abroad, they are only made for the British market, as nearly every Continental manufacturer will admit that he could not sell a six-cylinder car in his own country. In France, where the average member of the public is better posted on motor lore, people absolutely refuse to have anything to do with the six-cylinder, and I may venture to predict that, after the craze is over, a great many firms in this country will regret that they ever embarked on the construction of six-cylinder machines.

Mr. Edge accuses Mr. Jarrott of 'bolstering up a declining cause'. It looks to me very much as if the boot is on the other leg, and pinching badly at that.

In conclusion, the principal claims heralded week by week before the world in the correspondence columns of The Autocar by Mr. Edge for the six-cylinder cars are flexibility, smoothness of running, and wear on tyres. Now, I cannot refrain from stating that I am prepared to prove that on a 16-20 h.p. Chenard-Walcker chassis, costing one-quarter of the Napier chassis, I can get into my fourth (top) speed from rest in 8½ft. I will further drive the car at the speed of a walking horse on top gear, without the necessity of slipping the clutch, controlling the speed of the car by one pedal only, without any levers whatsoever. As regards tyre bills, I will invite the readers of The Autocar to give their experiences of the life of tyres on standard four-cylinder cars, as well as six-cylinder vehicles of Mr. Edge's manufacture, and I venture to predict that that gentleman will be sorry he ever threw out the challenge. I submit that there is nothing that the much vaunted six-cylinder can do which a well-constructed four-cylinder car at half the price cannot do equally well.

With regard to Mr. Edge's kind advice to Mr. Jarrott, I believe the latter gentleman is quite able to take care of himself; but is Mr. Edge really so innocent as to imagine that the two great British and French firms represented by six-cylinder chassis, if they had thought that such was really necessary, or superior to their present productions? Anyhow neither the capital nor the means are lacking in either concern.

In the same issue, SF responded to Jarrott's letter:

I read with considerable surprise that Mr. Jarrott is still harping and seeking to draw me into a correspondence with reference to the merits of six *v.* four-cylinder cars.

It has seemed to me that the day for this controversy has entirely passed. There are now ninety-five manufacturers copying Mr. Napier's six-cylinder principle, and it is quite immaterial to me whether one concessionaire more or less believes in the six-cylinder principle.

If Mr. Jarrott's four-cylinder principle is so much better, then I am surprised that at Shelsley Walsh the six-cylinder Napier, with a cylinder capacity of only 471 cubic inches [7.7 litres], completely paralysed the two De Dietrich cars which ran, the one with an enormous engine having 732 cubic inches [12 litres], driven by Mr. Jarrott himself.

If for a competition of this sort he could not with this huge engine beat the little six-cylinder Napier, I am quite satisfied that he cannot beat it for all-round general points, such as quietness and smoothness of running, ability to run fast and slow on the same speed without using the clutch, and general durability. It is no use for him, however, to continually flog a dead horse, viz., the powerful four-cylinder car — it has been a splendid friend to all automobilists, it will be still for small cars; but for big cars with powerful engines, for those who require the latest and best mechanical device, the six-cylinder car has come to stay, and I am only sorry that Mr. Jarrott should be lagging behind in his ideas of modern motor car progress.

In regard to his reference, I am glad to hear that he does consider it possible for good motor cars to be manufactured in Great Britain, and that he wrote some two years ago, saying that motor cars manufactured in this country were not as good as many of their foreign rivals, he did not really mean that we could not manufacture them in this country.

Personally, I cannot understand his subtle difference of what he actually said in words and what I understood him to say. They both mean the same to me. However, it is quite satisfactory to know that even Mr. Jarrott agrees with me that Great Britain can make perfect motor cars. The next thing will be when he agrees with me that six cylinders are better than four for powerful cars. It is something to have converted him to the British manufacture idea.

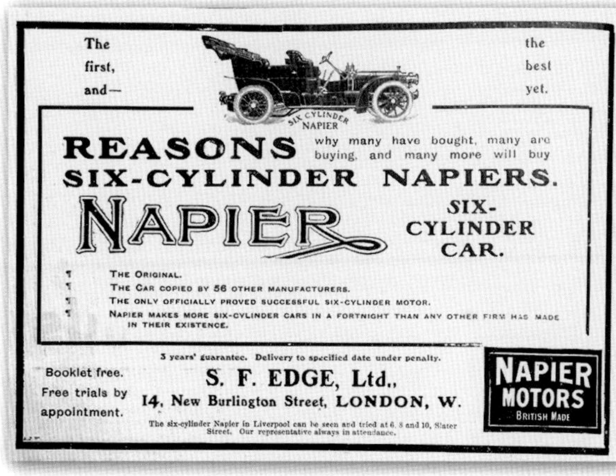

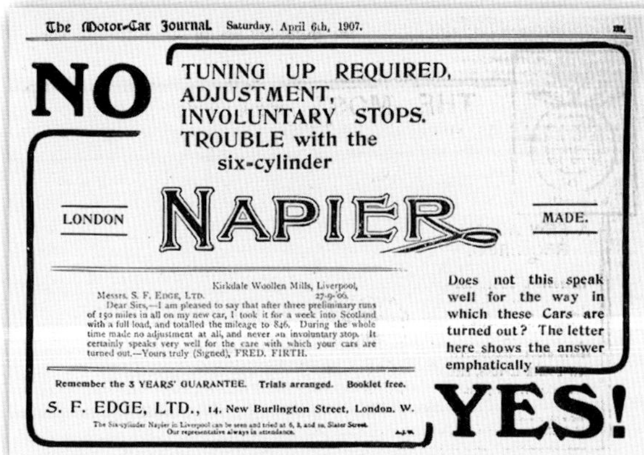

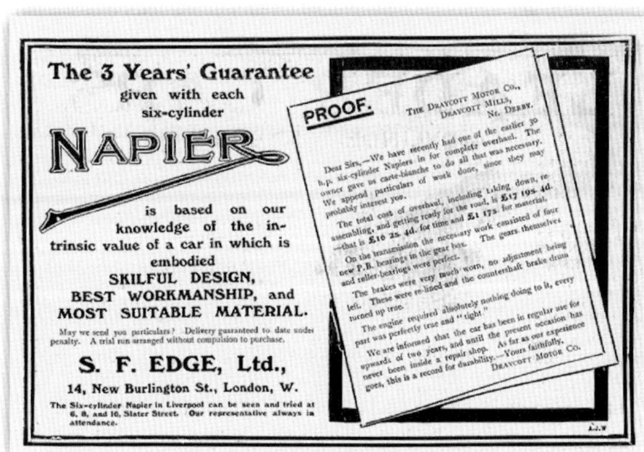

These advertisements show how tirelessly SF promoted the virtues of Napier's six-cylinder engine over the four-cylinder models of other manufacturers. *gracesguide.co.uk*

The Autocar, 29 December 1906, page 960. A week later SF responded to A.E. Cohen's letter:

> Mr. A. E. Cohen in seeking to assist Mr Jarrott's cause, really makes rather a strong case in favour of the six-cylinder Napier car. His statement that probably eighty per cent of the six-cylinder manufacturers are located in the British Isles is inaccurate, as I find the proportions are as follows, so far as my data permit me to observe: British manufacturers, forty-seven per cent; foreign manufacturers, fifty-three per cent.
>
> When he says that over fifty per cent of their productions have never been tried on the road, he probably understates the case and it is further proof of the merits of the six-cylinder Napier that so many leading manufacturers have thought it fit to risk their reputation with untried productions rather than being accused of being unprogressive.
>
> Mr. Cohen's argument that the French people refuse to have anything to do with the six-cylinder is rather concisely dealt with by Mr. Massac Buist in the *Morning Post*, who writes: 'Of course, in regard to the building of six-cylinder models, I am not surprised at the display of reluctance on the part of French makers, for, apart from the natural jealousy, caused by having to follow the lead of those English, who are so utterly hopeless at designing and building motor cars that are not traction engines, there is this to be considered — and the astute Mr. Edge has foreseen it all along — that now that a great number of the foremost houses are placing six-cylinder models on the market, intending purchasers of high-priced vehicles are saying to themselves, 'Ah! The six-cylinder car is evidently the thing for luxury, else all these important motor manufacturing firms would not be falling in line.' Let us look at each of them in turn, and what is the result? Well, of all these multi-cylinder machines, how many of them have been tested for a lengthy period in the hands of private owners as distinct from workshop tuning up? One make only — the Napier.'
>
> As the list of six-cylinder makers has to my knowledge increased from seventy-eight in a letter previously written to ninety-five at present, it can hardly be considered the declining cause indicated by Mr. Cohen. There are possibly some things that a low-powered four-cylinder car can do as well in proportion, but that is really nothing to do with the present case, as we are considering equally powerful cars and their merits, and if there are so many four-cylinder cars as good as, or better than, the six-cylinder Napier, it is rather surprising that some of them do not attempt to win the £1,000 which I have been offering for some time to the builder of any four-cylinder car which will equal approved performances of the six-cylinder Napier.
>
> The concluding portion of Mr. Cohen's letter is rather discounted by a paragraph in the *New York Herald* of December 7th, which I assume to be correct, that the directors of De Dietrich and Co. have decided on the construction of a six-cylinder model next year.
>
> A little bird has also whispered to me that Mr. Jarrott has undertaken to represent the interests of another French firm which made a specially strong feature of its six-cylinder car at the Salon.
>
> If, as Mr. Cohen contends, French buyers will not purchase six-cylinder cars of their own countryman's make, and as Mr. Jarrott could not be expected to push the sale of a pattern he does not believe in, it seems hard to see where the output of these firms, in six-cylinder models, is to be disposed of.

BIBLIOGRAPHY

A.C. Cars Limited *The History of AC Cars Ltd* (Fullerton & Lloyd, 1952)

Bennett, Elizabeth *Thousand Mile Trial* (Elizabeth Bennett, 2000)

Bird, Roger *The Birth of Brooklands* (Roger Bird, 2012)

Boddy, W. *The History of Brooklands Motor Course* (Grenville Publishing Company Limited, 1957)

Davis, S.C.H. *Memories of Men and Motor Cars* (Seeley, Service & Co. Ltd, 1965)

Du Cros, Sir Arthur *Wheels of Fortune: A Salute to Pioneers* (Chapman & Hall, 1938)

Duncan, H.O. *The World on Wheels* (Duncan, 1926)

Edge, S.F. *My Motoring Reminiscences* (Foulis, 1934)

Horner, Craig *The Emergence of Bicycling and Automobility in Britain* (Bloomsbury Publishing, 2021)

Jarrott, C. *Ten Years of Motors and Motor Racing* (Radclyffe & Hutchings Ltd, 1906)

Jepson, Andrew M. *Around the World in a Napier* (The History Press, 2013)

King, Peter *The Motor Men* (Quilter Press, 1989)

Lawson, Bruce *Charles Rolls of Rolls-Royce* (Bruce Lawson, 2013)

Lord Montagu of Beaulieu *The Gordon Bennett Races* (Cassell & Co. Ltd, 1963)

Lynch, Patrick *At the Greatest Speed* (Unicorn, 2021)

Lyons, R.S. *Sir Malcolm Campbell's Book of Famous Motorists* (Blackie & Sons, 1937)

Nagle, E. *Veterans of the Road* (Arco Publishers Limited, 1955)

Nixon, St John C. *Romance Amongst Cars* (Foulis, 1937)

Nixon, St John C. *The Story of the S.M.M.T.* (S.M.M.T., 1952)

Noble, Dudley and Junner, G. Mackenzie. *Vital to the Life of the Nation* (S.M.M.T., 1948)

Pulford, J.S.L. *The Locke Kings of Brooklands Weybridge* (Walton & Weybridge Local History Society, 1996)

Rose, Gerald *A Record of Motor Racing 1894–1904* (The Royal Automobile Club, 1909)

Smith, G.H. *Selwyn Francis Edge, The Man and Some of the Things He Has Done* (Smith, 1928)

Venables, David *Napier, The First to Wear the Green* (Foulis, 1998)

Vessey, Alan *By Precision into Power* (Tempus Publishing, 2007)

Watkins, Martyn *AC* (J.H. Haynes & Company Limited, 1976)

Wilson, C.H. and Reader, W.J. *Men & Machines* (Weidenfeld and Nicolson, 1958)

REFERENCES

Chapter 1

1 1881 Census
2 Lyons, Sir Malcolm Campbell's Book of Famous Motorists, pages 25 & 26
3 Lyons, Op. Cit., page 26
4 Ancestry.com
5 The Norwood Review, No 226
6 Article published on 28 May 1910
7 Smith, Selwyn Francis Edge, The Man and Some of the Things He Has Done, page 5
8 Edge, The Secret of Keeping Young, an article published in December 1927
9 Article in T.P.'s Weekly, 31 December 1927
10 Article in T.P.'s Weekly, 31 December 1927
11 The Times, 8 August 1883
12 The Times, 31 December 1883

Chapter 2

13 Irish Cyclist & Motor Cyclist, 8 June 1927, page 35
14 Smith, Op. Cit., page 12
15 The Anerley Bicycle Club, A story told by Members 1881-1981, page 61
16 Smith, Op. Cit., page 12
17 The Anerley Bicycle Club, Op. Cit., page 61
18 Smith, Op. Cit., page 46
19 Blackburn Weekly Telegraph, 9 September 1911
20 Article in T.P.'s Weekly, 31 December 1927
21 Smith, Op. Cit., page 12
22 Smith, Op. Cit., page 13
23 Smith, Op. Cit., page 14
24 Smith, Op. Cit., page 15
25 Smith, Op. Cit., page 16
26 Duncan, The World on Wheels, page 800
27 Duncan, Op. Cit., page 801
28 Duncan, Op. Cit., page 800
29 Smith, Op. Cit., page 18
30 Smith, Op. Cit., page 19
31 Smith, Op. Cit., page 20
32 Smith, Op. Cit., page 21
33 Cycling magazine, 17 November 1909
34 Smith, Op. Cit., page 22
35 Duncan, Op. Cit., page 801
36 Duncan, Op. Cit., page 801
37 Duncan, Op. Cit., page 801
38 Duncan, Op. Cit., page 802
39 Smith, Op. Cit., page 25
40 Duncan, Op. Cit., page 803
41 http://www.webgirl.co.nz/SharpHealy/theodosiahann.html
42 Ancestry.com
43 Smith, Op. Cit., page 47
44 Edge, My Motoring Reminiscences, page 19
45 Smith, Op. Cit., page 26
46 The Anerley Bicycle Club, Op. Cit., page 11

Chapter 3

47 Edge,.Op. Cit., page 10
48 Edge, Op. Cit., page 12
49 Edge, Op. Cit., page 18
50 Duncan, Op. Cit., page 672
51 Edge, Op. Cit., page 261
52 Edge, Op. Cit., page 24
53 Edge, Op. Cit., page 23
54 Duncan, Op. Cit., page 705
55 Ancestry.com
56 Edge, Op. Cit., page 35
57 Edge, Op. Cit., page 36
58 Edge, Op. Cit., page 41
59 Edge, Op. Cit., page 44
60 The Autocar, 4 November 1916, page 499
61 Duncan, Op. Cit., page 804
62 Jarrott, Ten Years of Motors and Motor Racing, page 26
63 Edge, Op. Cit., page 220
64 Smith, Op Cit., page 30
65 Jarrott, Op Cit., page 19
66 Jarrott, Op. Cit., page 19
67 Duncan, Op. Cit., page 805
68 Nixon, Romance Amongst Cars, pages 55 and 337
69 Nixon, Op. Cit., page 73
70 Jarrott, Op Cit., page 27
71 Edge, Op. Cit., page 215
72 Duncan, Op. Cit., page 807
73 Nixon, Op. Cit., page 109
74 Edge, Op. Cit., page 61

Chapter 4

75 Jarrott, Op Cit., page 81
76 Edge, Op. Cit., page 45
77 Jarrott, Op Cit., page 39
78 Edge, Op. Cit., page 46
79 Jarrott, Op Cit., page 82
80 Jarrott, Op Cit., page 84
81 Edge, Op. Cit., page 56
82 Edge, Op. Cit., page 58
83 Jarrott, Op. Cit., page 83
84 Jarrott, Op Cit., page 90
85 Jarrott, Op Cit., page 92

Chapter 5

86 Smith, Op. Cit., page 47
87 Edge, Op. Cit., page 20
88 Duncan, Op. Cit., page 803
89 The Daily Mail, 19 July 1911
90 Duncan, Op. Cit., page 827
91 Duncan, Op. Cit., page 808
92 Edge, Op. Cit., page 64
93 Wilson & Reader, Men and Machines, page 70
94 Edge, Op. Cit., page 69
95 Duncan, Op. Cit., page 812
96 Wilson & Reader, Op. Cit., page 71
97 The Automotor Journal, April 1900, page 367
98 Edge, Op. Cit., page 74
99 Edge, Op. Cit., page 75
100 Edge, Op. Cit., page 75
101 Edge, Op. Cit., page 83
102 Smith, Op Cit., page33
103 Edge, Op. Cit., page 89
104 Edge, Op. Cit., page 89
105 Edge, Op. Cit., page 91
106 Edge, Op. Cit., page 92
107 Edge, Op. Cit., page 96
108 Edge, Op. Cit., page 97
109 Edge, Op. Cit., page 98
110 The Autocar, 4 August 1900, page 741
111 Edge, Op. Cit., page 102
112 Rose, A Record of Motor Racing 1894 - 1904, page 119
113 Edge, Op. Cit., page 76
114 The Autocar, 14 July 1900, page 684
115 Edge, Op. Cit., page 94
116 Edge, Op. Cit., pages 214 and 215
117 Jarrott, Op. Cit., page 243
118 Edge, Op. Cit., page 222
119 1901 Census
120 Edge, Op. Cit., page 229
121 Edge, Op. Cit., page 103
122 Duncan, Op. Cit., page 834
123 The Gordon Bennet Cup conditions laid down by the Automobile Club de France
124 Edge, Op. Cit., page 105
125 Duncan, Op. Cit., page 834
126 Jarrott, Op. Cit., page 247
127 Jarrott, Op. Cit., page 107
128 Jarrott, Op. Cit., page 107
129 Duncan, Op. Cit., page 571
130 Rose, Op. Cit., page 144
131 The Automotor Journal, July 1901, page 507
132 Smith, Op. Cit., page 34
133 Edge, Op. Cit., page 107
134 Jepson, Around the World in a Napier, page 15
135 Jepson, Op. Cit., page 20
136 Jepson, Op. Cit., page 21
137 Jepson, Op. Cit., page 120

Chapter 6

138 Rose, Op. Cit., page 108
139 Edge, Op. Cit., page108
140 Edge, Op. Cit., page 109
141 Edge, Op. Cit., page 110
142 Edge, Op. Cit., page 111
143 Edge, Op. Cit., page 115
144 Edge, Op. Cit., page 116
145 Rose, Op. Cit., page 158
146 Jarrott, Op. Cit., page 132
147 Edge, Op. Cit., page 117
148 Jarrott, Op. Cit., page 135
149 Edge, Op. Cit., page 118
150 Edge, Op. Cit., page 118
151 Jarrott, Op. Cit., page 139
152 Edge, Op. Cit., page 121
153 Edge, Op. Cit., page 122
154 Edge, Op. Cit., page 122
155 Edge, Op. Cit., page 123
156 Edge, Op. Cit., page 124
157 Duncan, Op. Cit., page 839
158 The Motor, 18 March 1930, page 317
159 Edge, Op. Cit., page 124
160 Edge, Op. Cit., page 126
161 Rose, Op. Cit., page 165
162 Duncan, Op. Cit., page 840

Chapter 7

163 Rose, Op. Cit., page 193
164 Rose, Op. Cit., page 194
165 Edge, Op. Cit., page 141
166 Edge, Op. Cit., page 140
167 Edge, Op. Cit., page 129
168 Edge, Op. Cit., page 129
169 Rose, Op. Cit., page 186
170 Edge, Op. Cit., page 131
171 Edge, Op. Cit., page 133
172 Edge, Op. Cit., page 134
173 Rose, Op. Cit., page 198
174 Edge, Op. Cit., page 137
175 Edge, Op. Cit., page 143
176 Edge, Op. Cit., page 142
177 Edge, Op. Cit., page 142
178 Edge, Op. Cit., page 147
179 Jarrott, Op. Cit., page 190
180 Jarrott, Op. Cit., page 192
181 Jarrott, Op. Cit., page 223
182 Edge, Op. Cit., page 230
183 Edge, Op. Cit., page 168
184 Edge, Op. Cit., page 170
185 Edge, Op. Cit., page 171
186 Edge, Op. Cit., page 172
187 Edge, Op. Cit., page 174
188 The Autocar, 24 October 1903, page 528
189 Edge, Op. Cit., page 175
190 Edge, Op. Cit., page 176
191 Venables, Napier, the First to Wear the Green, page 55
192 The Autocar, 19th December 1903, page 772
193 Edge, Op. Cit., page 151
194 The Autocar, 21 May 1904, page 698
195 Edge, Op. Cit., page 159
196 Edge, Op. Cit., page 160
197 Edge, Op. Cit., page 161
198 Edge, Op. Cit., page 161
199 Edge, Op. Cit., page 162
200 Edge, Op. Cit., page 163
201 Rose, Op. Cit., page 212
202 Edge, Op. Cit., page 165
203 Edge, Op. Cit., page 233
204 Edge, Op. Cit., page 240
205 Edge, Op. Cit., page 236
206 The Automotor Journal, 13 August 1904, page 963
207 The Times, 9 August 1904, page 6
208 Smith, Op. Cit., page 38
209 Edge, Op. Cit., page 241
210 Edge, Op. Cit., page 242
211 The Automotor Journal, 6 August 1904, pages 922 to 926
212 Rose, Op. Cit., page 234

213 Edge, Op. Cit., page 175
214 rmyc.club
215 Edge, Op. Cit., page 246
216 Edge, Op. Cit., page 221
217 Anerley Bicycle Club website
218 The Automotor Journal, 3 March 1906, page 271
219 Duncan, Op. Cit., page 846
220 The Automotor Journal, 3 March 1906, page 271
221 Edge, Op. Cit., page 247
222 Edge, Op. Cit., page 248
223 The Autocar, 25 May 1907, page 773
224 The Automobile, December 2019, page 38

Chapter 8

225 Edge, Op. Cit., page 177
226 Edge, Op. Cit., page 179
227 Edge, Op. Cit., page 180
228 Pulford, The Locke Kings of Brooklands, Weybridge, page 53
229 Edge, Op. Cit., page 182
230 Edge, Op. Cit., page 183
231 The Autocar, 12 January 1907, page 64
232 The Autocar, 29 June 1907, page 979
233 Interview published, in German, in the magazine Neues Wiener Tagblatt on 31 May 1914
234 The Autocar, 6 July 1907, page 4
235 Edge, Op. Cit., page 186
236 Edge, Op. Cit., page 187
237 The Autocar, 6 July 1907, page 5
238 Edge Op. Cit., page 188
239 Edge, Op. Cit., page 191
240 Edge, Op. Cit., page 192
241 Edge, Op. Cit., page 195
242 Edge, Op. Cit., page 199
243 Boddy, The History of Brooklands Motor Course, page 21
244 Boddy, Op. Cit., page 16
245 Boddy, Op. Cit., page 17
246 Edge, Op. Cit., page 198
247 Boddy, Op. Cit., page 18
248 The Autocar, 1 August 1908, page 186

Chapter 9

249 Minutes of the Dion Dunlop Motor Company Ltd
250 Grace's Guide to British Industrial History
251 Duncan, Op. Cit., page 814
252 Horner, The Emergence of Bicycling and Automobility in Britain, page 152
253 Duncan, Op. Cit., page 823
254 Duncan, Op. Cit., page 823
255 Wilson & Reader, Op. Cit., page 79
256 Wilson & Reader, Op. Cit., page 80
257 Wilson & Reader, Op. Cit., page 83
258 Wilson & Reader, Op. Cit., page 71
259 Duncan, Op. Cit., page 824
260 The Automotor Journal, 7 October 1905, page 1230
261 The Autocar, 10 November 1906, page 650
262 The Engineer, 16 October 1914, page 363
263 Who's Who in Business 1914 (from Grace's Guide)
264 The Veteran and Vintage Magazine, March 1967, pages 224 to 226
265 The Times, 29 July 1907
266 Motor Finance, 13 November 1907
267 Duncan, Op. Cit., page 825
268 'Motor Finance, 13 November 1907
269 Duncan, Op. Cit., page 827
270 Duncan, Op. Cit., page 825
271 Duncan, Op. Cit., page 827
272 The Automobile Owner and Steam and Electric Car Review, January 1910, page 475
273 Wilson & Reader, Op. Cit., page 96
274 The Automobile Owner and Steam and Electric Car Review, January 1910, page 475
275 The Financier, 26 January 1910
276 Minutes of D. Napier & Son Limited
277 The Automobile Owner and Steam and Electric Car Review, January 1910, page 479
278 http://rememberjamaicaplain.blogspot.com/2008/01/american-napier-automobile-company.html
279 The Autocar, 3 July 1909, pages 21 and 22
280 Wilson & Reader, Op. Cit., page 96
281 Wilson & Reader, Op. Cit., page 96
282 Minutes of D. Napier & Son Limited
283 The Daily Mail, 19 July 1911
284 The Times, 19 July 1911
285 The Daily Mail, 19 July 1911
286 Wilson & Reader, Op. Cit., page 95
287 Venables, Op. Cit., page 119
288 Wilson & Reader, Op. Cit., page 79
289 Eventful Careers, article published on 28 May 1910
290 Pearsons Weekly, 3 February 1910
291 Weekly Times & Echo, 21 November 1909
292 The Chauffeur, 26 March 1910, page 448
293 The Autocar, 2 April 1910, page 458
294 Duncan, Op. Cit., page 851
295 Country Life, October 1900
296 Article by Tom Clarke and Will Morrison in Aspects of Motoring History, No 14
297 The Autocar, 13 April 1912, page 657
298 The Autocar, 13 April 1912, page 659

Chapter 10

299 Edge, Op. Cit., page 225
300 Edge, Op. Cit., page 225
301 The Car, 9 July 1902, page 224
302 The Motor, 2 July 1907, page 679
303 Wilson & Reader, Op. Cit., page 96
304 The Times, 10 December 1913
305 The Times, 10 December 1913
306 Minutes of D. Napier & Son Limited, 23 October 1912
307 Wilson & Reader, Op. Cit., page 99

Chapter 11

308 Smith, Op. Cit., page 7 and The Autocar, 22 September 1900, page 926
309 Smith, Op. Cit., page 9
310 Duncan, Op. Cit., page 847
311 Duncan, Op. Cit., page 800
312 The Veteran and Vintage Magazine, March 1967, pages 224 to 226

Chapter 12

313 The Daily Express, 30 October 1912
314 Nixon, The Story of the S.M.M.T., page 28
315 Minutes of D. Napier & Son Limited, 23 February 1913
316 The Car, 10 November 1915
317 Smith, Op Cit., page 11
318 Duncan, Op. Cit., page 851
319 Bird, The Birth of Brooklands, page 200
320 IMDB.com
321 The Bioscope, 12 November 1914, pages 650 and 652
322 Motor News, 13 November 1915
323 The Autocar, 3 June 1916, page 680
324 The Financier, 17 September 1915
325 1901 Census
326 1911 Census
327 The Daily Graphic, 8 January 1917
328 The Autocar, 17 February 1917, page 152
329 The Motor, 16 January 1917
330 Motor News, 14 April 1917
331 Hansard, March 1917
332 Motor World, 12 April 1917
333 Car Illustrated, 22 August 1917
334 The Motor Trader, 24 October 1917, page 103

Chapter 13

335 Grace's Guide to British Industrial History
336 The Automotor Journal, 11 March 1920, page 293
337 The Motor, April 1920, page 437
338 The Motor, 1 December 1920, page 920
339 The Motor, 16 March 1921, page 270
340 Duncan, Op. Cit., page 849
341 A.C. Cars Limited, The History of A.C. Cars Ltd, page 41
342 The Motor, 7 December 1921, page 901
343 Noble and Junner, Vital to the Life of the Nation, page 151
344 A.C. Cars Limited, Op. Cit., page 44
345 Boddy, Op. Cit., page 97
346 The Motor, 26 October 1921
347 The Motor, 25 July 1922
348 1914 Who's Who in Business
349 The Motor, 25 July 1922
350 The Motor, 3 June 1924, page 779
351 The Times, 5 May 1924
352 Ancestry.com
353 The Anerley Bicycle Club, Op. Cit., page 30
354 Motor Trader, 9 December 1925, page 328
355 Financial Times, 31 December 1926
356 The Motor, 29 March, 1927, page 421
357 Watkins, AC, page 57
358 A.C. Cars Limited, Op. Cit., page 50
359 Smith, Op Cit., page 52
360 Financial Times, 1 March 1930
361 The Veteran and Vintage Magazine, March 1967, pages 224 to 226

Chapter 14

362 The Sydney Morning Herald, 15 August 1903
363 Nagle, Veterans of the Road, page 23
364 Boddy, Op. Cit., page 294
365 The Motor, 14 June 1938, page 909
366 The Motor, 21 February 1940, page 55
367 The Motor, 21 February 1940, page 55
368 The Motor, 28 February 1940, page 113

Appendix 2

369 Duncan, Op. Cit., page 590
370 Duncan, Op. Cit., page 589
371 Ancestry.com
372 Jarrott, Op. Cit., page 23
373 Edge, Op. Cit., page 266
374 Duncan, Op. Cit., page 674
375 Edge, Op. Cit., page 261
376 Edge, Op. Cit., page 262
377 Grace's Guide to British Industrial History
378 Edge, Op. Cit., page 263
379 Edge, Op. Cit., page 263
380 The Veteran & Vintage Magazine, March 1967, pages 224 to 226
381 The Times, 28 January 1931
382 1871 Census
383 Edge, Op. Cit., page 266
384 Edge, Op. Cit., page 260
385 The Automotor Journal, 5 February 1910, page 141
386 Duncan, Op. Cit., page 897
387 The Veteran & Vintage Magazine, March 1967, page 226
388 Duncan, Op. Cit., page 899

INDEX